CHURCH
A Counter
Narrative

Gaz Kishere

Gaz Kishere

Church – A Counter Narrative

DEDICATION

I want to thank all the people I've met along the way who were just really wonderful human beings. Some truly great people whom it was easy to like and love.

I would like to thank those very rare and precious few who had a genuine desire to help me get where I was going, instead of asking me to build up what they were in. It's a privilege to still hear their wise counter culture voices in my head. I thank the people who encouraged me to fly, and those who clipped my wings in equal measure, for showing me the kind of person I would wish to become, and what I would never wish to be.

To my best friend and wife of 35 years Victoria, you are priceless. To my children Holly, Emily, Jesse and Jacob, they made me promise to never again take them to 'happy clappy poopy nappy church' and I never did.

You make me proud every day.

Special thanks to Kent, who has stuck with me throughout my long emergence and remains a wise, non judgmental friend and mentor. Steve Cole makes everyone feel they have something golden to bring. Tim Waldron, best boss for saying 'you can fuck up, I just need to hear it from you first, not someone else'. Mark Markiewicz for the best motivational 'you can do it' stories, some of which were even true.

Finally to Hailey, who tells me I have things that are worth saying out loud and was willing, along with Jo to endure proof reading all of the books 'Gazisms' into more intelligible English.

I am forever grateful to live in a part of the world where I don't have to ask anyone's permission to disagree or make a valid and hopefully useful contribution.

G

Church – A Counter Narrative

Table Of Contents

Church – A Counter Narrative

"Maybe the journey isn't so much about becoming anything. Maybe it's about un-becoming everything that isn't really you, so you can be who you were meant to be in the first place."

anon

Forward

A Normal Person Writes A Foreword

By Hailey Kilgo

Hi, I am Hailey, I am currently living in Maryland with my husband Andrew trying to work out what a meaningful life looks like away from the church world and those mercy orientated projects. I don't know about you, but I grew up in a world where some roles are seen as spiritual and of worth, while the rest of life is seen as 'stuff' of less value, which we must survive and get through. This is an unfortunate aspect of the world I grew up in because I am someone who likes the 'stuff' aspect of life.

It has become a cliché for someone to 'care too much'. The phrase has been co-opted into a meme, an overused indicator of self-sacrificing while onlookers applaud, or observe with concern, that you are potentially seeking recognition, affirmation, or adoration. As someone who would like to use that phrase positively and without the irony, I simply do not understand where caring too much about something or someone became problematic.

When I first met Gaz in Athens in 2017, I, like others, cared too much. I cared about people, what was going on for them, and their needs. I quickly found myself lost in the details, buried underneath the difficult stories. I cared so much that I gave up on sleep, I lost track of normal eating habits, and began to lose boundaries along with too much of myself. I worked for a faith-based non-profit in Athens with Greek co-workers. In theory I loved the idea of being the only

American, but that romanticized notion imploded after sitting through my third team meeting where the commitment to use inclusive English would drift back into Greek, never to return. I was burned out at the end of my first month, feeling isolated, and the demands of the work were not getting easier.

I moved to Greece to work with the large refugee community of displaced people who were fleeing war, persecution, and torture. There are currently 50,000 such people in Greece, stuck in a three or four year asylum process and enduring very poor living conditions. I arrived and did not know how I, as one person, could affect this global crisis. Each day I started rolling my boulder up the hill to work and every night it would roll back down behind me.

The first time I met Gaz he offered me this piece of advice, just ten minutes into knowing each other. He said, "you can't expect a person to trust you and build a relationship with you until their basic needs are met." A straightforward thing to say, but it changed my mind-set. I came to Athens to meet people, build relationships, and to understand more of what was happening. But I couldn't get there without a bridge. Meeting people on their terms, at their point of need was the foundation. It was not just Gaz, there have been other supportive challenging voices along the way, but this advice led to the creation of an English school in a densely populated immigrant portion of Athens. The community I lived in requested, well more like demanded that since I had this skill of speaking English that I needed to share it. I can't remember the exact moment when I was approached by someone at the project and asked if I could teach them English, but I do remember Gaz's advice ringing in my head. From then on, conversing with Gaz became a staple of my life in Athens. He and his incredible partner Vicky, whose voice also lives rent free in my head, gave me a resting place, somewhere to speak in my native tongue and to put my feet up, feeling acceptance. I learned early on in my relationship with Gaz that he, like me, also cared too much. Gaz was not, and still is not afraid to get mad and to express himself about things, which control, limit or oppress. He can cry and laugh and have a bad day along with the rest of us and it's all out there for the world to see.

We once sat on Mars Hill, the smaller hill and location of many Bible stories next to the Acropolis. It was here that he told me about 'cycle breaking' in families and how habits and coping mechanisms do not have to be repeated. Learning to care with healthy boundaries and no longer waiting for someone else's permission to take a break was a cycle breaker.

If you continue to read this book, which I hope you do, you will learn that Gaz and the Jesus person have been breaking cycles of behaviours and unhelpful inherited thinking in their own relationship for decades now. I had never met a person who thought to do that. Part of my journey of living in Athens and working during hardship and injustice was constantly questioning where this Jesus person was. Was he going to show up? Who was he? Was he looking at this mess, because hello, he really needed to be.

I was raised under the limitations of whatever the Southern Baptist pastor preached to us. Gaz will refer to my generation later on in this book as an age group that is "haemorrhaging on mass from the church organization." I left church while I was still in High School and have not been back. The stigma around people who don't go to church, in only church communities separated from normal life and people, is that when you stop going to church it means you're in rebellion, back sliding, or worse, you hate the Jesus person. For years before arriving in Athens, I carried this guilt that I knew had no real basis, but it was constantly gnawing away at me in the background. This guilt came from the idea that I was a bad Christian, that I did it all wrong, that Jesus was an indifferent critical parent figure only interested in where my bum sat on Sunday mornings.

Then, I met Gaz. As a side note, I'm not trying to paint Gaz as some kind of hero; he would be the first to reject any such elevation. He is a flawed human being, but it's the openness in sharing these flaws that makes him capable of writing a book like this. Gaz knows who he is and what he thinks, through living, through his own trial and error.

So, here I am. I have changed because of interactions with Gaz and with Vicky, along with the people we worked alongside (not forgetting those we had to work against to make good and healthy things happen).

My deepest struggle for the two years I spent in Athens, the further two that have followed me back in the US, and pretty much the last decade has been this; will I meet the Jesus person 'anywhere' in this world or did I leave him 'somewhere'? Will we have chance encounters in the bars, streets, back rooms and dark troubled places? Is it enough to just be an ever evolving me, in my real life chatting with Jesus, but removed from the organization known as church? Is that okay?

My whole life in church I was told we are not meant to be alone. We, as the body of Christ, are not meant to exist on a spiritual island being kept safe till we land in heaven. I always thought that meant I had to be seated weekly, face solemnly pointing towards a preacher, talking about all the sins I had not yet committed but was on the right track to. Now it is different. I know that for me, and others, the church as a building, as an organization, is the last place I will find a connection with this Jesus person.

I am just a normal person who met a hairy guy called Gaz and took the time to sit together and listen to his stories. This book is written for me, and for you, the normal person who is carrying their guilt, who cares too much, who wants to work out how to flow with the Jesus person, or has broken away from the church organisation and doesn't know what comes next. If you are not interested in any of those things, well, you will probably be offended but you should still read this book because Gaz is 'funny' as hell and who doesn't need a little of that in their life?

4

Proud of you Gaz, and honestly, honoured to be included in your brand of weird.

H

Free To Love

It is absolutely clear that God has called you to a **free** life. Just make sure that you don't use this **freedom** as an excuse to do whatever you want to do and destroy your **freedom**. Rather, use your **freedom** to serve one another in love; that's how **freedom** grows. For everything we know about God's Word is summed up in a single sentence: **Love others as you love yourself.** That's an act of true **freedom**. If you bite and ravage each other, watch out—in no time at all you will be annihilating each other, and where will your precious **freedom** be then?

Galatians 5:13-15
The Message

For The Biters & The Bitten!

Preface

The journey 'out' of organised Christianity is more complex and potentially more traumatic an experience than the journey 'in'. It seems that everything is geared towards getting you in and keeping you in, with little thought or process given to helping people leave in a healthy and supportive way. There is 'no' exit strategy.

I have been out of the church world now for more than 20 years, having previously been a detached youth worker and eventually a pastor. I have worked in multiple communities with justice-orientated projects. I have had some experience in supporting grassroots communities in different countries as they have sought to break with the norm and find a less conformist way forward.
I can see my Bible from where I am sitting in its black dusty vinyl cover. I have no urge, need or desire to pick it up as I have long since left school and in my opinion, graduated.

Part of my current work is giving therapeutic support to those who seek to continue a relationship with the Jesus person as the source of their spirituality whilst dealing with abuse, conditional regard, rejection and control from their Church experience.
As I have helped people re-orientate and have sought to re orientate myself, I have been surprised at the regularity with

which my reference points for helpful language is largely from the world of those recovering from addiction and cults. Phrases like:

Detox / De-programming / Recovery From Addictive Behaviours / Separation From Toxic Relationships / Undoing Controlling Messaging / Recovery From High Dependencies.

This will not be a historical or theological debate but instead will be from my voice as a practitioner. In fact, I promise to try and keep any bible references to a bare minimum. This isn't that book.

The narrative here will be of insight, shared perspectives and contextual experience, while also recognising the reality that the church organisation got me here. Like others, I found that church had a ceiling, an umbilical cord, a cultural bungee attached, which in the end would limit my growth, potential, journey, life experience and ultimately hinder my 'becoming'.

I like that in more simplistic and less competitive times, Christianity was referred to as 'The Way', because that is what it was bringing. A better way for what was intended to be a movement of people. I increasingly believe the movement, yes movement, was never about making us more competent and informed Christians, but instead wanted us to become more fully human, immersed as participants in society, what the bible book refers to as the created (you may have your own reference points for life, work, world)

For the larger part I won't be looking to explore or focus on what is working, as there are literally millions of things written, affirming and adjusting what 'is'. **Those have been the massively dominant voice, hence a counter narrative.** I will be confronting what's not so good in the assumed paradise, without trying to balance critique with kindness. **The church isn't a needy child** and it's only right to explore some of the poison that is mixed into its waters.

I am writing in solidarity with the voices of dissent that often disappear into the ether without being sufficiently heard or valued. Those who are seen as critics, when, in truth, they are often the ones who have found or regained the ability to bring healthy objective critique, but are rejected without finding open ears.

Stories Are Just Saying To Another Person,
"This Is How It Seems To Me, Is This How It Seems To You?"

This book is not intended to be balanced. Please don't message me saying 'Gaz you're not balanced in your views', because I am giving fair warning. Don't message me telling me how the church isn't perfect but has managed to impact millions of people over 2000 years, when it has little to no relevance for the 99% of the people living in your own street. This book will be very triggering for anyone wishing to protect what 'is' and it's misguided to feel that an institution hundreds of years old needs help to remain fixed on the landscape, it isn't going anywhere, but some people might be. Instead I hope to the best of my ability, to 'rage and scream' just a little on behalf of the marginalised, controlled and manipulated. Those who have exited the church construct feeling, or being indoctrinated to believe, that they have left God in the building. This book is almost entirely for them.

Reader Warning:
My favourite comedian of all time is a Scotsman called Billy Connolly who has a goatee beard of glory, the likes of which I can only aspire to. While travelling with a car full of kids to the south of France on holiday, I heard one of my sons giggling and laughing uncontrollably in the back of the car. In the days of audiotapes and personal tape players I kind of figured he had stumbled across my Billy tape, which is not suitable for young ears.
Billy was one of the first people in my lifetime where I heard someone confront religions that were able to get away with abusing children sexually. Billy used to have nuns with placards outside his shows asking people to boycott him for blasphemy, which I consider to be a positive reaction to his

provocations. The part I believe my son was laughing at was Billy's introduction to this live show where he said, *"Are there any journalists here? If there are, I would like to give you the opportunity to 'f$ck off'. Don't just sit there and then go and write 'Billy was insensitive about religion, He chose to leave out all the good that it does and Billy's language left a lot to be desired', I'm going to say f$ck and I'm going to say it a lot, I'm also going to mouth off any religion which cant stop itself from having sex with children, so if your a journalist, please f$ck off now!" ;-)*

This book is unapologetic in that it is not pro congregation or organisational Christianity in the form that is expressed most, a building called church.

Unlike some, or perhaps many, I have managed to come away from all the distortion and human invention of church world and still have a sense of the Jesus person. To be fair, that is more down to him and his willingness to sneak through the cracks, than me leaving a door wide open. He is still the source of some, but not all, of the wisdoms, which I try to live from. He is an evident, dare I say actively present source for my on-going spirituality. Sometimes I call him Bob, but because he is a mate!

I have not needed to pursue other routes for enlightenment, though I recognise there are other valued wells to drink from and affirm those who do – so keep becoming truly alive!

I would like to say as clearly as I can that I have every respect for people who have come away from the construct called church and found it all too tainted to continue with any of it. Where you are at in this journey is to be valued and affirmed, you have not failed, you did not lose a fight with the system and proved them right in their positions and judgements. Why? Because you haven't finished yet, 'we' haven't finished yet. You just have to accept that people will look out from a 2,000 year old system and tell you that something, which took its first steps of exploration twenty to thirty years ago, has failed already. Such observations do not come from a heart, which wishes to cheer on the saints to go further, wider, and deeper.

Can you imagine, just for one moment – the former generations saying, **"Run, Explore – Go Further Than Us!"** Gosh - if only!

Fortunately my mate Bob says that in my head frequently 'go – run – explore', as his own counter narrative to those who are stuck and projecting fear or their own disappointments onto their spiritual kids, us!

During my own journey out, a less than helpful parental voice suggested that we could **'deconstruct' ourselves into oblivion** if we weren't careful. It's a fascinating position to take from inside the church, that if your not careful, your going to end up just like all the unbelievers. It craps on the reality that most of 'those' people still find a hugely meaningful existence of love, family, friendships and a fulfilling participation in society without any contact with church, probably because Christians do not have a monopoly on love. It's a significant lie that it's 'all a bit shit and broken out there'. I'm not saying this is what he meant, but there are those who mean exactly that. That's part of the internal church world 'speak', telling us that if we leave we will be like the others out there, truly fucked and without God. Funny, because the oblivion guy would probably now identify as following Buddhist wisdom more than any other and I wish him every good thing in his journey.

For me, part of my journey involved the inquiry, 'will the real Jesus come forward?' In part, the figuring out of that question has been an experience, which has led me to state that I still 'do' the Jesus person. What I definitely do not do anymore is Jesus 'Plus' (and mate, there was so much 'plus'). I'm pretty happy with that and in no way think less of people who have arrived at a different place. Perhaps you're at a place of still being into Jesus, but working out the 'Plus' or because of crap experiences, leaning towards Jesus Zero. People are rightly finding that there is a lot of shit to sort through and lay down. In reality, a person's recovery may well result in there being very little of 'what was' being left but... I reckon you're going to be okay.

In trying to get my head straight and start writing, I shared an early chapter with a good friend and she said that perhaps I could offer more by way of alternatives, different options, or from my own experience some 'different' methodologies. I feel doing so would, in some respect, be counterproductive to the call for people to risk, to journey outward, to perhaps do things differently and have your own experience of a new way, or 'thee way'. All of creation groans and yearns for the children of God to be revealed. Half the battle is just showing up, being human, and increasingly being a participant in society as a whole as a worker, a friend, and a lover.

Speak Even If Your Voice Shakes
Speak Even If You Lack Eloquence
Speak Even If You Can't Recite Memory Verses
Speak Even If It Does Not Meet With Approval
Speak Even If People Will Be Offended
Speak Even If You Lose Friends
Speak Even If....
Speak!

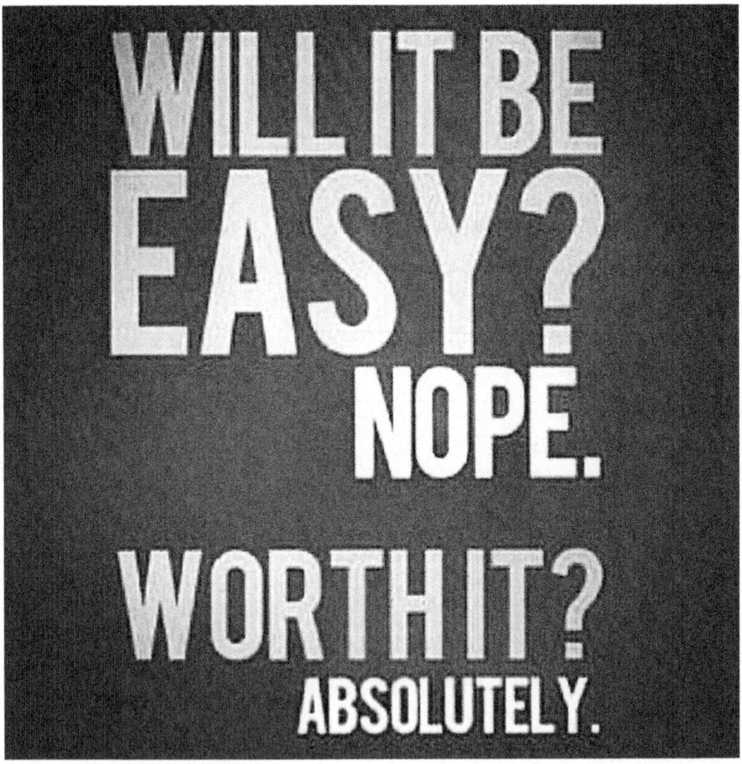
WILL IT BE
EASY?
NOPE.
WORTH IT?
ABSOLUTELY.

Introduction

Good Day to you fellow traveller :-)
Let me start with some mild comedy, as you will need to be able to cope with some irreverence if you are to take anything positive from the pages that follow.
Congregations across the world feel they are progressing, at least in part, and these radical PR campaigns will show you just how far churches have come… or not.
Roadside Sign:
Horsham Christian Fellowship
A Church Without Walls
(Someone had crossed out Walls and spray painted 'Balls')

I actually wrote half of a book around 20 years ago as I was exiting organised Christianity. I passed my embryonic scribbling's onto someone I respect, an author and thinker called James Thwaites. He was writing about life beyond the congregation while the rest of us were polishing chairs with our butts each week only just becoming suspicious that something was deeply and systematically out of 'wack'. It was his feedback that put a stop to my writing career for two decades saying, "Gaz it's interesting, it feels like a collection of blogs (not the end of the world) but it lacks a Golden Thread of Hope (not so good)". He was right of course, I was writing in a place of reaction, in a place of strong critique, which is okay, but also out of the pain and the pendulum swing of emancipation. I don't think I could ever speak badly of peoples' various experiences of leaving organised religion or the institution of Christianity. Each will have their own unique internal world, responses, and ways of recovering. However, we will share some of those common threads, which give us a sense of solidarity. There are a growing number of people who have a shared journey and a mutual respect for daring to disconnect and become dislodged from the immovable object, which is the church as an organisation. If only there was some consistency between the efforts placed on the love and regard invested in getting you in, and enabling you to leave with as much freedom, affirmation, regard and kindness. However, this is not the world we currently live in! So, it's back to those first attempts of sharing my thoughts that I go to now to get this sticky rolling ball of issues and enlightenment out of my head and into your hands. I've learned a lot since my first attempts at writing. My critique of church is still strong but my insides have rediscovered kindness, empathy and the value of all human journeys. I have also learned that writing everything you want to say, in an attempt to include everyone, does the opposite.

Whilst most churches have salaried admin and a PR people developing the branding and label to go on the public face of the organisation, let's spend some time exploring the chasm between the advertising and what's actually inside the church tin can. There will be those who feel they have explored all the corners of what 'is' and have found it to be lacking or restrictive to personal growth and to a sense of personal or collective movement. For people such as these, they have an internal desire to continue to pursue church beyond the inherited points of arrival. This book is really for those who are feeling or seeing the cracks in the institutional church, by which I mean, the physical place you go on a Sunday. It is designed to help your internal argument, which has, perhaps, led you to be on the fringe, where you have chosen to be or have been forced. I would like to help you explore the reasons for your internal conflict with your external environment and take the final leap out the door, if you haven't done so already, or if that's where the God idea, or life, is currently leading you.

Many of those who choose to move beyond the walls find that it is a painful process, one of guilt and rejection where there is no blessing placed upon them by the church. Or perhaps, what they feel is actually just the initial 'sting' of the umbilical being cut. If this is you, I hope it will be the last church, by name, that you will ever leave, as you join the community of the saints on a rather different journey. I hope to that you will find love and empathy for those who have lost all, on the journey out. If you have long since been out of the door and struggle to find the God of creation, of work and life where he always was, then I hope to help you to stop looking over your shoulder at where you were, and find delight, spirituality, faith and a continued becoming wherever you find yourself now.

Personally, I never left church (though I have not been part of the organisation's machinery in 20 years). I am instead continuing to explore as part of what is meant to be a global community of the free. Sadly such people are called many things by the institutions that they leave and its rarely anything life giving. It is unlikely that they will affirm that you're doing something positive and incredibly brave, since you were meant to build up what they are in, not stray too far outside of it.

"Movement Orientated People Cannot Spend Too Long In Something Which Isn't Moving"

This Is Me

Hi, I'm Gaz, I listen to soul and house music, I still swear from time to time, I am facially dominated by a now grey, once black goatee beard and have been collecting tattoos since I put the name of my fave band on my wrist at school with needle and ink when I was 15 years old and rather bored. With that overview out of the way, I want to fulfil part of a

personal dream I had when I read someone else's book.
I promised to myself that one day I would write something useful and would begin that book in the exact same way that this other author had done with the words...
"Ah fuck it!" which was followed by a long pause before his writing again, 20 years in my case.

Let's Begin...

A Golden Doorway - The Way In

I became a Christian at the age of 18 after several years of being part of a motorcycle tribe, living for the weekends, embedded in my culture and having a solid number of normal friends. My journey into faith began as a result of attempts to please the father of my then girlfriend, a deacon in the local Baptist church. My intrigue also grew as a result of my own father spoon feeding me repeats of Charlton Heston bible movies on rainy Sunday afternoons, in the days when the TV only had 3 channels.

Having said 'yep I am in' as a declaration of my list ticking acceptance of salvation at a youth camp, I followed it up with getting dunked in the official baptistery and immediately feeling worried that my bare breasted devil woman tattoo with the words 'Bad To The Bone' would show through my shirt. After the initial 'I'm a believer' I moved on to the stage of having a home visit from the elders. This was to explain in a sit down meeting that they would like a slice of my income if I come into membership. After that, having established my responsibilities, I was invited to walk to the front of the church building to shake the pastor's hand of 'Welcome Into The Full Fellowship of the Church' (a less interesting contrived version of Peter at the gates). This basically meant that I was elevated to places on high, like attending the Baptist church business meetings, where my role was essentially to raise a hand of agreement at certain points to sustain the churches charitable tax free status. Sadly, the Baptist minister's daughter Beth was not permitted to enter the quivering waters with the rest of us due to committing the heinous crime of smoking a cigarette.

Walking with the Jesus person is meant to be immersive, a package deal of good things - not segmented into steps of behavioural obedience, controlled as a passage of entry into another world.

My first business meeting didn't go so well, though on reflection it's pretty much an indication of how life has continued since then for me. There was a decision of what to do with the large multi bedroomed house next to the church building, which was now empty, since the pastor had the good sense to move away from his workplace. The decision was made to leave it empty for now, which didn't sit well with me. I raised my hand and asked if it could be temporary accommodation for the homeless and was told 'no' from a leader with a side tilted head implying 'ah bless this simple, young, inexperienced newbie'. I was expected to remain quiet at this point but instead said, *"If we are faithful with the small things, we will be trusted with even greater things"*. I would like to think that this comment is gathering dust somewhere in a church historians cupboard, alongside the later comment made by said girl's deacon father, that we, my wife and I, were, **"A cancer on the liver of the church which needed to be cut out"**. I'll leave that one there, as I said I was going to try and keep this book attempt on the shorter side. Said 'angry' deacon would have shit a brick if he knew we had been shown what he had said in the official minutes of the deacons meeting (I guess he knows now)

I actually ended up marrying the deacon's daughter's friend, my beautiful wife of 30 plus years Victoria. Being able to say 'the deacon's daughter dumped me and so I married her best friend' still gives me cause for amusement, it's a little bit rock n roll isn't it?

"A Critique Is Often Received As A Criticism To Someone Defending An Immovable Position"

Today I live with said beautiful human mixing time between the US, UK and Greece, where we travelled to do anti child trafficking work but have mostly been engaged in the refugee crisis. Now in our early 50's we have 4 wonderful grown up children in different countries (Holly Emily Jesse Jacob) along with 4 grandchildren... and counting (Edward Brandon Spencer Parker).

The Trickle Approach

It's funny how 'remembering' triggers things you long since forgot about. I was attempting to wrap 'entry in' stories in a tidy little candy wrapper in the above text, but I would be failing as a storyteller not to include this additional bit.

It seemed that in the era in which I was growing up, there were four places people could meet, run clubs or book it for a wedding reception; the church hall, the old men's smoking club, community centre or a veterans association of one kind or another. I remembered that I had actually gravitated towards the Baptists church hall for much of my childhood. Firstly, it was where kindergarten was, the local infant play place where my father would collect me on his moped and I would ride the half kilometre to my house sitting on his lap. Then it was also the venue for a youth club where at around age 10 we would play pirates and all the gym equipment and benches were all that would separate us from an invisible sea of sharks. Then finally it was the place of the boy's brigade, a Christian version of scouts with militaristic overtones, blue uniforms and caps similar to Captain Scarlet. I have no idea how this occurred or its context but there was a fabulous church member called Mr Spinney, who always seemed to me to look perpetually 100. He was the kind of guy who genuinely loved kids without any predatorial rubbish; he was a total gem of a man. For some reason during youth club days, the obligatory post playtime bible story led into a 'who would like to talk to Mr Spinney about believing in Jesus' and it seems I'd put my hand up and found myself in another room with Mr Spinney telling me he could see the light in my eyes. I recall he had a terrible stutter and so my ADD used to kick in if he was that week's bible storyteller with me offering a multiplicity of names beginning with the letter J whilst he was stuck on pause trying to say JJJohn. It seemed that conversion processes were sown into just about every activity-taking place in the church hall.

On another occasion in blue Brigade uniform I was to find myself at the front of the church on an obligatory annual Sunday attendance with some other staged commitment processes. Here I was to approach the minister to receive a badge and shake hands but with strict instructions to interlock pinkies! What I was signing up for at that moment is sadly beyond my comprehension, though I assumed something masonic without an additional need of rolling up my trouser leg.

Boys brigade ended in a bit of Gaz created disorder when I was around 12. There was a fellow there called Mr Lindsey who I found to be a little weird and we would clash from time to time, pure projection on my part of course. Most of the time I found myself obsessing about how he would always have white stuff forming at the sides of his mouth and this just bugged me out. Our clashes caused me to not want to go to BB anymore and in fear of my father (who as an ex soldier saw me in a uniform as a ray of hope to his struggling parenting), I thought I would create a small... white... lie to avoid my father pressuring me. I thought it appropriate to suggest that said Brigade leader had touched me in a way a man shouldn't touch a boy. I perhaps over shot there since I had not thought through the fact that my parents would now need to challenge him on said kiddie fiddling and they actually did. Parents - please don't pressure your kids, it makes them do some really stupid shit.

Anyways, this is a long build up to me highlighting some God ordained 'dropping me in it', since on my very first adult venture to church and turning from the street into a Sunday service, who should I meet eye to eye with but Mr Lindsey. He graciously shook my hand as he was on duty as the welcoming committee and said, " I feel we have met before and perhaps have crossed swords", which is Baptist pirate speak for 'you were a little bugger'. I think I got off lightly.

Foundations
Intro Part Deux:

As we began our early married life with a baby and moving between bedsits and local temporary social housing (deliberately crap conditions to check you're actually homeless and not faking it), we eventually found ourselves in an actual liveable home on a housing estate. This recent move was aided by my showing up at the local council offices with a press cutting from the previous day with the headlines; 'Arson Attack by Disgruntled Tenant' and pointing to the bedroom window above the burned out shell stating 'this is our room'. Our bedsit floor had felt just a little bit more toasty than normal as we were going to bed the previous night.

In our new home, I began that classic Christian journey of asking, "what is my calling?" It had to be dynamic, clearly spiritual and profound because, as we all know, normal work, simply isn't sacred enough, whether it was me as the then supermarket manager or perhaps you, a teacher, doctor or mother.

I really felt that my focus would be helping people get out of cults, pretty random I know. I really liked the language of detoxing or deprogramming and other aspects that would be involved in seeing people re-centre themselves, recover, and move forward. It seemed like a real 'something' and so I spent a good amount of time exploring cults, which ended abruptly when a matriarch of a large Roma family moved into the house behind us. This was followed by neighbours of three houses either side of us swapping council homes with the matriarchs family members. Suddenly, we found ourselves in the middle house of 4 related families which ranged from a well spoken house proud family with all the lace and frills of wonderful tradition of the Roma on one side, to the other side of us Robbie (name changed), a snaggle toothed Elvis impersonator (really). Urine soaked mattresses would be thrown into the back garden as new ones came in the front. Robbie would wash the dog crap from the two Lurcher hunting dogs from the children's feet in the kiddie play pool. He also stole our front garden, moving the fence to under our window so they could park their car off road. (we eventually got this back when they moved and I pointed out the flowers in our new neighbours garden were ours). I am clearly now meant to be working with Roma families and become what I was to later be called by one of the family; you 'is' a God man', but no, just a passing season of intrigue, learning, resilience and torment.

I think it's where I first discovered hyper vigilance, an aspect of PTSD, where you are constantly ready for something to 'kick off'. In this case, anticipating a confrontation and punch up. I watched as a group of males would run up to a removal truck, leap into the air and head butt it as high as they could, seeing who could make the highest dent. For the larger part it was a deeply enriching experience of a different culture and just plain bloody stressful. Greece can produce similar feelings just leaving your front door because so many people are angry about something.

Of all these seemingly oven-ready callings, our path instead led to becoming part of a large local youth work team working across two housing estates with the support of Youth With A Mission (YWAM) a discipleship training and mission's body helping us make a few less blunders. I'm going to skim that whole period of time though in truth, it is worthy of its own book. We learned a lot in that period as we sought to use the principles of cross-cultural mission to view young people as an unreached (unsupported) people group, tribe and tongue. We planted youth church into Rave culture and eventually found ourselves in the city running a community out of a bar in an attempt to be visible, culturally relevant, and at the same time, have a bloody good time ourselves. It is with great pride that I remember during the youth work phase, the local council safety officer throwing us out of the village hall (our rave home) due to causing structural damage from our 5,000 watt, 9 foot stacks of speakers - cummon!!

Perhaps one thing learned from that period which will keep us all in good stead: Beware the inclination to present yourselves as having a 'New Blueprint For The Church' or as we called ours, when we moved to the city bar: 'Bliss – A Brand New Flava For Ya Soul'. Don't go saying this stuff when in reality, all you did was move houses and adjust the inherited furniture, regardless of how others may applaud your seemingly radical approach. It was well intended, but it's not always healthy to believe that God trusted your gang 'with the new thing', or re-discovering an old anointed thing, you know the one, the mythical original we continue to pursue blindly because it doesn't exist. It taught others and me many things; one was **the pervasive nature of church world pseudo sacred culture and its control**. To explore beyond this structure and culture, even though we did not venture far, felt like we had climbed a mountain, and cost us all considerably to stretch the bungee that far. The motivation and desire was noble, it was embracing change for relevance, to us, and those we sought to engage with and a deeply appreciate those who pushed 'outward' alongside of us. I think those early explorations into cults, control, life and outcomes limiting inherited cultures, meant that my bursting out of organised Christianity was an inevitability, a soon to become painful re-birth.

Having read back through the above, I think I am meant to say a little bit more about me 'doing stuff', as if to qualify myself to join the conversation in some way or to get you to believe that I've been around. It's not going to help at all for those who already have their hand on their positional theological gun, so here is a bit called:

I've Been Around Doing Stuff ;-) - Kind Of...

My school education pretty much prepared kids for work in a factory or to join the army or generally 'middle' tasks. I think my first jobs were far more psychologically scarring than any childhood trauma, after all it is our first grown up place of working out who we are in proximity to others. After selling my soul to the supermarket devils, I found that I didn't die when I left the job of retail management, that there was life beyond the shop doors. Just in the same way that there is life beyond the church doors.

After several years I eventually went from the supermarket to doing community youth work with my wife and then church planting in some trendy form or another. Having left the congregational world behind in 2000, I was feeling very loved when someone chose to help support me financially for my work across town supporting projects (I was less enamoured by the church cleaning job which topped up our income). I spent seven or so years helping to find and fund grassroots projects thanks to a dynamic rich fellow who wanted to empower people and their visions beyond the limiting controls of the congregations. He also wanted to support projects, which involved people from more than one church to ensure that it remained a story about people, not how clever your congregation is. I got to be part of a national team where we were, by the time I left doing this work across forty towns and cities, giving a very local team a bucket of money and love to distribute in non-controlling ways. Money is power. It affirms position and narrative and it was good to try and get a handle on this early on, so that any power we did have, was to remain as footprints along the shore, quickly washed away by the next wave. Indeed on occasions simply saying, "here is some money, now how can we help or encourage you" was enough to kill some of the power dynamic though you can never ever really kill it completely.

Alongside this, I began to work with a small group of local people in my town on Counter Human Trafficking efforts having had a productive 'shared burden' conversation in a pub with mates (Steve and Marie) over a few beers. I was especially struck by how we looked at each other and said 'what do each of us bring to the table that's useful' as a real sense of using our already accessible resources. Four months later, we were working with an organisation in Moldova to launch a regular prevention magazine as a Trojan horse for exposing trafficking recruitment strategies. This magazine went into schools and colleges for under 18's deemed to be the most unaware and most at risk from recruitment and exploitation. This magazine later received government recognition as a youth development tool. I'm grateful for the 'Beginning of Life' group there for partnering us and continuing the work long after we left, just as they had long before we arrived.

So yeah, I believe Margaret Mead when she said, "*never doubt that a small group of thoughtful, committed citizens can change the world, indeed it is the only thing that ever has.*"

From there I got picked up by a US based counter child trafficking organisation called Love146 to help establish their work in Europe, which brought me to Greece at the epicentre of European trafficking and exploitative people movement across its borders. As it turned out most of the Love146 founding team were ex YWAM'ers working out of a mainstream project, which was pretty progressive.

Currently, we spend a chunk of our time in Greece. My wife helps in a community kitchen, which prepares up to 1,000 meals a day, free for anyone one who needs it. Co-operatively working alongside an amazing team of volunteers from many nations. She also helps clothe people through a funky free shop where refugees can come and choose clothing and hygiene items.

As for me, I give therapeutic support to volunteers who are burning out and advice to organisations on strategy and addressing internal culture, which is stopping them from achieving their objectives. I also do plumbing and other odd jobs, whatever the work need. I occasionally try to encourage Greek believers to explore new 'ways' but they are stubborn little beauties who will find their own path. I have helped refugee communities trying to make life work in squats, both practically, with buckets of love and doing parties as a DJ as my alter ego Mr Prof. Our squat community was 'Clandestina' and long after the armed police raid and the displacement of its occupants, we still consider many to be part of our extended family and visa versa.

I got to set up a Northern Soul Club in Athens with friends and found myself doing dance lessons which came rather out of the blue. I put one of the lessons on you tube and have 153,000 hits so far, not too shabby for an old fart.

I have travelled quite a bit but mostly with a purpose since as my wife will tell you, I'm a terrible tourist. I'm motivated to travel when I can work with emerging communities, trying to not repeat the cycle of building a construct or with individuals dreaming of life beyond the congregation. Sadly, in my travelling I have also had to see how inhumane people can be, in the commercial sexual exploitation of children.

Occasionally (rarely), I get up to speak which isn't really my thing, as I prefer qualitative cups of coffee and beers with people. In those 'speaking' settings where people get introduced as an 'expert' on something, I have to quickly demolish this idea by saying an 'EX' is a has been, and a 'SPURT' is something that happens quickly and is soon gone, so no, I'm not an expert, I am a co learner.

Oh and I've totally burned out three times over the years, once as a church leader, once during my third year of trying to study as a counsellor and in more recent years due to my inability to cope with our family table of six becoming empty as they grew up and left. These times were totally unravelling and I wouldn't wish them on anyone, I was the last person I thought would ever lose their shit but they were also opportunities to deal with old wounds so overall, I am grateful. I would say with my hand on my heart that I'm recovered now and am exploring the world through a different lens of 'I Am Well' instead of the debilitating idea that I walk with a limp, scars though are different since they speak of battles and healing.

I wish the same shift in self-perception for you as you read this book, of being free and of being well.

That's me. Welcome to my world, the much larger one that I found outside of the church doors.

Starting At The End - The Last Chapter

I was going to put a chapter in here at this point, a kind of a bombing run before you've heard the air raid siren warning you to head off to the shelter. But, I think it's too heavy as a starting point. Also, it is a long one, because it is a blow-by-blow overview of behaviours, practices and roles within Cults. I think I wrote it to challenge church leaders to understand that almost everything they do and say has a power dynamic for good or for ill. That all of our practices should be held gently and with a degree of caution, lest we control, wound and create a cultural trap. In that chapter we take a look at cultic practices, all of which exist within our normal everyday church world experience. But, I've decided to put that chapter in at the end. If you make it to that point, you can choose to read it or not.

I am about to start the book. What will follow are observations, ideas I have given names, and at times, had to create language for to make better sense of. I have also borrowed helpful reference points from fellow travellers, because we are not the only ones leaving organised Christianity behind and as such, there is learning to be explored with one another. My hope is that this helps you discover language and reference points, which make sense to you, reflect some of your own experience and dis-ease with the Church as an organisation. I hope to show how it holds goodness in one hand and irrevocable 'life and outcomes limiting culture' in the other, behaviour which hinders you from becoming an adult, full grown and healthily independent (self actualised as Maslow calls it).

Oh crap... here we go!

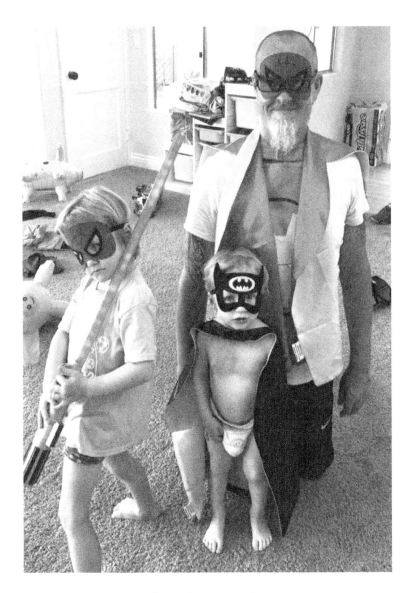

Brandon – Spencer - Grampy
Masters Of A Universe Somewhere!

Chapter 1

The Church of Elsewhere &

The Outward Journey

I used to have this concept where if I went and stood in certain historical places I would somehow supernaturally catch some of what was going on there, what those faithful folks from the past had represented and carried, a kind of divine infection. I've stood and prayed at John Wesley's statue where he began a sect, which would form Methodism in Savannah Georgia. I have photos somewhere of him holding a prayer stick, which I took on my travels and snuck into his extended hand when no one was watching. I've stood in a crater in woods in Texas where Keith Green's plane crashed and knelt at Leonard Ravenhill's resting place and other such well-intentioned weirdness. I guess I thought I was some kind of Jesus ghost hunter in the hope of connecting with some ancient anointing or some continuity of what happened there. Like some strange kind of pilgrimage, playing the part of a bee, collecting spiritual pollen to share. I don't want you to think I travel to death places, these were just things I felt a pull towards while in certain countries.

I'm aware that I've already said Jesus a few times; I hope it's not an irritant to a sore place for anyone.

Nothing in this book is trying to convert, re convert and there's no subtle conversion therapy, thank god... oh shit, now I've said god ... ;-)

So, I had a lovely friend called Zoe who signed up for a discipleship and mission's programme that allowed you to make suggestions of where you would want to move for a period of active mission. She wanted to join a dynamic bunch doing education in schools on England's south coast, but instead she woke up to see a cow outside her bedroom window in another country called Wales. Amazingly, this became a place she would stay and journey with people for more than a decade. The Jesus followers there were a prayerful, prophetically sensitive bunch called Antioch Fellowship in Llanelli. At times their prophetic insights were put into video format to be passed around the country like yeast. I liked their symbolism a lot, like this one that was a print of the sole of a boot saying **'dreams with tread on for new terrain'**. Their voice was an emergent one and soul food for those becoming dislodged from life limiting inherited thinking. I think this notion resonated with people because it rejected any idea that they had already arrived. It suggested that the journey was on-going and that we needed to prepare for new things. Perhaps the boots with fresh tread indicated that it was going to be a long walk out, in, and through the creation and its life spheres.

I felt I needed to connect with what they were about. I loved it when we got to pray together. I also loved walking down the steps of a local river where many hundreds would have queued during their historical revival to be immersed in the makeshift baptismal. I wanted some of the history to be carried on my feet and maybe take a few stones from the pool to put in my pocket. However, since they were a creative bunch, it would end up being one of their prophetic, poetic videos which would impact me the most and adhere itself like transformative glue to my journey.

'Outreach Language Reveals That We Operate Out Of 'Two Worlds' Thinking, Since You Can Only Outreach To A Place Which You Have Removed Yourself From'

The premise was that God had placed Jesus as head of his church, his body, which was the fullness of him 'in' and through the creation. ("And God put all things under Jesus' feet and gave him as head over all things to the church, which is his body, the fullness of him who fills all in all.") There are various versions and all speak of integration and immersion in the life places.
#jesusiseverywhereinfullmeasurewithus

It was a visit to those verses, which brought out the sense that the body was the mobile, integrated aspect of God through all things, through the creation and through the life and work spheres. This imagery seemed to be the opposite of church as I knew it and the one that dominates the landscape. What I saw all around me was what I had for a long time referred to as the Church of Elsewhere. Perhaps I can qualify that statement a little more by saying I had experienced several group settings where I would ask those gathered what they considered to be the spheres of society, each time it would be the same answers; education, healthcare, business, family, others and always church. The problem for me here is that it was my firm belief that "church" was never to occupy a sphere of its own, but instead, have fully embedded itself as participants in all of life's actual spheres. Simply said, the church, which is a people, should have remained in all of the actual spheres of life and society. The challenge, or should I say challenging question in the video was **'what does it mean to be the fullness of him in and through education?** (cue teacher's voice), healthcare? (cue doctor's voice), gypsy sites (cue Roma voice) etc?

This is a question I continue to ask myself, and perhaps one we could all explore concerning immersion into society through life and work.

I'm talking about integration here, a million miles from Dominionism, a thoroughly spurious, contrived notion based on power and position, or what I like to call, the opposite of Jesus in every way. I am pretty convinced that the Jesus person listens to Dominionists and thinks 'where the heck did they dig that rubbish up' as he shakes his head. Yeast was always an active ingredient, but just that, part of, not on top of. Dominionists have a theology that God wants Christians in all of the seats of power such as Government, a politicising of biblical narratives, the outworking of which is deeply counter to the nature of the Jesus person in every way.

We Messed Up The Collective

I used to be immersed in town wide church and pastors networks that I foolishly felt were a gathering of those charged with reaching and transforming our locality, towns and cities. I loved the idea of the Unity of the Body, the whole body, the church as God sees it. I would probably use the word solidarity these days, unity around a purpose. I worked hard on this stuff, which in retrospect, was well intended but ultimately a flawed strategy. As a friend said much better than I could, ' **We cannot create unity, we already have unity in Christ, we just need to stop_doing the things which separate us off from one another!**'.

What else could you expect from someone with the surname 'Love'.

Take A Moment, Pause Reflect On The Above.

At one such pastors gathering, after the ritual of the male voice choir worship session was complete, I was allowed to ask a question:

"Do we believe that our missiology informs our ecclesiology?"
That those we wish to be present for and love in 'the mission', shapes and informs how we 'do church'? Almost everyone nodded, in that 'but of course' kind of affirming what a 'stupid question' manner.

I then asked, *"Who of us has inherited an ecclesiology which directly limits our mission?"* ... I took the following silence to be an answer in and of it self.
It is problematic that we are operating out of something, which, even to our own thinking, is so foundationally conflicted and flawed.

'Thinking outside the box is not necessary once you lose the box'

The leader of the pastors network, a much respected man called Dave, once gave me a sound bit of wisdom; **'If we do what we always did – we get what we always got!'** – which quite frankly, isn't enough. His softly spoken Scottish accent still survives as a formative voice in my head. As someone who was working hard on the impossible task of bringing our institutions closer together, I am not sure he realizes what a critical role he played in my moving away from said restraints, nor how affirming his tolerance of me was as I began to advocate for things removed from his own experiences and perhaps theology. I think we were both aware of the imperfections and the flaws in our selves and in our ideas. I feel we managed to connect as people first, not our roles, and this was precious. Once over a cup of tea and some shortbread (very Scottish), we had a philosophical conversation where I was saying that I don't have any more energy to invest in changing a seemingly immovable object, church as organisation.

My heart had always been to see the church change. It was the only reason I ever considered taking on a pastor's role. My observation of church as an organisation was that it keeps **pinning its hopes on the next self-**

referencing book, that would help them deliver the changes the previous book had promised, but failed to deliver (press repeat).

I remember saying that I guessed he had seen the church go through 40 years of incremental, manageable adjustments already, instead of significant change to itself, so that it could finally become an agent of change in society. I didn't doubt that he had paid a considerable price for any and all changes he had sought to bring. I said that if this was the case, I'm not going to be sticking around. His answer, I felt, was deeply honest, "Yes, I am afraid that I agree with you, the church is likely to opt for another 40 years of incremental adjustments".

Often the biggest change seems to happen at that organisation's inception. The change, which required a group of brave people to break with the old, and explore the new, embracing and outworking what had been lacking. But sadly after this initial change, more change is rare and difficult to implement. Have we inherited a system that is capable of this kind of change? Change, which can see its primary function as supporting the Jesus followers to come to fullness in all the spheres of society? Has it managed this so far?

In my experience and also sadly in my practices, what we are good at is the opposite, as we recruit, praise and prepare people for work IN the service.

When church occupies its own sphere as it does currently, with it's building, its own world and orbit, it can only truly focus energy on perpetuating its own existence. It's priority becomes equipping a small percentage of the saints for works 'in' the service/organisation, instead of serving the vast majority who are unsupported as they stand in, and through, the creation (perhaps still waiting for a call to the seemingly sacred roles of pastor, youth worker, community worker, house group leader, missionary).

There was an excellent Willy Wonka post that was circulating last year that said:

"You Say The Building Isn't The Church, **But** *You Keep Calling That Building The Church."*

Covid was fascinating in this regard, allowing Wonka to become the wise elder of the moment. As churches across the globe sought to retain their members through online services, many were seen to say, *'Don't be afraid, church is still happening, church is also the people, not the building'.* The only thing wrong with that statement was the word 'also'.

The thing that excites me most about a different paradigm is that, if there is no separated off from life 'Church of Elsewhere', then there is no leadership and no ministry gifts of elsewhere.

Instead, we find those roles helping people come to fullness in all the glorious diversity of where God has placed them to be lovers, friends, creatives and participants in life. Suddenly, I feel hope that we can actually find ourselves engaged in systemic change in the world around us, more than topically treating the suffering, those broken systems create. What makes me despair is, that it takes that misplaced sphere of church to take on a John the Baptist mantle and become willing to decrease so that what is coming can increase. I don't mean more manageable, incremental or minor adjustments. I don't think the church has any capacity to entertain the idea that it might need to diminish in a kind of 'good being the enemy of something better' way. (That's a bible verse, which outlines a principle that it is possible for one significant moment, to give way to another more dynamic one)

It has to be a significant mind-blowing paradigm shift, and explosive change. Alternatively, it goes into the ground, or that the body, us, simply begins to stand in all of those awesome, life happening, glorious places that church as a construct is not. Those places where the farmer can't come out with his shotgun and shout 'Oi You, Get Off My Land' as some church leaders and Christian organisations do. I speak from experience having begun to develop an anti trafficking work in Greece and being asked outright 'what are you doing here and why have you not told us' by another group 500 miles way. Territorial extreme! This is a dislocation where we each need to avoid the pressure to pop it back into the socket. In reality it's a blessing that the church is in a container aside from society, since it means you can go and stand pretty much anywhere, freely far from the influence and destructive criticism or emotional absence of the church organisation

Welcome to the church of where you are, in the creation, where the earth has been crying out for the sons and daughters of God to reveal themselves.

'When we look outward and seek to engage with society, we should do so with humility and not a trumpet call hailing that we have arrived. Not unless you are equally willing to repent of your late arrival due to having spent several hundred years inside singing songs.' anon

The Art Of Killing Something Alive

I've been thinking back to our housing estate Anglican church, where I learned a profound lesson at the hands of an invasive red-headed New Zealander who seemed to have lost all sense of boundaries. He was part of a team hired into the three churches of what was called a team ministry, the parent church and its latter insecure babies (plants). They had come from YWAM at Liverpool's School Of Church Planting with the task of doing an audit. It is something I had never heard of but value deeply as I find myself increasingly doing similar organisational audits.

It looked like this:

-Meet with the current leaders and get a sense of the current landscape.

-Meet past leaders to assess any damage or repeating cycles of dysfunction they may have become subject to.

-Meet with some of the members and find out how things were stacking up for them at ground level and if there were any concerns.

-Take a detailed look at the vision of why any of these three churches came into existence.

-Take the temperature of whether things were on track, if they had changed the vision, improving it or dropping the ball along with any timeline measurements of progress.

I was employed as a youth worker at the time and the thought of external people being invited to see what has been swept under the carpet was both rare and exciting. Essentially, anyone faking it was probably feeling nervous at the time and anyone with imposter syndrome began feeling especially anxious and worried. I didn't know it was going to go down like this but each of the three churches would have a member of the visiting auditors summarise their findings on a Sunday with freedom to speak, as they wanted. I mentioned the red head with no boundaries, because he began to pace up and down the aisles looking at people causing a few bottoms to wriggle in seats, including mine. I felt we should have had a little bit of a warning that this stranger was going to break some rules.

It was a little, like the day my daughter Holly forgot her lunchbox, she was around 6 years old at the time and so I popped across the road to take it into her classroom.
It was one of the modern schools in a circle with all the classes facing outwards to the playground and requiring me to walk past several rooms to reach my objective. Unknown to me, the previous day a safety officer had spoken at the school assembly talking about 'stranger danger' both in terms of safety out of the school and on the premises. Sadly, this resulted in several children obediently disrupting lessons with pointed fingers in my direction and shouting 'STRANGER' as I quickened my pace, adding further suspicion. To finally crush my will to live, I held up my daughter's lunch box, having caught her attention, only for her to lift up a different lunch box she took to school that day. I felt a total idiot and had my young daughter been aware of such words, she would have confirmed them. I digress, but I'm sitting there in this church meeting I am pretty sure more than a few peoples insides were screaming 'Stranger Danger!'

What was said?

"There's a bad smell in this place (add NZ accent), something is stinking up the place and it's been around so long that you no longer even smell it. There are some dead things here which need to be let go of and be buried, which will need you to stop kicking them hoping for signs of life. There are some things here which need to die, and the problem is you don't know how to put something into the ground when it is still has signs of life and so you have stuff going on here which is in the way of progress and better things.

I mean, that's a pretty bloody awesome start to a talk in a middle class white church that felt they knew shit. What I got from that is this critical aspect of learning, that we don't in fact know how to put something to death when it is long past it's 'sell by date' and as a consequence, it remains a critical hurdle for any progress at all, especially for institutions to move forward or simply move. To this day, I'm not aware of any actions or changes taking place as a result of the audits findings.

What's around for you at the moment in the church world if you're still a participant?
Is there anything, which is stinking up the place and needs to have a funeral?
Is there anything which just continues as part of the cultural norm, but is getting in the way of progress and as such, needs discernment and real strength of will to put it to death?

This was a theme I shared in a community in Sheffield, where I told them to adopt the principle of the Greek plate smashing, that was before I had even been to Greece. My suggestion was that you have likely taken things from the food selection, which look good, smell good, and you hope tastes good. There is often so much more at the buffet to experience. Sometimes in real life, what church as a construct or what we as people have on our plate has lost its taste. We keep it there feeling guilty that we chose something that looks great but tastes pretty bad, causing us shame, and stopping us from going back for more. Perhaps we need to

ɩ the plate, even if there is still stuff on it, and ask for a
‿‿ᴜ‖ plate to go graze the buffet again and try something
clsc. It isn't best practice to simply keep doing something
when the moment, the season, the attraction to it has passed,
and you are now simply in programmed 'maintenance mode'.
The Church world is full of people deeply committed to stuff,
who have lost their ability to consider if they should even still
be there.
What is the plate you need to smash?

The Heart Of The Issue

I was told once that the heart of the issue is often an issue of
the heart. We can be pretty protective of ourselves as we
move away from the church as an organisation. This is in part
because we anticipate or experience a considerable amount
of rejection, judgement and criticism. Sadly, if you're moving
towards 'more' life beyond the current machinery, this is a
fire that you simply have to walk through. As you come
through and out the other side you will find yourself
discovering love and grace towards those who remain (less
so the abusers). However, until you find your own feet,
rediscover God in the creation 24/7 or have left it all behind,
you are likely to be looking over your shoulder to some
degree, anticipating the invisible but present stalker, your
accuser and carrying a need to justify yourself. There is
something deeply wrong in church world for so many to fear
being told it's not ok to leave. Worse still is that they need to
give a reason, which will be acceptable to someone in
authority.
It's a good job that we are justified through faith and it's a
faith in ourselves along with feeling that there is going to be
more life ahead - which eventually moves our feet.

"With An Unravelling, Comes A Revealing"

I am not looking to get people 'out', unless you want to get
out. If that's you, then it doesn't have to feel like your losing

42

your mind, that your insides will never untangle or that guilt will remain your closest companion.

I am not anti church as an organisation, I am not against it like it's the on-going focal point of my activism, **I simply no longer give it the name Church, which it has so confidently awarded to itself.** I'm not even sure what that thing is anymore. A mate said to me, 'whoever gets the name church wins!' What he meant by this was, once you have built your establishment, erected your remixed version of what you were in before, (something old, something new, something borrowed, something blue), agree to the mission statement, and have the sign over the door, you now occupy a space of elitist superiority. Having arrived and ticked all of your inherited legitimising boxes you can finally state 'We Are Now A Church' and nobody can say otherwise. Probably because literally anyone can start one.

The outward flow or bungee cutting of many in these days is actually more towards the unknown than the known, and certainly not towards a destination of absolutes, which is why people tend to reference what they are participating in as **a journey.** Don't get me wrong; I'm not saying I don't see colour or I don't see gender, which is a foolish way of trying to not be racist or sexist. I do very much see the church, but as a human construct rooted to the landscape with their gravitational pull of people towards them like a tractor beam (I didn't say the death star, did you think of the death star? That's entirely your fault if you thought that LOL).

Ultimately, I do not like what I see, what it does, and what it does not do.

Standing in the space, breathing a different air, exploring faith, perhaps for the first time, and not what was handed to you pre-packaged, it all tends to heal the abuse as you simply keep moving forwards and towards a far less known spot on the horizon. It's ok to follow your senses, perceptions or simply the end of your nose in the direction of something that is smelling good. It's not about writing a thesis on what you will find there or a book at each and every stage of discovery shouting 'This Is It' - like MJ. It's certainly not about writing a book about somewhere you haven't gone yet, projecting yourself as an authority on the new. I like to think that's not what I'm doing. I'm instead attempting to leave the 'what's next' entirely in your capable hands.

"We have to get post rebellion, where we are no longer being driven by what it is we are moving away from, but by what it is we are moving towards"
James Thwaites.

As I've been writing, I'm online video chatting with another ex pastor friend who is also taking stock of some of the misinformation we have preached. My wife is in the other room shouting over the top of my voice, "20 years, 20 years, can you imagine if we had stayed in that stuff for another 20 years? I'm so glad to not be in that stuff!" Not having church as construct in my job description anymore has given us freedom, not only not being in it, but also not looking in my rear view mirror constantly with memories haunting me and learned behaviours limiting me.

I can say this next bit because it's not just me, it's also a story common to some of the people I have walked with; My life simply got better when my actual parents died! There was pain and loss and grieving, but my capacity for life and other things grew significantly. The reason for this is that I was no longer emotionally tethered to them nor parenting the parents, in hope they would become the parents I needed, to give me what I should have had, to grow and be the person I could/should have been. It is a sad but true comparison that it is freeing, not to keep investing in something which is likely incapable of change, waiting for it to become as it should or could have been so you yourself can be fully alive. Progress exists beyond this and some of us are just too damn movement orientated to stick around.

"Time and time again, when people who have left the church construct tell me they have lost their faith. What we quickly discover is that they are simply 'working it out' as was the original idea"

44

THE FOLD
A Dedication - Lovely Savannah

Chapter 2

Shepherding the Field

The year was 1993, I was told that I had a face like a slapped arse when Roger and Sue Mitchel prayed a Pastoral anointing over me. To me, this anointing seemed like I'd been given a 'Mrs Miggins Pie Shop' printed tea towel during a secret Santa instead of one of the good presents. The notion of anointing sounded pretty cool but nothing of the title "pastor" spoke of daring adventure or dynamism.

The last three years of my life in organised Christianity were spent as pastor of our ragamuffin crew of co-workers and people we had helped navigate away from the institutionalism of church, only to find that, to me, we had only travelled a few metres from such ideas. It's pretty common to think you've built something entirely new when in reality you've only moved the cultural and religious furniture around. 'This new lounge feels wonderfully different', an improvement for people who came along with us, an improvement on past less creative contexts, yes it was certainly an upgrade.
It took a beautiful human being from YWAM called Jeff Pratt showing up to hammer down the final nail in the coffin. He was one of those troubling empathic Jesus types who asks

real questions, ones where the wild horses of feelings stampede to your mouth and you share where things are really at. ``How's things with you guys?" he would ask. ``Awful" I'd reply, "we are burned out and feel total fakes, do we wait to be found out or just confess that we can't really do people right now?" A common symptom of burnout is withdrawal.

We had considered stepping back for a few months now, a 'smiling face handover' and polite process masking the trauma. Jeff asked, "How long do you have left in you"... Our answer was suddenly ``two weeks!" An answer that came from the raw truth that escaped out from under the disguises of responsibility and reason. But, I would not discover for another decade that it was simply the wrong context, the fold. We had overstayed beyond our shelf life and my memory of it is that we left with our hair on fire, running for the nearest fire extinguisher. You get to a point where some things just finish you off.

It was disappointing to sit with an alleged 'apostolic' support person who has come in to help, asking you to stick around for a checklist process of a handover. My response was, "I know how this should go, but I've got nothing left so simply cannot". I'm then hit with some classic controlling proof texting bullshit of "For him who knows what he should do, but does not do it, then for him it is sin".' Oh Fark Awff!!!' - but I didn't say that, I just cried and experienced further emotional trauma at the hands of a someone projecting positional insight but actually just being a product of the system with little to no empathy. I've met so many people over the years who are waiting for someone else, to recognise they are hanging on by their finger nails and just not in a place to say out loud that I'm 'fucked'.

A young lady in Athens who has been working in refugee camps for several years posted on Facebook recently for all to read, *" dear friends, please don't tell me about anyone in a crisis, or in need, or in hospital without being able to tell me the whole story. I now have PTSD and these things are very triggering to me".* I wasn't this brave or mature sadly, but I was also part of church where not all honesty is welcome.

Our having gone from a team of 14 full time volunteers in the youth work to only two of the old guard sharing an office and running a church full time and transitioning leadership took too much of a toll. The co-founder /previous leader and I were both very different animals and not natural bedfellows. I think the breakdown in our relationship was perhaps inevitable, at times our viewing things from different perspectives was deeply eroding, no doubt for both of us. For less thick skinned sensitive Gaz it contributed significantly to my heading for the door, along with an accumulation of other stuff you pick up when you no longer feel safe to be known and are descending into pastor syndrome (head down arse up getting on with it).

In the chapter **Unconditional Love - Conscious and Unconscious Positions**, I unpack some of the complex dynamics and interplay between leaders and followers, parent figures and those who have initially found a place of rest and recovery with someone as I did, only to find that those roles become unable to transition well for both parties and essentially become counter productive, life limiting, and increasingly broken.

I've empathised greatly with others now that I understand just how difficult it is to confront and challenge significant others when they are getting things wrong or simply missing 'it', whatever 'it' implies. Those who occupy seats of privilege and power afforded them by followers will often find themselves trying to fight their way out of a corner, armed with little ability to own that things are going wrong. Perhaps our platforming of people as heroes of the age, as keepers of the flame and the primary story tellers, all contributes to the culture of fear of being known, human and fallible, where anyone is capable of royally fucking up, me along with the rest of them.

I am much more able to look back with empathy and understanding as to how some of it played out. We thought we were going to radically impact a shift in church culture in the 90's. We had people affirming that God had put us together for such a purpose and yet, for much of it, we were kids getting to play adults. External groups telling you repeatedly that you're the dog's bollocks is affirming but contributes to self delusion as well, so in the words of Public Enemy; "Don't Believe The Hype... Don't, Don't, Don't, Believe The Hype."

Brother Beyond

It's really interesting to begin again, to re-explore life beyond the familiar reference points, and to explore what is transferable from church world or what should be left behind as remaining only relevant there. I would like to suggest that this dislodging from the known, and the inherited, was just me continuing to follow the Jesus person. At no point was it born out of a desire to leave this thing called church, especially cool bar church. This was a continuance, my on going exploration. It was a revelation to me what constraints I have had to cast off along the way to have a continued journey. This was a conflicted time for me as I was trying to live more holistically, moving forward, and not looking to pull church apart as an ideology. I've continued that forward focus for more than 20 years and now find it is time to pass some comments on that system primarily because I see it restricting peoples potential and for some, actually doing harm.

What Comes With Us?

My first formal meeting in our main context of Athens to discuss 'child protection from exploitation' would set the scene for most of our time spent there. I met a young lady in a coffee shop to discuss doing a workshop on human trafficking and exploitation and fifteen minutes into the conversation she became emotional, talking about burn out along with other conflicts and dysfunctions in the team and project. I had nothing but empathy for her, but also hope for her personally and the work, having been through such poop. Have you ever felt made for a moment? I felt like the accumulation of everything I had done, every season I had walked through, my dislodging from inherited thinking and structures was for this.

I simply said. "I can help with that, I can help with all of that if you let me".

Since that moment I have been working with grassroots projects, workers, leaders, and founders in what I can only refer to as helping people, come to fullness in terms of ability and identity, employing some of what I experienced when those church auditors used honest reflection to hold an uncomfortable and helpful mirror in front of us.

I help to identify challenge and uproot 'life and outcomes limiting structures and organisational cultures'. Read that again, it's quite a long tagline, but I think it sums up so many issues faced by people and projects. It's worth mentioning that none of the projects that I currently work with are faith based and so I find it amusing that my understanding of dysfunction and the need for change came from church world but could not be 'realised' there.

Around two years ago I found myself in the north of Greece hanging out with some people at a youth gathering and with some folks from YWAM. I like people from YWAM, and having done their discipleship in my early days of faith, I like to think I can smell them out, that they have a particular DNA or have passed through a cultural context making them focus a little more upon coming alongside others.

I had been observing this bearded guy who had come from the USA to work with the gang there. He seemed inseparable from his guitar, as though at any moment he might be called to lead the people in a song or that divine inspiration would have to be captured in song writing. As such, my inner grumpy old man had determined this was someone I was not looking to spend time with. During this trip I had nowhere to stay for one of the nights, and was given the opportunity to stay with an intern in the YWAM accommodation, only to find that it was this guy.

I thought to myself, 'well that's just sods law isn't it' which is essentially code for not being able to avoid this guy you're avoiding and knowing there's likely something to be learned there.

As it was, we ended up praying for one another in his kitchen for an hour after having a strangely honest and deep conversation for two strangers. I had some words of insight for him and he had some for me, as though we were sharing sandwiches with one another from our intuitive lunch boxes. What he said to me was, "you are pastoral, you are a shepherd", to which I replied, "yes I am!" It seemed a reversal of my rejection of the term when I had been prayed for some 25 years before. The reason for the turn around? Context!

I don't encourage people to reconfigure old Christian roles and labels in a new place as I want to encourage people to normalise and integrate, but for me it was important coming from a leadership context, to identify what those kind of roles look like in the real world alongside people, not stuck in a building waiting for people to come to me. Also I no longer work with Christians, I work with people, whatever their worldview or beliefs might be, so old labels are pretty useless. I have found that 'values connections' trump faith connection for me these days, where I can gather with anyone around justice, standing between the oppressed and the oppressor, and seeking to challenge systems, which fail people.

It is in this 'field', I can finally accept the words 'pastoral and shepherd'. I include this to say that my caring role has been re-imagined in a new and better fitting context. Though, what I am really trying to say is that I have found myself to be a more life engaged and integrated follower of the Jesus person in my own personal outlook and spirituality. Everything, which is both right and wrong about organised Christianity, has prepared me to arrive here and be useful. Having said this, it is my current opinion that very little of organised Christianity can help me stand here. It is not the well that I drink from, nor the context of my learning.

I have deeply embedded myself amongst those who have not needed to re enter the land nor have come from such an alternative universe as the church. They have only, always, dwelled fully in the creation, responding to its groans as the visible children.

I have undergone an immersion, a re-baptism back into culture, back into society alongside a much more inclusive Integrated people. The reality of those I see, and what they do, screams to me that these were their works, prepared in advance for them to do at their conception (a bible reference concept concerning each having a purpose). What I mean is I am around people, mostly of no faith, though many are spiritual, and you can tell from every part of their being, they were made for this stuff, this moment, and for a great many other things I am sure. I know there is no kingless kingdom in our 'Christian speak', but I cannot ever say they do not flow from the same king, the same source as I (as one still identifying as a follower of the Jesus person). I get to stand with ordinary extraordinary people in solidarity. People who are simply 'getting on with it'.

My days of being on the inside looking out are over. This is the field and it is a space full of boots with tread on, comfortable shoes with your name on.

THE FIELD
My Beautiful Afghan God Daughter
'Maria' Day 1

Chapter 3

Leadership Paralysis

& The Death Of Submission

When I stepped out of congregational leadership and away from the church as a construct (human creation), I didn't step fully out of the church world. Freeing myself and my energy from attempting to build the organisation, enabled me to **spend a lot more time in 'the space'.**
Space is a term used by people exploring new ideas, new projects or community initiatives. It is almost a discipline where you try not to jump into something, create something too soon, put in structure before you know what that structure is there to serve (lest we serve a new structure). Our orientation is to name something, bolt it down like clear, fully realised ideas before it's even fully born. This includes you as you journey outward.

I remember when I was worried about who I would continue to vibe, connect or walk with when someone said ``*don't worry, we will find one another in the space."* and it has been true, though I've tried to restrain myself from too many faith connections, things simply move and progress more productively when the connection is one of values. Shifting to immersing in some faith relationships but mostly values connections has been incredibly enriching and I know that some of my journey friends across the world have found themselves shifting similarly. I've also found an ability to simply be a friend, hang out and talk rubbish, which is awesome, essential even.

For me at that time of moving further away from congregation all those years ago, my 'space' then, was to align myself with those who were engaged in community projects ranging from night club chaplaincy to working with addictions. It was a really positive time of walking with people who were actually doing stuff. I want to point out that my passion remains the 97% of the saints still waiting for a call to the ministry or seminary, congregation leadership or the mission field because we have falsely presented them as 'sacred'. We have to turn our attention and resources to the body as a whole. I've no interest at all in people stepping into more church construct roles; there is a big world for us to participate in as whole people, not waiting for a ladder to climb the in-house roles to find meaning.

I am desperately committed to those who are seeking to find meaning in the life and work settings as a prime context of their faith or spiritual journey. I cringe at those creating more sacred roles for themselves or perhaps removing themselves even further into deeper priestly, deeper sacred everything spaces (still constructs, internal and external). I do not hold with the idea that our purpose is found through removing ourselves. I am not a fan of those who are exploring New Monastic in their emergent journeys, an attempt to bridge the old and the new. Monastic was about withdrawal, the ultimate quiet time, and we have mostly lived too long in a state of withdrawal. Also the monastic was a highly centralised model, which provided some care recourses to the wider community when such things were scarce. That's where things are at today. **Trying to pull the past forgotten, into the present, instead of stepping into future unknowns perhaps allows us to explore things of meaning left behind, but not if they sustain the idea of the church of elsewhere or church as centre.** I digress just a little, more on this in the chapter on Dualism.

After stepping away from congregation, stepping into space with other local community focused 'activists' was a positive time for me. I was delighted that the conversation was never about who did or did not have something to do on a Sunday morning. The larger dialogue orientated around peoples community engagement, and was solidarity around people 'doing shit'. It was a gloriously imperfect, ragamuffin bunch trying to find a way forward together through cheering each other on with the dynamics of **'a win for one was a win for all' and a spirit of 'how can I help you get where you are going',** which I see as a positive reversal of the old thinking and congregational inward flow.

This was an interesting time for me as I found myself struggling to engage in much of anything to do with leadership. It's a common right of passage for those who move away from organised Christianity to have to work out what comes 'with' them. The questions of what is no longer toxic, what is still based on control or based on an insecure need for position. I think it's pretty important not to jump from one context of dysfunction straight into another without first exploring in some detail what beliefs and patterns of behaviour no longer fit your purpose and possibly never did.

If this is you, I encourage you to 'hold space', like your arms are stretched out in a hoop in front of you, a field, your field. Keep exploring what it means to walk with the spirit into that space, without pressing the 'default setting' button as many sadly do. **As you 'hold space', be really careful whose voices you permit to come into that place with you while you are recovering.** You will experience more life as a result; more sensitivity to what is toxic, controlling, positional and disempowering for others. If you have had a leadership role in organised Christianity, this space, in my view, is essential, and in some sense, considered a critical period of time spent in 'rehab'. Seriously, I make no joke about this, people who simply transition from one to the other, before the dust has settled, usually find themselves in a repeating cycle. The result is to have missed deep work on the self, and equally deep change. There is a saying in the addiction community, that if you have an addictive personality, and you stop doing cocaine, you had better damn well have something else your going to be addicted to, even if its reading or sports. But that's an <u>illness</u> and I think jumping from one role to another, one position to another, one Christianised purpose to another, could also be viewed as such.

A friend disclosed just this week that she is visiting a traditional church. She deems it to be of less threat, with it having a low reading on the bullshit 'o' meter. We chatted a little and she shared that she wasn't worried about it having a negative influence (she wasn't asking if she could, cause she's a grown up who can make her own choices). She knew what she would be walking into knowing that it doesn't need to be problematic since we have now seen that the Great Oz (priestly construct) behind the curtain is not so great after all, and it is unable to help fully with your heart, brain and need of courage. When my friend shared her plan, I reminded her of a church song that feeds the idea that God is near or far. One line is 'within the veil, I now would come, into the holy place, to look upon your face', but this separating Veil was torn down in theology more than 2,000 year ago with that re-defining cross event, and despite organised Christianity often seeking to put it back up, my friend now sees clearly what is what, and can take it or leave it. That doesn't mean that it wont be triggering.
To come out of something requires an element of recovery and personal reconfiguring. I have at times been accused of throwing the baby out with the bathwater. In reality, I think I have only done this once, where it was clear that what I threw out was something that was still intrinsically part of being me. It's an imperfect recovery as with all unhealthy

lifestyles or injury. The paralysis I felt was part of my need for recovery, it was an important time of being around people who really didn't need anyone to lead them as they stepped into adulthood, and to the same extent I didn't need to lead anything, other than my own self.

If you have been around displeasing or toxic behaviour think of David when he was anointed king but still remained around and under Saul. It seemed unfair, other than it was a perfect way to get the 'Saul' out of David' and break the dysfunctional cycle. Time around dysfunction may have been painful, but it hasn't been wasted. What once was tolerated now disgusts you and repels you, symbolizing the first break in the cycle.

Don't worry too much if you feel exposed in this season. With no altar to prostrate before, and no ritual to appease the saints or your measure of yourself, perhaps God's voice is more likely to be heard in the stones, a movie on TV or at the cinema or music at a club or on the radio. In the thick of it, my nourishment was in screaming along with Linkin Parks 'In The End';

I've put my trust in you
Pushed as far as I can go
For all this
There's only one thing you should know

I tried so hard and got so far
But in the end it doesn't even matter
I had to fall to lose it all
But in the end it doesn't even matter

I used to sing this in my lounge at the top of my voice with tears rolling down my face in the first few days following my exit from congregational leadership. Sorry, I mean when I 'ran' away from congregational leadership and as I laid down everything where I had, up until that point, misplaced my importance and worth.

It is necessary to strip down and be at ease in your nakedness, or to cry it out and feel it all. If in this process you still feel you have a connection to the Jesus person, that's more than enough. If you don't feel you've come through with any sense of that connection, then feel the solidarity, and know that you are very much in a shared journey across the world with those undertaking a necessary rebirth into the real.

If you can't stand to hear any of that God stuff spoken by men concerning the concept of the divine don't worry, the stones will cry out (or Linkin Park), the creation will speak and sooth you in a purer less tainted voice.

"It's Still Funny/Not Funny, The Residual Need Of Going Back In My Writing And Adding A Capital Letter G For God When I Forget And Not For The Reason Of Any English Language Etiquette."

I would say that it took me a decade to begin exploring how to bring leadership to things again. The exploration happened, in part, as the result of two insightful words, from two people, in different cities within a few days of one another, both saying:

"Gaz, I see you on a soccer pitch, the goal is open, the ball is at your feet and the crowd is cheering you on, but you wont kick the ball".

I don't identify as being prophetic anymore, though in old money, I would have been viewed as having that ability. I sit much more comfortably these days with seeing myself as an empath, an intuitive empathy. Words and language have garnered armies, won and lost wars, do not underestimate the power of reframing and slowly finding words and expressions which better reflect who you are now and where you're going.

Language can be limiting, alienating, or releasing and relevant. The ability to translate worldviews or complex ideas into accessible language is an important aspect of social movement theory, which we would do well to embrace.

It's when you try to transfer 'church speak' into 'real world speak' that you realise how much of your time has been spent living in two separate worlds. Some of us always found that the language of one world was mostly useless as a means of communicating relevantly in the other.

"If You Find Yourself In A Context Where 'Deconstruction' Is Dirty Word ... Just Keep Moving In The Most Freeing Direction, Trying To Be A Smart Arse To Justify Yourselves To Critics And Those In Positions, Is Mostly A Fruitless Distraction."

I think some of my learning during this time revolved around how to be a leader, and to use leadership as a gift into the mix, not a right, an imposition or a position. Essentially, I was created to initiate things, to interpret stuff, which means working out how to work with others and of course, healthy succession (helping others surpass you). It's a discipline that as the 'caller' (initiator) for a project or initiative you are being hierarchical because unless it was an 'open call', you were the one who got to decide who was invited/recruited. It's just what it is, but, after the initial call to gather, you can dissipate much of that moment of 'temporary hierarchy' into the collective. I have seen this often in projects like Khora, a largely anarchist run refugee engaged project which uses consensus decision making in Athens. Such decentralised approaches are imperfect, but are definitely progress, and exist in a world far away from pyramid approaches and are a healthy safeguard against ego and controlling voices.

Words Words Words Words Words

I feel lucky to have spent some time with a global community of learners called The Art Of Hosting, a collective all of you can 'learn' with if you wish. Please seek them out and connect if you have the opportunity. They played a deeply significant part in my unlearning, learning, and self-management. I attended their School of Participatory Leadership where there were people from all walks of life, pagan, wicca, business, life coaches, politics, and activism. It was a space where in all of my years exploring faith, I was most welcomed and encouraged to be fully present and share my practices.

So much of what they helped you learn there is the need for managing the self and enabling the power of the group. Lessons like how to self manage your participation in group dynamics and how to host 'conversations which matter'. I guess that's now an intrinsic part of what my leadership looks like today. It is an attempt to have or host conversations, which matter and actively dissipate any power in doing so. If you need to work on how you show up in life, how you show up in a room, and how you greet others as peers whilst viewing leadership as a gift, the Art of Hosting Global community of learners and practitioners really gets it. It has become a guiding voice in my head, especially when it comes to this idea of needing to first host your self.

Another aspect of leadership is how to connect with others and show up not as a specialist but instead as a co-learner. It is a strange but deeply freeing thing to explore faith without a desire to place myself at the front, centre, or on top of something. This approach deeply counters the default behaviours in Christendom and where we place meaning / authority.

It is not my objective to gain a profile or to be invited to speak in front of people. I would probably decline in all honesty, since that is not a qualitative context nor is it a dialogue. But I do hope that by writing some of this, these experiences and thoughts will lead to meaningful encounters, coffee table conversations, alongside support for those whose heads and hearts are a mess on their way to places new.

I find helping a conversation happen or participating much more enjoyable. If I do have to speak, I feel a need to deconstruct myself a little at the start, to address expectations, and to undo the power of the platform. My narrative is simply this, "I am not an expert, if I have anything to offer then at best, it is something from the next page of our collective book or from my failings. I am not here to tell you stuff, but I will share some of my journey and then hope that we can communicate together as co-learners and come out of our time together all the richer for it. "

I find this helps me be fully present in the room, and I hope at least for a moment, that it closes a gap between people and allows for them to experience/participate in a different way. There is a need for deconstruction of the self, but also for those we gather with who come or participate from a place of learned or adopted worldviews and behaviours. We bring our own preconception and learned behaviour into the room, and so does the listener, especially if we are from church world.

"If you lead, it should always be in the spirit of working with others as they grow, mature and hopefully surpass you.
Never to sustain your position."

Lets not forget that being in leadership can suck, it's a two way street, its not just having to recover from other leaders, or recovering from being a leader, there are also elements of recovering from those you lead. Actually my ride was a pretty smooth one in this regard apart from a few entertaining lumps in the road I simply did not know what to do with (other than keeping private thoughts, private). A prime example would be that were are a young, hip, bar based community, 80% of us are under 30 and the oldest person was older by a small leap of years being in his 50's. So, the guy is feeling left out, not included, not catered for and so his preferred means of communicating this is that I receive a hand written letter, not saying much at all really, other than he felt marginalised, and either had the creativity or sarcasm, to write all of said letter at the side of the page, in the margin. Some things you can't fix, they are simply realities that need adjusting to.

My history as a leader still prompts some of those aspects of helping something to 'happen'. The primary aspect of leadership or management is the management of our selves, that 'hosting the self' idea again. There is a constant and growing sensitivity to how we bring our part and our regard for the 'whole' of something as a peer gathering around a table with others. If people appear to express a need to be led, then you're doing so could actually significantly hinder a potential need for them to grow up and find healthy independence. You might feel useful, but your feeling of value is not the object of connection.

A couple of years ago I was invited to run participatory workshops in the Khora Project, which had a large number of volunteers (in fact all were volunteers). I was using some of the tools from the Art of Hosting to ensure I was not positional. The objective was to explore what we felt around the concept of hierarchy and why a different approach was both valued and practiced. The key discovery for me was a degree of redemption for the idea of what hierarchy means when it is not about power or position. The root of the concept is:

Those who gather around the precious object or idea, and feel they are the guardians and midwives to such things.

It's a good idea to progress what non-power based leadership looks like. Personally, I am not drawn to people who think they know what this looks like, as I don't feel we are in any way at the end of processing and exploring different, uncontaminated ways. Perhaps that's a good thing since most of our problems arise when we think we have arrived, or that we have 'got it' before all of the detoxing and reframing is complete.

Caveat: I know good people, friends even, who are still leaders in the church world. They actually understand all too well that it is a huge responsibility they have undertaken since it is a developmental and caring role with people. I'm suggesting that the greatest responsibility is to who you are in any role involving people. You have to continually revise your world view and practices, to keep check of power and the projected expectations of 'the other', and to remain professional and self aware, just like my wife has to do as an Occupational Therapist.

Dirty Words

Submission

/səbˈmɪʃ(ə)n/

def;

'yielding to a superior force or to the will, authority or control of another person'

Submit to your leaders or wives submit to your husbands and so on... are not the meta narrative, submit to one another out of reverence for Christ 'is'. Pause, read that again, a few times even. In the latter, submission has been brought down to an idea of making ourselves available to one another on equal terms, where the other versions above are seen as positional, unquestionable, and the submission can be experienced as form of psychological and even biblical slavery, not to be questioned lest we find ourselves 'uncovered', another spurious 'fear inducing' notion. In terms of how it weakens or removes the rights and values we place upon others, submission is a repeating narrative in the stories of those struggling in the church world. It is the same for those in recovery from submission 'experienced' as over parenting, over leading, and overwhelming. Where this is utilised in church structures, and with related personalities, we are simply now in cult territory. (See the final chapter.) I find the submission Bible passages to be on unsafe ground.

It reminds me of the line 'Guns don't kill people, people do'.

Submission in the hands of our broken humanity, become positional inequality and utterly un Jesus like behaviours. I saw a post recently about how 'grace doesn't give us position over others; it makes us siblings of one another'. In itself a really positive comment, but the family roles, names and ideas taken into an organised Christian setting, places us in the same dynamics and those abused in cults, of being in a family with family roles. My comment was 'can't we just relate as people?'

It is these submission texts, which seem so often to be in the wrong peoples hands, used out of context to perpetuate power, discrimination and the subjugation of others. If they come across as power play, usurping of the 'submit to one another' equality, well then we are almost certainly reading them wrong and using them to support an existing out of date paradigm.

As a grown up human being, you are increasingly in a place of deciding these things for yourself when you feel they do not resonate with your view of the Jesus person. Lose the mysticism, the power of suggestion and the fear of displeasing your idea of people or perhaps God.

All of the submission texts, funnily enough, must themselves submit to the spirit of submitting to one another out of reverence for Christ. Read that again, all of the submission texts, which indicate someone as superior, must be placed underneath the texts of submitting to one another in Christ. End of sentence!

Let's just say the Bible told us that God wanted human rights for Africans, human rights for Mexicans and then also said, 'I want human rights for all mankind' We wouldn't make two nations any more important than the rest of the nations. Yet when it comes to submission, we act like some specific parts were what really mattered and not the all encompassing 'everyone'. This kills the seductive nature of submission as leader and of being under leadership. In exactly the same way that all of the commandments can be summed up in the greatest of them, Love Each Other.

How we twist and weave and bring our brokenness to positions of responsibility leads to subverting texts to perpetuate our own un-wellness, which is then, in turn, inflicted upon others. Jesus is the opposite of this, and I can hear him as a projected voice in my head saying, *"You think it's this, but it's actually this. You think submission is this, but it's actually this"*. Until now, most of us have no bloody clue what the right way up looks like, what Jesus's own counter narrative on submission looks like, because we have some seriously flawed ideas about leaders. We have an adopted, broken human version, a distortion that counters Jesus' true freedoms with oppression, captivity, and control. There will be people reading this being accommodating with, 'but there isn't much control, not as much control as before or like in that other place' - that's so messed up - a reduced sentence is still jail time.

It's the prime reason for much of the wounding and usurping of power in the church construct. If it's undermining and wounding, the text is wrong, or our understanding is wrong, and we're buying into a toxic shit show. Our distorted accommodation of dysfunction means we say stuff like this; "Yes, but there is more good than bad, when it's bad it's bad but when it's good its really good, the church does more good than harm, the leader is mostly caring" is actually the same 'splitting off' thinking of every abused partner who remains in a violent or abusive marriage. If a person treats you good and then bad, they are broken and need to get well. If a system loves and rejects, heals and wounds, we shouldn't separate one off from the other for some false reason of loyalty. We should say it's broken and we shouldn't stick around ('but it needs us to remain and make it better' - oh please – stop it!)

Cognitive dissonance is a psychological term to describe where a person begins to compromise with conflicting beliefs or worldview in order to cope or make poor choices. It can be something that is present in our submitting to leaders, where their actions and behaviour do not marry to your own values and beliefs. The dissonance happens when we rationalise their, or our behaviour, so we can continue down the current path to God knows where. It could be said that we are splitting ourselves off from our true self, which is why much of this book is an encouragement to **'gather your self, back to your self and become centred'.** Someone I used to know was given a 2-year sentence for domestic violence against his partner. The choice to remain in that relationship would have required a disconnect from common sense through such rationalising as, 'but he is also a really good person'. Such is the power and reach of a conflicting emotional connection. He was actually let out early on the condition that he committed to regular group meetings for several months which were created to explore how men have developed their broken and distorted view of women. After the course, 25% of those attending will still feel that women are second class citizens who exist to meet their needs. We cannot assume that people have the capacity to change beliefs and behaviours, which are harmful to others, which unfortunately means we find ourselves having to exit such contexts.

"Someone is going to wake up shocked to find they are superior to no one"

Gifting is cheap, in-fact; it's so cheap that it's free, a free gift given to people without repentance. The passage is said by others to mean those gifts won't be taken away if your naughty, but I think it is more that they are not 'only' given to believers. An anointing is said to be God being 'on you and around you' doing something which is maximum G man and minimum you, so taking these things into account and coming back to earth a little; **The gifts didn't require good character, repentance or change, and the anointing is God operating and not really you, so take the stick out of your arse and well done for being an available conduit**. In reality we shouldn't be surprised if the holder of the title turns out to be a narcissist with vested interests, deep-rooted insecurities, and an ego to feed (or a variation on a theme). Choose to be around good people. *Find People who are a good unconditional mirror reflecting back the best aspects of yourself,* building you up, telling you you're meant to be here in life, living it to the fullest and affirming you are worthy and loved. Don't simply accept the good with the bad nor afford power to broken people, as those stuck in abusive relationships do.

The Waterboy

If all else fails, then we can find ourselves in the world of Adam Sandler's movie *The Waterboy*. There are two American football (foosball) teams in the deep South and two coaches, one is Coach Klein played by The Fonz and another is Coach Red Beaulieu. Some years before as younger men, Coach Klein kept winning games and had a secret 'play' book. He was a real visionary, and he kept the innovative game playbook with him at all times. That was until Red stole it. Since then, Red has had the power, which he uses to intimidate and mock Coach Klein who has now lost all confidence in his abilities. You will have to watch the movie to laugh at the journey of both teams, who end up being at the superbowl together. To win, coach Klein would have to face his deepest fear of his adversary, the one who stole his power and ideas.

Eventually, Sandler's Waterboy (Bobby Boucher) tells coach Klein a secret, "you just need to look at him and see something you're not afraid of", and so Coach Klein looks over at Red and suddenly see's he has a huge gurgling baby head. Klein starts calling, 'coochy coo, does baby have a poo poo' and the fear dissipates. Suddenly, Klein gets his mojo back and **starts writing new plays, new positions, and ideas for his game play book.**

We are children at play in the garden of the divine, applying such ideas to people who are truly not divine. As such we make them more than the flawed human beings that they are. This is one of the major toxic fallouts of celebrity platforming culture in some parts of the church world. Until we stop doing this, we are complicit in welcoming and keeping these people in such roles.

What we need to find is the ability to take away the platform, take away the awe and re-humanise people. I don't like to call things sin, but since we are talking christianese, if it is a sin to dehumanise someone, it is surely a sin to afford them a divine, superhuman position that God does not.

Let's play with this humanising thing a bit more. I was in Brighton, England with my friend Suzanne, who had told me this prophetic woman was likely to be present at a local funding team 'get together'. I knew she was not a superfan of being cornered by such gifting and so, as we left the gathering, Suzanne and this good lady were walking together and I could hear them talking behind me. Suzanne was saying something along the lines of, "I'm ok actually' why don't you go and 'do' Gaz."

It was very funny, as she did come and 'do' me. What she said was that I was going to find myself talking to people in positions of power at a national level, but it would not bother me, or worry me, since I had died to myself. I told her that I was already meeting with members of parliament, and yes, it didn't bother me. It would have bothered me greatly as the dancing monkey, performing for acceptance and affirmation in my former years, but I credit the Jesus person with having centred me over time.

Losing our 'fear of man' is Christian speak for feeling comfortable in our own skin, and realising that those who have position are people, flawed, failing, trying, hoping just the same as us. We no longer afford them power which is not theirs, but instead we claim and draw into ourselves the ability to flow from the power which is ours.

The surest way to deal with the fear of man, of the power and influence of another, is through self-acceptance. It is knowing that regardless of what they are doing, **they are as human as you and of no more nor less worth or value to God than you**.

You have a comfortable pair of house slippers somewhere, look for the ones with your name on and walk in them.

As a disclosure, I'm choosing to generally refer to Jesus as the 'Jesus Person' in my writing. I am doing this in my own efforts to re humanise him, since it was not his divine healing powers that first drew me to him, nor some heavenly status, but the humanity of the persons feet I saw, as he stooped down to give Ben Hur (Charlton Heston), a dying slave, a drink of water. I am doing this in my writing as part of my own personal reframing.

A friend called Martin Scott has just put out a book called 'Humanising The Divine', which I'm told is excellent and I'm sure contributes something relevant to our emergence along with his other utterances. Martin has been a progressive voice in my head for a good many years and I have always valued his contributions. All we need now is for someone to write a book on how we can 'Un-Divine The Humans'.

Maybe that's the next project for one of you folks.

Finally, Stop it. Stop it now. Just stop giving people power which is not theirs, and take back that which belongs to you, your right to disagree, your right to walk away, your right to not take their advice, your right to make mistakes and think for yourself, your right to be you, a unique individual. You are no one's clone."

DJ PROF + DJ KASRA

Chapter 4

The Mission Statement

'Poison In The Well'

When my wife and I were good Anglicans, living on the same housing estate as our church building meant that we were never too far from its orbit. I remember being told that something of significance was happening and that a group of women in the membership were going to meet and pray about how to progress this. I am not sure that it required the gravitas that it was given, since these ladies were meeting to discuss what should be written on a fabric banner that would be hung at the front of the venue. It took weeks, maybe even months for them to agree and create it. I'm aware that there were even some arguments about the various ideas. Eventually, it was launch day and the side of the platform suspended from sticks hanged a small drape of cloth. I can't remember exactly what was on it, but I do remember it was as simple as He Is Risen or Jesus Is Lord and probably had an image of a communion cup and perhaps some grapes, you get the idea. As humans, we are very good at getting stuck on the

ls of things, like everything we do has world shaping
_tial or might be the one thing that brings Jesus himself
back to earth. One of the critical places that we fall into the
'detail pit of despair' is at the very beginning of a new 'thing'.
I say 'thing' because people generally connect over
something they wish to start, spending their time
on preparatory work for a launch instead of the much
simpler notion of hanging out and being in a relationship or
journeying together. It is here, that more often than not,
there is a desire or panic to create a mission statement.
Without realising it, there is a point in the inception of the
new, what they believe to be pure waters that they begin to
put the first drops of poison in the well.

I will talk about sectarianism and elitism in another chapter,
but generally, this is where those things begin to creep in,
right at the beginning. I feel that the reason for this initial
poisoning is that in the process of moving away from
something we feel is inadequate, the ball has been dropped,
or perhaps what we are leaving behind is too traditional, too
stuck, too stubborn and resistant to change. It may be that
you have a new 'practice', perhaps an aspect of spirituality
that is enriching, but the previous context could not embrace
it or even simply reject it along with you. So there is
something we clearly want to be, or become, and something
that we no longer want to be, or be part of. I don't want to
suggest that there is resentment, but it usually costs people
dearly to finally squeeze out the door of something else to
begin something new. It is difficult to not include some
aspects or focus on what or whom you are moving away
from. It seems natural that to play a part in shaping what you
will become, part of the re-shaping will flow from being
against the past things, and the forward focus on the
perception of a truer truth or more profound practice. These
notions can be full of toxic undertones guiding you to repeat
the broken cycle.

The first step in the process is to extract your self as
painlessly as possible from the former situation. This
immediately transitions into step two, the need to define

what you are now, and your own mission statement, not just as a justification to others but also to yourself. You are now officially re legitimised as having or being part of a 'thing'.

In the same way that the group of ladies took the matter of wording on a cloth banner to the most extreme level of importance, the mission statement becomes a critical aspect of beginning something new. You could say that it is foundational, that until some things are asserted and scribed into a constitution, we may even fear that we are at risk of drifting, regressing or worse still, losing the people who came with us. The ones who are anxiously waiting to know 'what are we now?'

The questions that you have to perfectly crystallise in this mission statement are; Who are we? What aspects make us different or unique? What revelation was received that needed us to create a different space to implement it? There is not always a mix of push and pull. There may not be something significantly different in what you now form, which is the likely outcome. So it's likely that you feel that what you were in was not progressing quickly enough or not releasing sufficiently.

The mission statement requires thought and consideration, which may be a solo venture or it may involve several people, the embryonic team perhaps. Once the mission statement is formed and we now know what we are, we can relax a little, perhaps silence our fears as we now know clearly where we are heading, even before the sun rises on the third day.

The critical error here, in my view, is that we remain addicted, needy of form, structure and programme. The 'WHAT' of who we are quickly needs a framework for delivering said ideas. It may begin with a household as you get deep down dirty organic and into the unquantifiable 'authentic'. It may even begin with fundraising for that essential multi million pound building that your new mega growth intercontinental ballistic vision necessitates, but it is nonetheless about shape, form structure and renewing beliefs that all present can agree on. Your own version of the apostle's creed, attempt 137. The problem with needing to nail down the mission statement is that you have predetermined too much of who you are, when you have only taken tiny steps, and often a short time frame to journey from where you were. In a sense, more than a sense actually, you arrive before you have in all reality actually journeyed out. *In thinking about this, I had a little giggle to myself as I imagined leaving one house, noticing it's raining outside, pushing up your umbrella and running with haste into the next house whilst reciting 'it's bloody awful out there.'* Tell me this isn't so!

I think people like having this mission statement in place because it brings the safety of relative certainty, but also grossly limits movement, and because of the lack of movement, we frequently find that we have just adjusted the cultural furniture in the same limited container (even if what we have created feels dynamic). We are often complicit in regression, in our haste to re-instate the comfort of something familiar. Actually that last statement is often what limits a great idea from becoming a movement. We are held back by our retreat to, or need to rebuild the 'familiar'.

Did anyone ever watch the 80's TV show called Fantasy Island? There was the little guy in the white suit and he used to shout as guests were due to arrive, "Boss, the plane the plane!" That's kind of the voice in my head when I think of this modern parable;

There were several people out on the asphalt of an aircraft runway. The runway was very short and so everyone had spades and pic-axes in their hands and were dripping with sweat from the labour. Every so often there was a buzzing sound of a light aircraft above and people put down their tools and cheered as the plane landed bringing them gifts, which caused them to become ecstatic. They would periodically shout, 'the plane the plane' and put down their tools. For a great many years the people laboured, but the runway did not progress, because every so often the buzzing sound would appear and they would stop and were grateful for what the small plane would bring them. All of this time they had failed to see the large Hercules transport plane, similar to the ones which bring jeeps and tanks into the theatre of war, circling high above which waited for the runway to be extended so that it could land.

At times, the people speaking from the new platform with the new idea could be seen as this, shouting with great enthusiasm 'the plane the plane' and feeling that they have arrived at something amazing but missing what the dislodging, the sweat, tears and the labour was all about. The mission statement, the fresh dynamic statement of intent, is often a considerable hindrance to significantly moving beyond toxic behaviours, operant conditioning and the love of the familiar. What we know is that the cycle continues just as it has for hundreds of years.

You can't run, before you have learned to walk, that is simply where some of us find ourselves, not rushing off to anywhere, but simply walking and exploring with a sense of personal and divine permission to do so. It reminds me of Kill Bill 1 where our star Uma Thurman (aptly called 'the bride') has been in a coma for years and when she finds herself suddenly awake and trying to move, she finds that her legs have muscle loss due to atrophy and so she painstakingly drags herself to freedom.

Going back to basics, or even the beginning, it isn't a bad thing, it might even be really important.

Someone once told me that it doesn't matter what politician you vote for, they still only have the same deck of cards to re-shuffle, so in my mind why don't we simply play a totally different game? I think its part of our operant conditioning as part of church world that we can think the re shuffling is deeply meaningful and radical, at least in our own experience. To those outside, they didn't even notice, because they weren't looking in the first place. It was always the saying 'will your group be missed by the locality if you disappeared over night?' The answer for most is, probably not, since your being there mattered very little to them.

I know some good people who are still trying to reconfigure the box because in part, they are part of a wider institution who hold's their leash at differing lengths and that's what they have to work with. 'Missional Community' has been a buzz word for some during this time and if you hear the subtext as I did, it should make your head literally explode, here goes... 'Church With A Purpose'. The church as a movement always had a purpose, a bucket full of purposes so the title is a little laughable or painfully disappointing. So what's the difference? The main one is that the community either forms around a project or objective, or the community forms and then picks a focal point. Some if this is a distortion of the concept that unless a group is of one heart and mind, one focus, they will be divided and fall. Such words are usually spoken by a visionary leader trying to keep the flock basing their sense of purpose around a top down vision. Im not sure gathering around a project or objective is missional church, that just feels like a made up concept to further stretch the institutional leash or to feel like your being dynamic from the starting point of a very small world where little changes. If your gathering around a project, you're a project team and their may well be some dynamics of relationship which are improved by actually doing something together, as with any task based group.

My eldest daughter, our first, had to endure birthdays when we had very little money. One morning she came down to a bicycle wrapped in gift-wrap and quickly pulled it off asking 'Is it new, or is it new to me', meaning is it second hand. She didn't really care either way. Its entirely possible that in our 'small closed world' of church, that something can seem dynamic and exciting, and yet to the wider world, those things already exist and are part of the norm, without anyone saying, 'hey, see, we are doing a new thing'.
Also, does this shared work focus around an agreed task, place the same value on the life and work contexts of its participants? It is leadership, coming alongside, enabling the masses in the diversity of their passions or labours, seeing them all as having significant value, a paradigm shift, a different game, and not a card shuffle.

Shopping Lists & Compliance

In my hometown there was a group of friends who were either living in a large house together or gravitating around it as a social friendship hub. It was fondly called Jesus Street with a degree of humour in the title. I recall there being some tension in the relationships due to expectations and ideas around what the house was for, and the nature of the relationships that existed there. It seemed that they had different expectations for one another in terms of commitment or openness or some other such thing. Perhaps those ideas were never specifically stated or agreed - help! To my memory there wasn't a mission statement, but even without it there seemed to be some engrained thinking which had come with people from the church world. I remember one young lady saying 'if this is just about friendship, I don't really need it, I have enough friends already'.

This situation in reality was pretty minor, but it caused me to ask a friend of mine called Heidi a question. We had worked together in prayer networks regionally and I valued her discernment and less constrained perspectives. I asked her to tell me, when we 'step out of the church box', what does community look like?

Her response has stayed with me and I think speaks to the issue of the mission statement but also the question of the young lady asking if it's just about having more friends.

Heidi, "I don't know if there is a definitive description of what a community is, since it is applied in so many contexts both rigid and fluid. What it definitely isn't is a list of things on a bit of paper which eventually become something we are to conform to or comply with. To do so is like listing the fruit of the holy spirit, love, joy, peace, patience, kindness, goodness, faithfulness, gentleness, and self-control and making them objectives, tasks to be accomplished and behaviours to conform to. Those things are not a list, they are anticipated evidence of the life of someone who is walking with the spirit. Whatever community is, it isn't a list, it's evidence of our walk with Jesus and the overspill of this into our relationships."

Personally I've never heard a better explanation or health check for the expectations we place on one another, based around ideologies, or the expectations we place upon ourselves for which we may feel we frequently fail.

I wanted to say that I have felt thoroughly privileged to work with various grass roots groups of people who have broken with the old and set out into the unknown, physically at least. There have been a full spectrum of ideas between conservative regression to shiny constructs and loose/fluid where it is primarily relational and without rigid form.

I really did not know how to help one group of really lovely people who were reinventing the wheel. They soon had larger group gatherings in a hall with song singing and a sermon along with smaller group dynamics where there was a desire to outwork 'authentic' community. Authentic is that concept where we are in search of the somewhat mythical original and instead of being more fluid, despite a more relational start we evolve into something with a more rigid check list than what we left. Before too long there were apostles and disciples, pastors and elders all amidst a core group of less than 20 people. It had, in a very short space of time gone from journey to arrival with much of the same issues, just up close and uncomfortably personal. I could not doubt that some of the relationships were close and supportive, but there was very much an increasing critical sieving of who was 'in' and who was 'out' defined by proximity to the group, the elders and pastor, not to mention the small and larger gatherings as 'centre'. I also remember in answer to one of my questions about where they were making meaningful connection beyond the new construct, that ' they needed to work on feeding and strengthening their faith as based on the scriptures before engaging with others/outreach/the world'. To me this concept of getting it right 'in here' before being 'out there' indicated much of the old had been re imagined into a new old.

Whilst having been given permission in relationship to speak honestly into such groups, I just was not in a place with my own insecurities to challenge what was going on and so confess I simply withdrew, which I am not proud of. Also I think the leadership paralysis thing played a part because who was I to tell another that they were screwing up.

I think my sensing that they had this idea that 'they were doing it right', doing it biblically, doing it hierarchically, that it was already past the point of hearing anything counter to what had been put in place. Regardless of the invitation to speak into, my aversion to strong shape and form left me looking like I had little credibility to critique. Again, this is why this period of 'holding space' is critical to allow detoxing, changed thinking and behaviours, is why I feel that **this is not a journey in search of an original template but instead a reaching much more into the unknown**.

"New ideas, rejected by the old, become the new mainstream ... and so it repeats"

Quantity V Quality

Another aspect of the poison in the well is the idea of numerical growth being a main indicator of success, growth coming from addition or through multiplication of an idea or model. 5,000 immature human beings in high dependency culture kept safe until heaven is not an improvement on 500.

I've had the pleasure of mentoring and being a friend to an entrepreneur in Athens called Jonny. He is very gifted at going to a place, observing an issue in context, such as deficits in care for refugee minors and finding meaningful solutions. We have talked at length about the measure of productivity and how irritating it is that growth looks like success to outsiders since his focus is on quality of care, and silencing that inherited inner voice of 'big is better'. It takes effort and will power for any of us to keep that in check.

I just wanted to say, along with Khora, that his work is one of those places where refugees indicate that they feel treated like a person, a human, not a label, a number or an issue.

Another friend, Hailey, wrote an excellent article to prepare western workers for working here in Greece called 'My name is Hamid'. Her article is about how being a refugee is a transitioning state caused by external issues and is not the identity of the person. Quality!

There seems to be this inner default setting around growth, scaling up, and getting bigger. Do you know where it comes from? I've not really explored it yet but I recognise that it is out there. Those working at grassroots, doing the dynamic work, are so often overlooked while the big boys get all the funding and most funders are often unable to distinguish between size and quality of service. Rarely, do any of them inquire of those who receive the care (which would be empowering). How often in organised Christianity are you asked why you are there, where are you heading in life, and what is it **you** need to get there?

I have met several people over the years who have been 'starters' or founders of some faith based community exploring back at the grassroots, who now find themselves setting out generic plastic chairs in a large school assembly hall 'lamenting' the good old days of meeting in a house. Maybe that's the starting point. We ask the question of 'why are we doing this', and if the answer is that nothing significant has changed, then we have to begin again, but what we don't do is repeat the cycle that got us there.

Hindrance To Movement

Part of social movement theory is the element that violation plays in mobilising people towards activism. It is said that the nature and depth of personal violation or a sense of violation on behalf of others determines the longevity of a person's engagement with change. It goes alongside that comment that it is often our love of the familiar, which inhibits our sticking around long enough to persist in seeking change. An example might be the Occupy movement, or other activist happenings against things like consumerism and capitalism, camping out in streets or cities in protest. At the same time, the trappings of capitalism, the feel good factors of our normal consumer lifestyle are said to have called some back to the 'norm' and to 'comfort' prematurely. Some of those who backed away from the frontline of actions may have also had a limited sense of violation around the issues they were 'standing' for or against. I feel this has relevance since in my view this global group called church are meant to feel a sense of violation for a great many things and position themselves accordingly, but they remain in, or retreat to, the programme, or the comfort of the fold.

The Problem Of Common Union (communion)

I've deliberated over whether to include this or not since it stems from a conversation I had while at some activists prayer gathering in Prague. It was a free space in which people could share concepts without getting shot down and this section concerns one of them, a particularly interesting one. It's not something I'm advocating, or suggesting you do, but I do feel it has value, that you go where there is life, not empty ritual or hocus pocus.

In our own attempts at experimenting with meaningful community based in a bar, the concept of taking communion simply slipped out of the window. I am pretty sure there was never a conversation or a decision made that we would not do the communion thing, it just seemed that in pursuit of the real, it was forgotten, and nobody complained.

From my Baptist days, individual cups were handed out and chunks of bread passed along each seated, prayerful line. A piece of bread torn off in a rugged earthy manner before someone shouted 'Go', we chewed and swallowed perhaps extra slowly and then we all went up to people near us, shook them in a pre covid manner firmly by the hand whilst saying, 'the peace of the Lord be with you' 'And also with you'.

Then there was the formation of civilised solemn queues, one row of people at a time, attempting to look reverent and sincere in the Anglican set up where the priestly amongst us would afford us a sip and a wafer. It simply never ever felt ıre than something contrived. Perhaps it seemed progressive when compared to the bell ringing transformation of the bread into flesh and the wine into literal blood undertaken by more conservative church orgs.

It is perhaps a relevant context for 'ritual' conversations since being in Prague, there had been considerable loss of life in the history of its church. Some earthy radicals had sought to give bread 'and' wine to the lay people at a time when both were only permitted amongst the priests. At the Prague gathering someone posited the suggestion that the actual context of last supper was as significant, if not more so that the act of the bread and wine. Someone suggested that there was perhaps something more literal taking place in that Jesus was eating with his nearest and dearest journey friends, all of whom I have no doubt had been brought closer together by their solidarity. In this setting the premise was less of a 'Do This' often and more of a 'Can You Do This?' Can you sit as I am, amongst those you have felt a desire to walk closely with, to risk being known deeply by? Can you sit with others in the days ahead and say " I pour out my life for you?" or " I would be broken for you!"
I think that scales it up, making it about the nature of our relating to one another. The idea that at least we have gone deep with someone in our regard for one another, much more than trying to create a meaningful moment through the bread and wine, which in this context could be viewed as symbols of the relational. Is that a principle that we can bring with us beyond the administering priests and the constructs? Somewhere, we have relationships, at least with someone, which go that deep, where perhaps inconvenience or cost would be volunteered (the opposite of invasive forced relationships).
I can't think of anyone I'd take a bullet for (well my family I guess)... though there are those I would travel a great length of time and distance to sit with them and say 'you matter to me' on days when it is needed or even when it is not.

If we choose the less relational focus, the sacramental, the notion that something sacred is taking place, I don't see that in the text, I don't see it suggesting that something spooky, super spiritual or otherwise is meant to happen when they, or in turn us, eat the bread and drink the wine. Could it be, that it is simply remembering, centring, and identifying with the significant others of our lives... If the focus was relational then at which point did it become sacramental and who or what would have benefitted from that? Much was created to place the only legitimate manifestation of church and priesthood at the centre and to instil in you, the follower, a pseudo spiritual need of it and of them and their governance. There are still people writing and writing and writing seeking to make the sacrament of communion even more spooky, to seek to find the divine again, within something which may of possibly been a deeply human affirmation of our relating. I don't see anywhere that it say's do this, and XYZ things will happen as a result of it, nor does it say that if you neglect this eating and drinking ceremony XYZ will befall you.

"The church seeks to make cultural things sacred, but culture is in constant transition. There are likely very few things which could be deemed sacred, eternal and of eternal worth"

When thinking about the passage that, **"no greater love has someone, than to be willing to lay down their life for a friend"**, perhaps consider that it's not about dying, but instead saying that the highest level of our love is to be able to pour ourselves out for another while we are still living. I would also like to wave a red flag and point out that this doesn't say 'Christian' friend or other paid up club members. It seeks to draw out a depth in our friendships, our relating.

It may come as a shock to some, since it was to me... but one of the light bulbs that has gone on for me since leaving organised Christianity, is that I have found out that I actually love some people and I genuinely miss them when we are not able to be around each other. I consider this to be part of my on-going becoming alive, but also something which happens when relationships become more organic, less 'organised' or contextually prescribed.

I don't want to challenge the communion passages, so take that which is meaningful and move on, but in the absence of the sacraments having meaning for you, reframing the concept in more relational terms seems to lose nothing.

In early post construct conversations I had with people who were worried about losing relationships I would often ask; "In terms of relationships, what does church look like for you now? What do you consider are the core elements where you could continue to place meaning value now? What is being left behind, what still has meaning? Now take those things, and as you lay in bed tonight ask yourself with whom do those things exist? Where are those values in play and present in relationships? If they do not exist, dream and imagine with a degree of delight at who you might want to walk those things out with, both with believers and with non believers (if you still place yourself in a Christian frame). If legitimising is important to you, then I think church, as 'people' is happening."

In reality, following my asking that question (and with considerable repetition), people could only think of one, perhaps two people, with whom their relationships seemed to flow from those core values, which is either enough, or a good realistic starting point and that's ok.

In therapeutic circles **the 'should or shouldn't' voice is said to be the residual parent voice, we are seeking to mature away from,** its not really your own voice. There can be a lot of this around, a lot of what you think you should or shouldn't be doing in relationships.

Remember that relationships are not a task, nor an externally pressurised objective, they are a lifelong exploration of our humanity. So do yourself a favour and dump the guilt. In psychobabble, guilt is considered to be your punishment of yourself, in the absence of others to do so.

If I give everything I own to the poor and even go to the stake to be burned as a martyr, but I don't love, I've gotten nowhere. So, no matter what I say, what I believe, and what I do, I'm bankrupt without love. Love never gives up. Love cares more for others than for self. Love doesn't want what it doesn't have. Love doesn't strut, Doesn't have a swelled head, Doesn't force

itself on others, Isn't always "me first," Doesn't fly off the handle, Doesn't keep score of the sins of others, Doesn't revel when others grovel, Takes pleasure in the flowering of truth, Puts up with anything, Trusts God always, Always looks for the best, Never looks back, But keeps going to the end.
1 Corinthians 13:3-7 MSG

I think the last few lines of that need revising, along with any bible text, which permits others power of us. Until we become centred as people, we are often conditioned by our own development as children, to make sacrifices of ourselves, which can border upon self-harm. So put up with anything? Nope!

'FLAWESOME'
When you embrace your flaws and still know that you are awesome

Gaz Kishere

BLISS CREW – BRAND NU FLAVA FOR YA SOUL 1995

KHORA CREW 2019

Chapter 5

Stepping Back Into Culture

(Or finding it for the first time)

It's taken a good few years for me to re-connect meaningfully with my own tribe and culture. What is it about the church of elsewhere that seeks to save you 'from' stuff and primarily supports you to become part of its world? It seems to do this whilst ignoring its own inability to come and stand meaningfully alongside you in the real world, the cultural context in which you already reside. It helps you spend less time with the people that matter most to you, a counter kingdom flow, back into the church of elsewhere, keeping you safe till heaven.

My tribe was based around the motor scooters we rode, Vespa's, and Lambretta's, which came to fame in 60's Britain with the mods and rockers fighting their way through holiday weekends (see THE WHO movie Quadrophenia). The way we dressed and the music we listened to, from 60's beats and 70's northern soul to ska and psychobilly. My own local club was called the Modrapheniacs, these were my people who I had hung around with from age 15 into my 20's. We used to meet in a pub opposite my house, my older brother had been a founder member in the 70's (no 4) Since joining church world, I had ever decreasing contact with anyone from my old crew and this remained the case for the next 17 years or so.

Coinciding with my eventual exit from church world, the scooter club was holding an annual weekend scooter rally at a holiday park, not far from where I lived. My brother Ricky and I went to check it out. Several thousand people showed up from all over the country for the first get together of the year, braving the rain and chills on their scoots. The main summer gathering would be an invasion of the Isle of Wight back in the days, off the south coast of England by 10,000 riders, filling the bars and clubs and having a beer, or 6, while dancing to their favourite tunes. Life was happening! The first time I showed up at one of these gatherings it was illuminating and invigorating for me. I remember lodging in one of the mobile homes on the site with my brother and some mates, getting all smart and in the right frame of mind with our friends Jack and Daniels. We walked towards the main event arena and while I was still a 100 metres from the doors, I could hear the sweet sound of soul music, the resonance of the familiar and the hairs on my neck stood up while my insides moved with the rhythm, soon to be followed by my feet.

I can only describe it as a feeling of coming home. Actually, take a moment to listen to 'Julian Covey - A Little Bit Hurt' on you tube and you might even catch the vibe that I'm talking about. I walked onto the dance floor and someone I haven't seen for more than a decade shouted 'Oi Sproggy - It's Your Favourite Song', how the heck did he remember that for all these years?

I spent the time drinking, dancing, and reconnecting with old friends, while making some new ones, and it was all just really nice. In this scenario, I was the absent friend. My nickname used to be Sproggy, earned for being the youngest in the club way back when. Just then, a bleary eyed ex-girlfriend called Annie walked past and a mate said, "Hey Annie, you remember Sproggy don't you?" She continued to walk by without even looking up and said, "Yeah, didn't he go off and become all religious?" I had the strong sense of being someone who had left and was coming to terms minute by minute of my own loss at having been absent whilst their world continued without me. Friendships had grown, losses had been shared, weddings had passed and babies had been born into the clan of the beloved.

I was experiencing and self-reflecting all at the same time. I'm walking around, listening to people sharing all these recent memories, hundreds of them, with joy and laughter and joking, memories I am almost entirely missing from and I am thinking to myself, **'these guys are meant to be a bunch of hurting, failing fuck ups!'** These are the people the church world tries to keep you safe from, but you know what, safe sucks and safe can be an incredibly contrived concept from the religious keeping you in their exclusive elusive club.

"Jesus didn't come to create Christianity or make better Christians, he came to make humans more complete."

Along with the church worlds dualism of 'in here is good and safe and out there is bad and unsafe' was the idea that everyone else was a mess. Their lives were not rich or meaningful, their relationships were shallow and they needed Jesus to find any meaning at all. They were meant to be unspiritual, un-centred people, who have a far greater need of you than you have of them. This was far from true, in fact, it was actually total bollocks.

All of this is going on in my head and at the same time the mirror is cracking, the curtain separating us off from the land of the real is being torn, and I'm being caught up in a heady mix of lager, love, laughter, stories and joy (perhaps even making new memories which I actually feature in.) All of it is confronting deception, betrayal, truths and half-truths, even untruths and years of operant conditioning (let's just call that behaviour modification). There is this idea that people without Jesus or Church cannot know Joy or Peace, do you think that's true?

There were, without doubt, some utter lies in the narratives within the church machinery which I had inherited, opted into, and even became conditioned by. My world was about to get so incomprehensibly big that I could only see the human constructed world of the church as a suffocatingly small. A subculture, primed to make me feel like I'd arrived and yet, it exists away from where the action and life genuinely is, constantly trying to create its own version of things, attempting to find credibility from outside of society.

While I am writing, I am aware that I am putting pen to paper or finger to keypad for individuals who are in some kind of conflict with structures, transitioning away from inherited thinking and practices. I am not writing anything for the church as an organisation, as I feel that would be time that is wasted, like speaking to something that is not listening nor capable of the kind of change that is necessary. The ability (in the words of John the Baptist) to decrease, so that that which Is coming, can increase. What is coming is not a re-shuffling of the card deck but an entirely different world. A new life game to be lived out, not observed at a distance. I am also aware that some of my readers will have been in the church as a system as an extension of, or as a replacement for a biological family. Church may have been their life so far. For them, it is not so much re-engaging with things laid down, the babies we threw out with the bathwater, but instead one of experiencing the world anew, relationships beyond the club, friendship, and the concept of God in a wholly upside down, or right way up way world. If nothing else, I hope some of what I write does in fact 'rub you up the right way' regardless of your starting point on this journey.

"Don't leave the old, to join the old, spend some time away from the complexity of the church and rest in the relative simplicity of Jesus."

I appreciate that I have lived through a rather progressive period during some of my time in organised Christianity. For instance, I was working with Dj's setting up their own mainstream club nights in town as part of their re-entering into society. In a way, that was meaningful to them. However, the reality was that this was the 'disconnected', or never truly connected, trying to find a credible way of reconnecting with the world. There was often the confusion of folks needing to call it a ministry to validate their journey in some way, perhaps to themselves or back to the construct, which to be fair wasn't really looking but expected you to still explain yourself and show up on Sunday. The transition and exploring frequently meant we still created our own versions of things, like club nights for us to meaningfully connect with people. There was a complex 'missing' of the fact that those things exist, in real life, and we just need to integrate. There is still a place for projects, it's just not an alternative to, nor of greater value than actually living in the real.

Suddenly it became hip and trendy to say that young people don't fit the rhythm of church because you can't expect this guy Dj'ing till 4 in the morning to get up for church a few hours later. These felt like dynamic statements of activism at the time, fighting for space, changing the culture, and predisposition of the church. Yet, perhaps they had actually travelled very little from the status quo (myself included). I guess that's part of the dysfunction in fighting and wrestling for scraps off the table, searching for some degree of acceptance and an understanding of our taking baby steps back into the world of the real. Don't get me wrong, such things seem vitally important when you're inside the system and are often concepts that were hard fought for by some poor sod, long before they became trendy. Believe me, in your town there are 50 to 100 guys who want to become a Dj, and many of them will, but your journey out of the box into the normal world seems far more earth shattering, and that's because your cultural starting point is often far removed from theirs.

These early attempts of re-joining the world should be applauded, these were brave wanderers, forerunners exploring beyond the fold, desperate to be part of world culture. Kill dualism, kill the secular/sacred life limiting nonsense and kill Platonic pseudo spirituality, and you may just discover life, in all its fullness. Don't let a largely created and still partly colonial system, rewrite what was beautifully indigenous about you.

TRIBE

Chapter 6

Kingdom Flow

What nuggets or ideas have helped you take healthy control of your own situation? What ideas or statements have been useful to you in reframing how you view what church is and what that means for you as a unique individual?

One grounded intuitive voice, which has stood the test of time, is a guy who just said in passing, "I'm worried about the Brazilian revival and that it is flowing the wrong way, back towards church congregations." I worry about things like if my bodged rip tie repair on my car exhaust is going to get me home, or if my adding coconut milk to my curry is going to reduce the heat of over spicing to a bearable level. I don't tend to have much of a reflection about what is happening spiritually in other people's nations. I asked this thinker to explain what he was talking about, and what came next has been a finger hold and just one of the reasons that leaving behind organised Christianity was the last church I'll ever leave. It was a long time ago that I first considered the concept, but the core themes remain with me just the same.

He said, *"I feel there is such a thing as a Kingdom Flow. I think how we understand this will determine what we think the church is and our relationship to people and the world. It goes like this: Jesus shows up in the world that we might be reconciled to the Father and in so doing, become part of an outward flowing people movement as his body on earth. Telling people, about who he is, in the hope they too connect to the father, come fully alive and contribute to society, even to the ends of the earth.*

Alternatively, Jesus shows up in the world that we might be reconciled to the Father and in so doing we become part of an organisation in a specific location and building called a church. In fulfilling what is required of us, we do outreach and visit the world to tell people about Jesus, in hopes that they will be reconciled to the Father, come into membership of the church and be kept safe until heaven". Depending on how you view the above, it could be said that what we have in place with the name church is a real problem

He ended by saying *"You see there are two flows, one down from heaven and outward, ever outward, where church is a people that inhabit all things. The other is that the world becomes a place where God is not, and the church a place of safety and sound doctrine from where we visit the world and bring people back to the safety of the church. The problem is the Kingdom of God only ever flows downwards and outwards."* He didn't say this part, but I remember reflecting on the story of The Tower of Babel as a reasonable metaphor for a wrong kingdom flow, which didn't go too well as an approach.

"Another problem is whether we have a kingdom approach or a Christendom approach. In the kingdom there is a king, who is still working and leading the church. In Christendom, God has gone on a long holiday and left some special people in charge to carry out the family business"

Reaching For Narnia

Around 12 years ago I arrived at a London wide gathering of church leaders who were exploring new paradigms of church. It was really interesting that while it was still happening in a church building, from the outset they sought to unsettle us and challenge our expectations. Having entered the building in order to gain access to the meeting room, you had to fight your way through an old wooden wardrobe of hanging clothes to come out the other side. A deliberate Narnia 'esque' new world awaits scene setting. On arriving as a consumer and listener at the gathering, I found out much to my surprise that I was on the speakers list and began to fill my underwear and sweat a little more than normal. I remember thinking to myself ' Oh crap, I can't pull something new out of the hat, I can't put together something smart and clever, I can only speak out of what is already in me'. At the time it was this kingdom flow concept that was most current to me as part of life beyond the wardrobe, so that's was what I shared, but in a slightly more animated format. In the absence of music, visuals, and a dancing bear, which others had prepared, I felt the need to move my arms and legs more than usual to sustain people's interest. As a result of my speaking out the different aspects and stages of kingdom and non kingdom flow I managed to walk sideways like a crab, from one side of the auditorium to the other, using the wall as a good spectrum reference point for stopping. We all have to stop somewhere; I'm not an extremist ;-)

In the hope of not simply making a statement or asking them to agree with my frames of reference, I simply asked this, "whatever it is that you have, which you call the church, in what direction is it flowing?" and then I sat down. I ask the same question here to you now, the reader, in regard to what you are currently in or were in. What direction was/is the flow?

PROTESTING SOMETHING OR ANOTHER

Chapter 7

Finding Our Way Back From Dualism

I have excluded the word secular from my language for many years now. I have found it to be a wholly unhelpful term that fuels the separation of church from society. If we have the language of separation, it is quite likely that we have the practices of separation too.
I have swapped out the word secular for the word 'mainstream' in an attempt to try and normalise things in some way. Despite other uses of the word secular, it has come to mean somewhere God is less or perhaps worse, somewhere that God is absent and should therefore be considered unsafe, also known as the realm of 'the others', the lost or toxic.
I want to illustrate how dualism works in a real life setting and story rather than theoretically, I guess this is my version of drawing with a stick in the sand, my attempt to explain this idea.

For 6 years I worked with an international counter child trafficking NGO based out of the United States as their

European Operations Director (a title I was asked to create for my business card). On a visit to one of the nations in Asia where we were funding projects, and contributing a few initiatives, an amazing co-worker took me to meet a guy who was working in the nightclubs there. It seemed to me to be a gathering of people who were 40% people selling sex, and 60% 'johns' going there to buy sex. These interactions were set against a backdrop of a syncopated house music beat and flashing lights. There was a mix of girls and guys who were working in the sex industry, some were clearly there because they were pretty and young, and exactly what predators are shopping for, a source of considerable discomfort to me.

On a previous trip to another Asian destination, I had been offered a 15-year-old girl in a shopping mall by a lady pimp, in a mall just like the one in your own city. This place was full of shoppers, but that didn't faze her. The pimp stood by the children's slot rides, the horses and cars swaying back and forth and the girls for sale were sitting on them. Having initially been approached, I did a loop of the mall to deliberately approach them with a voice recorder ready in my pocket. I haggled with the woman; lowering the ages of the girls year by year until she promised me a 12-year-old girl could be sent to my hotel room. I was sick to my stomach asking those questions, but I was able to pass the details onto the City police who said they were already monitoring the situation. Monitoring what exactly I will never know. Anyways, I'm just highlighting that all of this stuff is nasty, ugly, and really shitty. It needs a lot more people to engage with it, but from a strategic point of view, not from any limiting Christian ideologies. It is simply far too important, which transitions me nicely back to my story.

So, back to the bar in Asia where my co-worker friend thought that the club worker dude and I would get along, since he was under the judgmental spotlight of working somewhere Christians refused to go, and as a result, they gave him the 'black spot' of suspicion and exclusion. He would raise funds for a specific girl to exit prostitution, either from donors or by teaching English locally. He would get them out, one at a time, while helping them gain livelihood skills as a means of sustainability. In the club we talked to a few of the workers but I mostly remember one girl. She was so beautiful, and seemed like a lost bird, this was clearly not her normal source of income. She had to have been 15 at the most, and as we talked, she explained that she was responsible for her mother and her own education. She had come to the city for a week to sell her body to mostly (really bloody old) American expats who had no other reason to be there, in the hope of her financing another term at school. After we left the club I went back alone, having taken what I could from my bank account. I walked into the club, found her, and she automatically assumed I was going to buy sex from her. I made it clear I was not back for that and put the money in her hands. She continued to look confused as I bowed to her with clasped hands in full Namaste honour/humility gestures, feeling a degree of male shame. I animated and gestured as best I could to the words 'now go home'. I never saw her again, she was just one amongst the many.

I don't get involved in the sex work is 'viable empowering business for females' debates. I have a reasonable sense that no little girl ever dreamt of a life being masturbated into by men for money when they are a grown up, or worse, when they are still a child. This was a country context where, if the bar had been a cross section of its own sex-exploited society, 37% of those being exploited that night would have been children.

Since I was a stranger in a strange land, and as naive as anyone could be, it seemed the best that I could do to express love and regard to at least one of those there. On top of this, I wasn't meant to be there, in that place where apparently the Jesus fella wouldn't dream of going (I've been told that about bars on too many occasions). What a crock of shit.

If you would like to read more on trafficking, you can find an article of mine online published in Relevant magazine called: 12 hours with a sex tourist.

'Blessed are those brave enough to make things awkward, for they wake us up and move us forward'
Glennon Doyle

The Real World And The Church World

The following night we went to a gathering of Christians from different groups. They were going to go and do outreach (a word for us to review) to the white males who were spending their pensions on trying to resolve loneliness and feed a predatorial nature. I should have been suspicious as soon as the word outreach was used. We walked off the busy main street where all the action was and into a small side building. We sat in a circle, we sang western worship songs with the aid of a tape player, and then we broke into confession groups. Men and women were separated into two so we could talk about our 'thought life' and any brushes with porn. This was supposed to help us so we could be cleansed and worthy of the work that was waiting for us 'outside'. I was feeling increasingly angry. There is no other word for it, in fact, I would say I felt offended by just about everything that was taking place. I am mindful of this because a preacher once told me (well, everybody) that having offense is a sin hmmmm. However, I tend to feel at times that feeling anger and taking offense is simply being tuned in and feeling exactly what the Holy Spirit is feeling.

The best was yet to come... strap your selves in!
It was time to put on the full armour of God. I mean like in full Marcel Marceau mime mode (the Frenchman). One item at a time: the belt of truth, the breastplate of righteousness etc.
Now this is where I need Jesus to answer this for me, why do I have to do all of this seeming nonsense to go back onto the street I had just walked off of?
Think about that. Think about where that comes from and if there is any of that crazy split world thinking in your world.

I bit my tongue and tried not to make eye contact with my western teammates. I would have hated for them to know I needed rescuing, and it would have been so disrespectful if a fit of nervous giggles suddenly struck us.
Finally, we reformed into mixed gender (now cleansed) groups and went off into the world, you know, the real one. I was with two of my female co-workers from the USA and a

lady from Central America. The Central American lady was full of learned charismatic behaviour, literally oozing everywhere, like it was read, or at least learned from a behavioural script

We were given the task to go and pray into the darkest areas of the city. My heart hit the floor when we pulled up in our van outside the same nightclub I had been in the night before. Not that we go looking for obvious stereotypes, but the club was called the Heart Of Darkness, so bonus points for that.

It became clear that like the CIA, we were to remain unseen, staying in the van and we were to pray as the Lord led. After 10 minutes I thought I would explode, seemingly stretched on the torture rack, roped in between two realities, and I just couldn't cope. Perhaps this trip to Asia was poorly timed in my personal 'life and religion' transition. A therapist would say I was 'in feeling' at that moment but I would just say I was thoroughly pissed off with how institutional ideas were impacting important work.

However, the comedy of errors was not over yet. I found myself explaining to my co-prayers that I found it very difficult to be praying outside a club at a distance when I had been in the same club the previous night, engaging with actual people, responding to what I saw, and connecting relationally for a moment with at least one beautiful human being.

You get me? Right readers? Well, this charismatic Central American lady in the van didn't - God love her!

She assumed that I was full of shame for what I had seen with the prostitution and the things that I had been exposed to. She began to pray in tongues, shumbarakumbarawantakawazaki over me and cast out the heeby jeebies of lust or something similar. (I joke, but I can speak in tongues, yup, though I am not sure what I think of that, as we reframe and move forwards?)

I was just about to break religious protocol and cultural taboos by saying, "good lady - please stop what you are doing, there is a misunderstanding," when suddenly I was saved by an angel. It was definitely an angel, albeit in the form of the biggest mother loving winged bug we had ever seen, excitedly diving its way around the vans occupants. The intercession turned immediately into screams of panic and wails from everyone's inner child and I was saved. I love it when our humanity comes back through to the surface to save the day.

This was probably one of the most internally vomiting experiences of my Christian life. I still feel so embarrassed that I felt that strongly, I hadn't planned it but I could not pull the robes of religious constraint off of me quick enough. I'm shocked by just how much I found it to be otherworldly and counter productive. I really did, and do, love my co-worker who was hosting this trip and introducing us to project partners. He is a dedicated activist working on behalf of sex exploited boys and girls and was supporting, perhaps even initiating some of these projects, all of them doing good stuff, but I just had to say 'Dude WTF'. I didn't enjoy doing that and didn't know if it would be hurtful, which, looking back, I sense that it probably was, I was most likely being a total dick.

It was a clash of paradigms and practices, not of values, love and shared hopes.

If dualism is really that hidden, that subtle, and that invasive, then once we become part of a separated off from life church culture we can no longer see the absurdity of it in our practices and we are not only stuck, but increasingly limited or even irrelevant. Dualism more than informs us that the church as a building is a refuge, a petrol station, an anchor point to where God resides 'most' to help us survive in another world where God is less, or even not at all.

Was it wrong for me to be as offended of the dysfunctional Christian works and their practices as I stood in streets and witnessed the sex abuse that was all around me?

Perhaps I felt it more deeply because we were meant to be their hope, and yet, here we were struggling to walk out of the door of our safely curated world back into the creation we live in, where the Jesus fella resides fully and always has.

I think this is why I spend most of my time with people who aren't Christians and who don't have to navigate two separate worlds before they find their place in life and in helping others.

After previous years of working with young people, a demographic that still haemorrhages out of the church construct in droves each year, perhaps this is the subtle 'splitting off' indoctrination, which leads them to feel that they have left God in the building. As my dad might have said, *"if I had a penny for every time I have heard that"*... I would have, well, I would have quite a lot.

How far reaching, life limiting, and dangerous is this dualistic thinking?

This stuff was not an accident. This separate worlds mentality is rooted in Platonic thinking, sown at the inception of the Western Church as it came to us through Greece, the creation of the sacred and the secular world. At this point you have to imagine some arrogant Muppets entrusted with a new religion in their hands, re-creating priestly roles as intermediaries between the naïve newbies and the God in the sky. In this scenario, to draw a picture of dualism, imagine them creating a church as a sacred space somewhere in the air, above the fallen earth and closer to God. This is their office, their place of business, and the earth is a hopeless irredeemably sinful place where God is absent. At its core, in its function – church today still occupies this place, even if its physical building is visible to us and tethered by gravity to the land. It acts as an in-between place, self labelled as sacred, with its priests (vicars, pastors, preachers) doing their job of letting you know that the church building and its programme is an essential place to be inhabited if you are to be closer to God and survive the worlds filth.

I was told that the greatest lie ever spoken was; 'the devil making you think he doesn't exist', but I would probably suggest that what I have outlined above is the most significant deception we face, rendering many to be hidden, disempowered, passive and superstitious addicts.

If we can eradicate this idea in our thinking, and from our very being, I feel our 'practicing the presence of God' as ever present, instead of 'near or far', 'here or there', will enrich us deeply and help us stand fully as his image bearers, wherever we are. I think we can actually move towards an integrated worldview and become increasingly centred as people. I will leave you to dig your own tunnel deep down into the impact of Platonic dualism, which has coloured your practices and thinking probably from the start, and you might not even realise it. I believe that as an outflow of this, there will also arise much deeper questions for us as individuals about the church as a centralised, high dependency human construct, with its mediating middle men, instead of his body, an integrated movement for love and change in society.

PS: I twitch when people say "I believe that bla bla de bla ", so if you catch me saying that, it simply means "I have an idea".

I think that 'I Have An Idea' is a wonderful explanation of 'faith' by Rufus, the 13th Apostle in the movie Dogma, where Alanis Morisette plays God, which is also awesome.

Im going to borrow a story I heard recently to have one last push shining a spotlight on dualism and it absurdity. It goes like this; One Sunday morning the pastor thought it would be good to honour the people who do the children's work each week since they are largely contributing to the programme out of sight and behind the scenes. A group of women and a few men were invited onto the stage and a time of heartfelt prayer was given in gratitude for their contribution. It took around 10 minutes and the now applauded helpers began to leave the stage full of smiles, all except one of the guys. He asked if he could have the microphone for a moment to share something and began by thanking those gathered for praying for his work in the Sunday school. He then said " *I have valued these prayers for my work with your children on Sundays, but I have never been prayed for, concerning my work as head teacher, actually for my work as regional coordinator for 5 schools and being charged with the education and care of almost 4,000 children!*"

Boom – Drop the Mic - Obama style!

A FRIEND 'BECOMING'

ATHENS NORTHERN SOUL CLUB

Chapter 8

High Dependency Culture

"Are You Not Entertained?"
Maximus Decimus Meridius
(Gladiator)

At some point in the emergence of church across the globe it shifted from organic to organised, which is simply a point of historical fact, regardless of who you blame, and most blame Emperor Constantine. Though in truth it seems we carry the need to structure, organise and control within us. At another point we went from just singing, perhaps more in the vein of how people carried oral tradition and story telling, to having musical accompaniment, and then onto musical group 'front led' singing. We moved from solemn observance in a man made sanctuary of wood and stone to a highly competitive show which needed to entertain you, followed by unpacking a scripture in a more interesting way than when you last heard it, telling you what the future will be without a crystal ball, diagnosing your personal destiny and causing you to feel that 'God is very Big and you are very small'. This is enabled through a captivating feel sad then feel good music corridor, befitting the very best church version of what Disney, Broadway or the West End has to offer. More amazing, it has to do this for you every Sunday morning, though thankfully there is no shortage of Christian musicians serving the construct with their wings clipped from using their skills to contribute and create in society.

It didn't used to be like this, so was there a tipping point toward becoming culturally relevant or perhaps a slide toward consumer appeasing and marketable product creation? When you consider the church missed having any cultural relevance in the 50's and 60's having deemed Rock n Roll and the Beatles to be the devil's own music, something significant has arisen, mimicking instead of rejecting the mainstream in the half century that followed. This cannot be denied.

I remember being at a youth church conference where, because we used Dj's both on our club nights and as an element of our song singing, we were asked to participate in a seminar on the progression of church music. Our guitar-playing singer James and Martin, one of our Dj's joined with Graham Kendrick of March for Jesus fame and Martin Smith of Delirious. Overall it seemed that even with those present there as a ' brief generational age span', there had been a significant progression from the worship leader, through to full worship bands and everything in between. Essentially this relatively modern approach to worship in the gatherings, continued to, well, modernise, but for whom and for what purpose?

Lets face it, you would be pretty miffed to show up on a Sunday and have no 'hymn sandwich' to cushion the blow of the academic sit and listen session with the inclusion of 'make sense' metaphors and visual aids. Imagine it, if you go to the building you give the name church, and all you had was the sermon and the notices. Imagine Hillsongs saying that they were not going to play any of their now generic music ever again. Whilst I don't really see a biblical narrative of people singing 'To' Jesus when he was alive, my critique is not one of 'should it be part of the meetings', since I don't really place much value on said meetings or their existence anyway. The issue I take with this is the part that it plays in the theatrical nature of the gathering, the consumer orientated programme, which has been diarised for your enjoyment so you can say 'we had a good time of worship'. My issue is that it creates a feeling orientated relationship to God that has to be sustained like a comforting addiction or worse, a **'God Is Close' addiction.**

For further context regarding theatre and emoting a feeling, I have often pointed out to my wife the soundtrack to teen thriller The Vampire Diaries as being an almost parallel universe to modern church songs. They are there to make you feel sad, be drawn to certain characters, catch the tension in a love triangle, celebrate and even share in their loss. Today I was watching Legacies (an offshoot of vampire diaries and originals) where Hope Mikaelson a Tribryd of Witch, Werewolf and Vampire was feeling rejected and dejected until her Originals series Witch Aunt 'Freya' comes to comfort her... all to the soundtrack of Lauren Daigle's alluring and beautiful worship track 'Rescue':

I hear you whisper underneath your breath

I hear your, your SOS

I will send out an army to find you

In the middle of the darkest night

It's true, I will rescue you

I meet a lot of post-construct people (by which I mean they don't go to meetings anymore and have cast off many of the rituals) aged 18-30 yrs. Among them are wild eyed and bushy tailed pastors kids and those brought up in the church as an organisation, who found the gap between the culture of church and the culture of society simply too vast to bridge. In the healthy independence journey of flying the family nest, there is often a strong aspect of flying the faith family nest. They really truly do feel that they have left God in the building either fully or in part, largely based on the reality ur dualistic approach or default to separate church from society, means **we have resurrected the temple and placed God theoretically, or experientially back inside of it.**

The reason I add the word 'experientially' as an adjective in regard to song singing is because I meet far too many people caught up in **a toxic mind-set that God is near or far based on an experience.** He is with them or away from them, based on an emotion or feeling and not the facts as the bible seems to present them. After all, we are meant to walk with and flow from the ever present spirit within us, essentially to never feel like orphans, abandoned or distant from God ever again.

Need a language adjustment much? What's the underlying agenda for God being more in the meetings and rituals than elsewhere, more present through a feeling than not?

The problem with how a great many people come to experience faith and step into a Christian journey is often highly experiential. I don't mean the personal encounter that they may have had or a miraculous healing, I mean the highly emotive activities which take place afterwards, in the gathering and in particular the 'lets meet with God' 'lets come into his presence' song singing session. You can probably add some of your own phrases here, which imply you are going nearer to god or he is closer to you. I'm sure there are many such terms used and perhaps in your head as a measure of how well you are doing, how obedient, how in attendance you've been to the faith measuring proximity meter of the meetings.

Some of this idea is based on the rather spurious proof texting of ' God inhabits the praises of his people' which is really again implying the 'more than anywhere else' aspect, which isn't what's written. God is either always present through the indwelling of his spirit or he isn't.

"If worship is not primarily about you feeling good, you would be singing laments, expressing travail and sheer misery, like a third of David's psalms"

For me this places or creates a narrative for believers that God is more in the building than outside of it, more present in the activities and shows up in a special way as you sing songs. This for me is where the construct builds, or perpetuates a perceived need in you, so that 'you', have need of 'it'. This is why it's important to give some critique to what may be building in you a high dependency and not allowing you to mature, stand on your own two feet and come to the God person, **not for what you need, but solely because of who he is**, which is actual worship.

I believe this to be one aspect of organised Christianity, which perpetuates the suggestion that God's Spirit leaks out of you as you endure un-sacred work in the week. You endure life between the higher sacred place of the gatherings and the world with its work, that you have need of the spirit fuel 'gas station' at the weekend, to be 'filled', to come 'near' and to 'meet' with him.

My Chemical Romance

I do not want to scorn where I have been, I sang as loud if not louder than everyone else. The songs were frequently emotional in nature and I responded accordingly with tears and sobs. There is nothing wrong with the beauty of a song whose words were, *'by your side, I would stay, in your arms I would lay, Jesus lover of my soul, nothing from you I withhold'* (thank you Noel Richards), such is beauty and the craft of the artist. I loved to sing such things, I was just happy to sing and it resonated with my desire but truly, *there is something about* **the culture of where such singing sits.It causes me concern, that we are hindered from progressing into the 'what's next' mature relating** with the divine because we seek to perpetuate the early days of our dating, our falling in love, the rush of chemicals and the intimacy of love making. But even in human relations, if we constantly seek to revisit that 'with all of our being' seductive, intoxicating stage of entering into intimacy, the foundational moments of becoming a couple, we risk living in disappointment. It isn't meant to be something constant, it's not meant to be

113

sustained. We aren't meant to keep trying to mimic that moment to 'feel' as we did. We are meant to bring some of that with us, but those early days of heady falling in love, are not the place that a relationship grows and matures. So, that's me rambling a little about that point, but I think there is something funky, not quite right, about trying to revisit as a constant, the emotions and chemical enhancement of our beginning an intimate relationship. I say this as I have met people who do not get past the high emotional and intoxicating euphoria of falling in love with another human being, and going from one relationship to another solely to perpetuate that experience, but still inwardly craving a place of rest and belonging. I have to say, any relationship requiring this amount of investment to re-invigorate things as constant or simply to maintain things is a pretty shitty relationship, right? I do recognise the healing nature of some songs, a salve for the soul, perhaps speaking to wounds and perhaps the first few times its heard and sung, it's a mantra contributing to wellness, but after a while, it just becomes self indulgent, feel good entertainment.

If our desire is to keep a God person/idea as part of our journey, its important that this finds increasing substance, as we any relationship. This means its going to have to go through a shift, whereby we no longer go to this entity for what we can get, no longer come in need, no longer come to sustain a feeling, but instead we are coming because of who that person is. The same way in a functioning relationship, we know them, they know us and were sticking around because of who we know them to be. That's what happens when we get past emotion driven foundation laying, beyond the hype, dopamine and surge of oxytocin.

Temple Mentality

My personal passion has always been for the generation behind me, those coming after me, or what the church often calls the 'rising generation'. There is a substantive fact that what we call the church, haemorrhages literally thousands of young people year in and year out with those leaving being primarily church kids. As they reach their late teens and early 20's, regardless of how cool you feel the programme is, the vast majority of them will leave and never return. Their leaving is not my concern, their leaving a gathering place and feeling that they have left God there, based on indoctrination and the emotion of theatre, well that should concern us all. Some parents draw consolation that what their kids have been taught in the meetings or from the bible 'will not depart from them' (bible verse), which seems pretty irrelevant if they feel that God didn't come with them.

I remember being at a gathering in the UK called Spring Harvest, which was said to be a reflection of the church in the UK across the cultural or denominational divisions. Many thousands would gather in the winter months in closed 'summer holiday sites', where a vast circus tent would hold the masses who had been scattered during the days across a wide selection of seminars and workshop programmes. In one daytime youth programme, the evening speaker had prepared several hundred young people to participate in the main evening's gathering. On cue, they were to get up and leave at a pre-arranged point, the meeting would continue as planned and nothing would be said. The evening event happened, during the talk, the 'cue' was given and the mass of young people got up and walked out. The speaker then continued as if he hadn't noticed but at the end said, " this is numerically representative of the number leaving the whole church in the UK, this is the number of young people who leave us every single year, those who were already part of us. They leave, and we give no attention to why, nor do we mourn their passing."

We fail to have any strategy which can affirm their on-going relationship with the God person now they have stopped attending the meetings``. He continued, "If those who leave the church in just one year, simply remained, church growth would exceed that of any past revival in Britain".

I say "Run Little Ones" but take the indwelling spirit with you and work out your faith in the Real, away from the Upside Down (for fans of TV show 'Stranger Things') ıve zero interest in keeping young people in anything other than a walk with God if that's what scratches their itch. If it's not, I still want them to live a full and rich life. I have maximum interest in their journey, their spirituality and meaningfulness continuing onwards and outwards as they seek to live out life in the real world. For me there is something deeply disturbing in the culture of the gatherings and the church as an organisation, laying foundations for damage such as this separation from the God of the meeting place. I'm not sure I want people to have too much contact with Christendom and a need for later deprogramming or restoration.

I don't say any of this to throw song singing in the bin, but to cause you to ask what part it plays for you in your walk, and if in any way it creates in you a sense or feeling that God is near based on an experience, which implies he is more distant at other times. The role it plays is likely to be one you were conditioned into thinking or inherited without even asking why. I don't feel this in any way presents a theological reality of our access to the God person.

For me, it took me reading the first few chapters of Practicing His Presence by Leanne Payne, to appreciate that aspects of church culture perpetuates a connection to the divine which remains a relationally swinging pendulum and that, dear reader, is just pure dysfunction.

If there was song singing in the early church, it is likely to be along the lines of oral tradition, expressing in words the nowness of now, of suffering or delight and what a therapist would call expressing gratitude. If the message in the world of the unwritten cultures was to be carried by the bards, they were the glue between the generations carrying the history and story across the generations of a tribe. That's not what we have today or the same 'useful function' context of what it is we are doing.

The reason for calling out what I deem to be the high dependency culture of church world, is that I think part of what it contributes is counter productive. Even to its own aspirations, but it's difficult to stop doing what you told people was important. The congregation does not want to lose you and as such perpetuates a need, which is not meant to help you grow up and fly the nest. The church construct talks endlessly about family, yet follows no natural model of how a family is meant to work and does not enable you to self actualise, reach maturity and go have children of your own. It doesn't 'launch you into life', enabling a new relationship to the mother ship to be defined or simply left behind, such is life when your children grow and make free will choices as adults. We don't get to keep them, we can only hope they want us around.

``Whom the son sets free is free indeed", but somehow the church perpetuates a considerable list of risk averse activities that you perform to be able keep that freedom. The narrative of church is one of destiny and fully becoming, and yet its practices are not aligned with this. I have often heard pastors infuriated that their members are not maturing with a sense of them projecting blame upon the member, while not even beginning to inquire to the nature of the inherited system that is in reality an obstruction to this growth.

Much of my work these days is helping projects and organisations identify inherited thinking or where an organisational culture has developed which is counter productive. Projects often use business speak and in principle can at least make the suggestion 'Lets Blank Canvas' this or that, implying let's think about what 'could' be, without any restrictions of what currently 'is'. For the organisation which has the name church, this is an impossible concept and as such, it is the reason that people eventually have to spill out, simply to keep moving forwards, to try something new, to flee constraints or remove a once immovable object from their lives. As leaders or members of the church system, what have we inherited without question and what have we adopted which was explicitly or implicitly communicated needs consideration. Is any of this counter productive to our faith, our journey, our time to invest in friendships outside the construct or our coming to fullness?

(Disclaimer: Fullness is a word I inherited as a positive term about what might occur if we get unstuck. Fullness does not mean perfection, or an end product, but instead being free to be the best version of ourselves in the moment, in the now, without hindrance, self harming beliefs or life limiting inherited thinking).

Personally, I have not been in a song singing worship environment for two decades. I do not miss it, I continue to 'feel' and the concept of God being present has entirely lost its counterproductive, near or far thinking.

ACCORDING TO WHOM?

OUT OF TOUCH

Chapter 9

Dialogue Versus Debate

The Art Of Communication

I remember talking at my daughter Holly's wedding and using the most bizarre analogy for why we may not be right about something, even if we really think we are.

I 'outed' my eldest son Jesse, sharing that he, like me, was a 'plucker'. He was blessed with the mono-brow, which means that unless it's separated in the middle, your brow is pretty much a furry caterpillar separating your eyes from your hairline. We should have bought shares in eyebrow tweezer production, that's how serious these mono-brows were. We had bought so many pairs of tweezers over the years, necessitated by the females of the house removing ours (the boys) from the bathroom to use in their own beauty regime, never to be returned.

I had come to the end of my patience after having bought a new deluxe, pink rubber gripped, matted black world shaping pair of tweezers. I mean this was serious business since I had never spent more than two pounds on a pair before. Two weeks later, they disappeared. I was wholeheartedly convinced that this disappearing act was my daughters and wife disrespecting the facial hair needs of the male members of the household. I thought I had to be right in every conceivable, logical way, and I told them so, as nicely as I could; "Stop Bloody Thieving My Tweezers, I'm Sick Of It!"

Two weeks later I was humbled by a new piece of information. We had two cats at the time, and being chilly wet England, we had a cat flap so they could come and go from the house at will, without, as my parents used to scream, 'letting all the bloody heat out!'.

What we didn't realise is that this flap also enabled the neighbourhood cats to come and go, helping themselves to the cat food and finding a cushion to sleep on. There was a growing amount hair tufts of an unusual colour, which was a dead give away.

Solution? We bought a deluxe 'catmaster' auto lock magnetic cat flap!

My wife was leaving the house one day and saw our cat rolling around in a neighbour's garden and wrestling with something. On closer inspection she found that the cat was wrestling with a pair of tweezers. To operate the new cat flap the cats had a magnetic grey mouse attached to their collar that lifted the door latch as they came and went. Consequently, they had moved into the scrap Metal business by attaching to random Metal objects and thus, the tweezers were spread throughout the neighbourhood.

You can be oh so right, and at the same time, oh so wrong because there is stuff you just didn't know or see yet, "you took my tweezers" - "no I didn't" - " you must have, since I have a good argument as to why I am right and you are wrong"

Needless to say that after my public family disclosures my other daughter Emily is not rushing to book me as her wedding speaker.

The Shift From Modernity

I'm old enough to remember modernity as an inherited worldview. Essentially, it was a time when we believed that science and human effort would end world hunger, end sickness, and all things could be accomplished. The prolonged period of this not happening gave way to a time when critical questions could be asked. In between the absolutes and the non delivery was a period of patriarchal positioning where a new generation would, with concern and intrigue ask, "Why should we believe this or that", and the former generation would reply with, "Because you should" or "Because I said so". The former generation would mask the fact that they didn't know the answer, while requiring your submission and obedience to a greater authority and wisdom.

I remember being asked to speak at a Youth Church Conference called REMIX on the subject of Post Modernity This topic was assigned to me after all the 'cool hip' topics had already been cherry picked. The senior leader from another organisation seemed to think I was up to the task and after my driving 70 miles to meet with him in hopes of gaining helpful insights, it became clear that he was none the wiser himself. I understood this to be the case after I said "but I don't understand post modernity" and he replied "exactly, and that's the point." Ever been left to dangle? Eventually, I fudged my way through the conference session (which he had the nerve to sit in on) by focusing on post modernity's impact upon communication styles.

One of the critical aspects of the shift between the time of modernity and post modernity might as well be a new generation. A generation who feel absolutely free to ask critical questions and enter shared dialogue as the means of learning from one another. I feel this is a critical aspect of people leaving organised Christianity, having as a generation the urge to ask questions and find realistic answers. For too long the norm was to debate as the primary style of formal communication, which, in some respects, leaked out into our daily lives and our communicating with each other. The way that debate works is from the outset it is positional and, to this day, remains a learning style in many places of education, where the purpose of the discourse is to determine through superior knowledge and argument who is the winner and who is the loser. My patience to listen to people who start from a position of believing they are right has worn thin.

A friend posted this question, "What is wrong with us as Christians that we don't see the healings and miracles in the Bible happening in our lives or on the streets?" I posted some thoughts I have about living in 'post' Christian contexts these days, where people have had a faith, which is personal, and many have lost it. Not a faith as the result of national identity or a faith as the result of kings or colonial imposition. Most of the bible stories about miracles are about Christianity coming into a new place, city, country. Jesus being brought into new spaces, new places, and such 'signs' being a positive expression that something good has happened (perhaps in the absence of a band and video projector, 'healings' were what brought all the boys to the yard). The Bible doesn't really speak to our reality, the reality of what happens in a place after people have ceased to be interested in the Jesus person. We need imagination for this, not historical models.
Another reply was posted from someone from YWAM;
"No, what you need is more faith, more authority in the Holy spirit and courage to go onto the street, to preach the gospel and pray for healing'." I left the conversation with a post saying 'this is no longer a dialogue". I don't really 'do' people who know shit, who think the solution to everything spiritual is 'Try Harder" #thingsjesusneversaid. This debating or positional method of communication is alive and well within the constructs of Christendom. It most serves the perpetuation of established positions and doctrines, which are not up for critique or alternative views.
The emerging method of communication, which completely undermines the positionality of debate, is dialogue. Differing greatly from debate, it offers a framework for people coming together as co learners. A place where both parties are

willing to 'offer' their perspectives and views in a context where they may come away enriched or with a different outlook.

I saw a cheeky Facebook post amongst the recovering community, which was a play on Nike's 'Just Do It', It said No amount of belief in something makes it a FACT - 'Just Doubt It'

My youngest son Jacob hosts a podcast called SenseSpace and was actually on the debate team at his university. Exploring other forms of connecting and learning is something he is passionate about. He has created a space where the concept of shared learning is taken to other levels of revelation and appreciation. His 'practice' is a million miles away from debate.

The term he would use is 'Dia Logos' which means there is a considerable love and appreciation for what other people are bringing, a respect for what you are hosting and contributing. That in coming together, learning can be shared and appreciated. There is also the capacity for new insights and wisdom to emerge, which prior to the discourse, neither party was in possession of. I am deeply intrigued by this way of communicating which he refers to as flow or flow state. I have experienced this with him on occasion as we talked without agenda.

It is difficult to convey this next point in writing as it lacks tone, and this part is all about tone. I wasn't aware of this at the time, but perhaps it was a fun aspect of my own detoxing and also an opportunity for my own family to tell me when I was talking out of my backside or being positional. This is something you may wish to adopt. In short, there are two ways to say 'You Know Shit'. The first is in a way that implies or applauds that someone has some interesting, unique insights, as well as wisdom. The other is geared more towards 'you have no clue what you're talking about'. The fun part is when you use a tone that is less obvious and the recipient is unsure if you are affirming them or taking the piss. Nobody said that deconstructing couldn't be fun. Try it out next time someone is inflicting a monologue on you.

It is still problematic in the church world to have enquiry or dialogue in a system, which prides itself on knowing answers, and when pushed, is a system defending what it knows like a hungry dog protecting a bone. It is not a context which steps readily into dialogue, or makes you feel safe with your new found confidence and comfort sitting with 'what you don't know'. **Knowledge is not king in a world where an unknowing is a valued aspect of faith**. Church is the domain of oral tradition (in regard to narrating that which is written), the up front specialist, and the lecture style, regardless of where it sits on the dull as dishwater to charismatic rant spectrum. It has never really made sense to me that in this modern age, where we have a much better understanding of how people learn or receive information that we still stick to the platformed talking head and the passive listening audience.

"Debate in church world is an attempt to cling to the illusion of control provided by a point of view designed to prop up an ideology and ego"

It has been a while since I looked at this information, but the last time I did, these were the dynamics of learning styles in society and how people learn things best:

Audible/ Listening 30% - Visual 65% - Kinesthetic (practical/touch/ feel) 5%.

Dialogue starts with the willingness to have our own thinking challenged.

The most important aspect of this shift from modernity, in my view, was the permission to question anything and everything, especially if it does not deliver what was promised. Also to critique that which comes with a cost not explicitly stated in the small print. The church generally keeps to the specialist model of a speaker disseminating information to the passive. This partly happens because it does not sufficiently question the model it has inherited, and feels that the introduction of the sacred OHP and now video

:ctors are tools from heaven, helping us to retain this approach. This shift was not good for the church as an institution, with the new era of critique and of 'questions which matter'. This is part of why many are feeling more comfortable with walking away. Not leaving one place with inadequate answers to a place with better answers, but into a space where they can sit with the intrigue of the question, the place of asking, seeking and knocking which remain central tenets to the core of what faith is. 'Blessed are those who do not see and yet still believe', should have the addition of 'blessed are those who's faith is not based on knowing stuff'.

'Biblical accuracy, in harvesting the spoken word? Like us, those reporters still probably only remember 10% of what they heard with no audio recorder or laptop to improve on that.

Again, dialogue starts with the willingness to have our own thinking challenged. In the world of 'followers' there are many who will shoot you down if you even begin to challenge their 'known' positions. Those moving away from fixed beliefs, behaviours, and systems have little to gain by trying to explain themselves to those who fearfully remain, unless they come as co learners.

INTEGRATION

Chapter 10

Commodification

"I'll Take That!"

Commodification
noun
1. the action or process of treating something as a mere commodity.

Whilst working with a team, trying to release finances and support to projects, I learned about the commodification of the church and **bastard initiatives**. That's the honest name to what the centralised church calls projects that the organisation did not birth and does not control. It is often the case that, whether we use this language or not, the unifying vision of the church organisation comes top down, from the 'anointed appointed' of the group. While some space may be made for ideas from the members, or some willing members are sought to deliver the top down stuff to youth groups or lunch clubs for the elderly, anything that doesn't fit the norm or the existing framework often remains un-affirmed and as such is on its own. Some will be permitted to progress an idea while others will be so controlled or discouraged that they will no doubt join the many hundreds of initiatives aborted close to conception or soon after they begin.

The church has had to create a term where it allows and accommodates, without causing too much damage, those projects born outside the fold. It calls these Para Church groups, which simply means 'not from the legitimate church', therefore damning them as illegitimate or in solid English, the Bastard child. I've found this concept to be incredibly offensive for many years. I feel it is one of the most condescending and cruel reference points, which the church has adopted along with all of its accompanying behaviour and distancing. Lets not mess around with placations and niceties, whenever you hear the word Para it means illegitimate. So go on, hear the word bastard and feel the anger that you should and the pomposity of those who justify it. I've actually tried to challenge this para idea with pastors and have had the issue pushed home, "these are not projects of the church, we recognise them but they are not ours." Commodification occurs when the church changes its mind and wants that project for its own.

Commodification in governments is not uncommon either. It's when the state and those in positions of power do not know how to progress with an issue, and then something outside the norm, which has been faithfully birthed at grass roots, by people seeking to address community problems comes into view. Those wonderful, contextual explorers have discovered through doing the hard ground work, creating an alternative economy, ethos, or approach, have responded creatively to a human need not met by the state. Something fresh, with bucket loads of contextual and 'alongside' learning has been birthed. The state then takes the idea, with little appreciation of the cost paid by those who gave it life, re-brands it a little to make something more palatable, and then makes it their own. Sadly this occurs often without any of the dynamic learning, which came from those who founded it.

This happened in the UK not so long ago when the state noticed how much responsibility local charities and community groups were taking in their localities, contributing to change and needs. It launched something called 'Big Society', essentially milking the social solidarity and volunteerism in communities whilst removing government funds from the charity sector. It is not too cynical to suggest that the commodification primarily takes place regarding ideas and initiatives that make the hierarchy or organisation look good, life engaged, and dynamic.

The Church as an organisation can do the same with ideas, people, and projects. I had a good friend who developed an aspect of support work in health-clubs. I guess in some respects it was still flowing out of a traditional pastoral way of **doing stuff to and for people**, but the context was dynamic. This person began to gain national attention for the work and some articles were written. In addition more workers were sought and work was rolled out in other health clubs large and small. Essentially, this baby had legs and began to walk. There were some beautiful aspects of synergy to the efforts, such as those who were recovering from surgery or injury were sent to the health clubs under doctors orders, perhaps even funded by state healthcare. At the clubs they had people caring for their bodies but not their hearts, minds, loneliness, or the trauma of changes they were facing. There was an evident human need.

The project found life, without practical support from the congregation. All of this progress was happening seemingly without the human invention of 'spiritual covering', which is largely an aspect of church conditioning that means submitting to authority and control. This manipulatively suggests that something is being developed outside the will of God and the devils 'gonna getcha'. Yuck.

The example goes like this. Generally, I think they were tolerated for doing something off on their own because nobody could question the sincerity of the work. The work began to grow in such a dynamic way that it was occasionally mentioned in prayers on a Sunday as the work they were doing, and then after being offered support from the leaders it would be spoken of with the royal 'We', the work 'we' are doing as a church, even if funding or human resources were not yet forthcoming. There were concerns expressed as to how the work was placing time pressures on some of her church responsibilities. I'm imagining that there was likely a presence of 'counter affirmation', expressing more gratitude for the 14hrs they gave to helping with the worship group and far less for the work outside, but I'm guessing.

On the flipside, sometimes commodification is not about resisting potential control from the church organisation. Instead, such affirmation and inclusion is sought out, or comes as a great relief. The work is succeeding and finally the church has taken notice of it, brought it under its banner/covering and dare I say, legitimised the previously illegitimate. That person can relax as the work now has support. They are essentially 'in from the cold'. The greatest risk in the latter is that being a co-opted project of the church means their reputation is now also caught up with the project's success. It is now a story of the collective and is likely to be pressured away from experimentation into the safe world of the risk averse. Sadly, it is also the nature of the work pioneered beyond the church walls that it may not do well in the hands of congregational leaders. The leaders who have been trained to know certain stuff, to teach, to replicate or grow 'what is' and run an engaging programme of meetings. Most pastors cannot help people to stand effectively in community projects or the workplace, as it is a place they left some time ago or never truly stood.
Be in no doubt that commodification can be overt and unashamedly part of the agenda. One faith based prominent organisation in anti trafficking work had brought some aggressive behaviour for multiplication of congregation to its multiplication of justice works. I remember seeing a celebratory PR communication in some of the organisations press, where it communicated having 'personally contributed' to the rescue and recovery of hundreds of women in forced prostitution in Romania. I immediately knew this was, well, bollocks. This was startling to me as I had been working in Romania for some years and nobody I worked with knew the mega group was even

working there. It was only then that I realised this group had employed (co-opted or released) a woman who had been a frontline pioneer in Romania for many years. Overnight, her work, efforts, and stories became the success story of the new organisation. It can be unclear as to whether a group is truly interested in change, or able to 'buy' change and re-label it as their own. I just find Christian groups employing people for their skills but also as a PR asset, somewhat unpalatable. Possibly it is an insufficiently critiqued element within organisations, and the privilege of those with money, to support people or buy them as part of organisational growth and to feed the narrative of organisational 'wins' as a constant. Worse still is that those who work under the umbrella and fund such organisations, have an expectation of constantly providing a story, and with that comes the pressure of hierarchical goals.

Commodification needs to be anticipated and understood as one of the patterns of organised Christianity under which some, not all, but certainly some have been burned. Sadly there are likely as many projects thrown under the bus as there were that progressed.

Competition and Duplication

When working as a group to find, encourage, and perhaps fund grassroots people and projects, we would have a keen interest in what else might be out there in the person's community.
In my hometown of Bournemouth the pre existing competition and duplication of the church is self-evident, it is also helped by the historical pseudo-spiritual mind-set of wanting to occupy the geographical high places. From some positions in the town you can see a myriad of church spires close to one another and a short walk from one another. Some of them were even breakaway groups starting new competing churches within the shadow of the one they had left. Each with a desire to brand lost souls as their stock, their family, their tithers, their wins, their flock and their future. I

know from experience this is even worse in the USA where you don't just have competing diversity you have competing numeracy, 1st Presbyterian, 2nd Presbyterian etc.

One chunk of research I read about had been taken with the permission and participation of most of the local churches in a large city. There were something like 27 employed church youth workers, who, after the maths, were looking after an average of 9 young people each, young people from its Christian families which we used to refer to as 'maintenance' youth work keeping little Billy and Ginny safe from the nasty people out there!

I did hear one redemptive story of a church which had financial resources but no young people, funding the youth worker of a neighbouring church which had several (though I now get less excited about such in-house progress as it can only be limited).

Another aspect of research showed considerable progress across the churches in having projects serving the elderly, though there was not one church in the town serving those who were disabled or having limited mobility.

If church connects with the wider community at all, it is a general theme that little research is done into what actual needs exist, or if they, the church, are the people who can best meet them. Engaging with community needs should never be about giving your brand a success story to sustain the feel good factor of a community that is 'doing'. Just because you can, doesn't mean you should. Actually, in the UK over the last 20 years, most church organisations will have a community-serving project, like an awakening occurred where we felt the conviction to serve non-members. There has been a considerable increase in either community projects in the church building (come to us) or placed in the community (done for you and to you but not with you) but these are infant steps and a nominal aspect of the church focus, a box ticked even though it may have come from genuine compassion.

Competing with each other is not a good use of resources and it is so often not coming from an informed place of reaching a need or contributing to change, this is rarely a truly person centred or community engaged approach.

Shoots and Roots of Change

In recent decades, the UK has seen widespread poverty become exposed, though it was always there to some varying degree. A lovely, not so little project called Food Bank has come to the fore in response to this need. It came out of a fundraising gathering where I believe the English founders of a feeding programme in Bulgaria were seeking to increase their reach and impact through fundraising in the UK. One of those attending, having heard the presentation on the needs of those in Bulgaria, spoke out and said "but we have those same needs in our own community, so why aren't we addressing that problem here."

It was such a transformative moment that the founders responded with a food-bank initiative where they would begin to interact with local social services to identify needs, people would be given a token and they could go to a food-bank to obtain a box of goodies based on the size of the family. The food initially came from individual donors who would buy a little extra with the weekly shopping. All of this then grew into a nationwide initiative being supported by major supermarkets who direct 'almost out of date' food to the banks.

This is to be applauded. It has certainly done a job of meeting an identified need and multiplying the work, it has also been the 'go to' organisation for when the national media wants to comment on the state of the nation regarding food poverty. Were it not for their work, I would not know that there are London nurses regularly using the service since they cannot sustain adequate living conditions in the city on their wages. As a young family we were also relieved to have been recipients of such basic support except ours was called the Love Box and was distributed to families of faith and of none, if you were lucky enough to know someone in the church.

So let's go to the bit that is not quite so good about all this.

Trailing Leg Syndrome

This is a phrase that I often use in therapeutic contexts with individuals or as an illustration with struggling projects. Essentially, when something progresses or takes a step forward, it is to be celebrated, but progress often serves to highlight the trailing leg, causing us to address what needs to happen next, for that leg to follow through and enable us to find momentum, to walk. Such is life! The church is often 'needs' focused and not change focused. What the food banks highlighted was a need, but whose responsibility was it to actually address poverty, low wages, and unemployment at a national and local level? Surely it's the state?

We can do some incredible work in bringing change to a family and they no longer have to endure hunger, but we can be incredibly weak in addressing why that poverty exists. Where are we engaging in the roots of an issue? Where are we participating in systemic change.

I'll take another example out of my work in counter child trafficking. Having visited safe homes for recovering adults and children sold into sex slavery in several areas of Europe and Asia, I can say with confidence that these bring amazing change the lives of those affected. However, they change little in terms of the reasons those children were exploited, such as addressing demand of buying sex or implementing criminal laws to punish traffickers and to asset strip them. A trafficker could make 200,000 USD in a single year from the forced sex work of just one girl or boy and yet they could be sent to prison for four years, out in two and still be rich.

My observation of the church organisation globally, is of them being strong on compassion and mercy responses, but weak on strategically effecting change. Compassion can be how we respond to emotive stories of the trauma people who are trafficked have experienced and the need to recover from the exploitation. Perhaps the emotional hook for us is simply getting them out, fuelling the work of those doing rescues. Essentially, this gets 90% of our attention and donor funding, and yet it does little or nothing in terms of long term systemic change. The majority of prevention work in anti trafficking comes from funds raised through stories of rescue and restoration; prevention is virtually un-fundable which is simply crazy. The church can also be naive and ill informed in its approach. I actually met someone who collected money from Christian businessmen to buy slaves from their traffickers, without any clue that the trafficker just procures another victim and their compassion is contributing to the demand/profit and produces more victims. Compassion is a very strong driver for Christians but we are pretty weak on being strategic or looking at contributing to bringing change to the big picture. Using pictures of victims and pictures of children is increasingly seen as a re-victimisation of the individual and for some also a sign of their voluntourism, selfies of their meeting a need of others and also that of their public ego. Our need to be moved creates or perpetuates other problems.

"Safe homes are the ambulance at the bottom of the human trafficking cliff, and quite honestly there are not enough of them and never will be enough of them. Yet no-one is building a fence at the top of the trafficking cliff to stop the next generation being recruited and being pushed off."

The ambulance is our mercy and compassion, creating the fence is prevention and strategy, those things, which contribute to change as we connect at the root of issues in society. Sadly, something which to date still needs challenging and a paradigm shift. This and many other things are the trailing leg behind our good, compassionate works, which must be explored and helped to travel through.

How can our contribution in society be both merciful, generous and strategically contribute to systemic change? **Systemic change 'out there' is something that is important to explore but will be very limited while we are unable to change our own restrictive 'separated off from life' church system.** We may also need to unplug, pull out the wires and stop our conditioned behaviour, again, like so many other areas, based on feeling and emotion.

Cookie Cutter Ideas

I remember driving around different communities in the USA while our daughter and husband were exploring where they would move to next for schools and other things. Some communities were full of colour and diversity whereas the homes in other localities were identical, generic, functional and unappealing. Replication is easier, but often not enriching.

Church organisations can get pretty excited about models from other organisations, which have been implemented in different cities or countries. The 'new model' approach often arrives as someone's next book on 'How To Reach People or How To Keep People' is often the way in which the construct arrives at new things. The problem is that **a model isn't meant to show you how it 'should be done", but encourages us that something 'can' be done.** Perhaps there's a sharing of values, contextual approaches and learning (often lost in commodification and replication).

How many models are adopted from elsewhere? How many models have you participated in as they are explored or outworked in the programme of the church organisation? How many national campaigns have you participated in? Some UK campaigns were called 'The Decade Of Evangelism' 'Ask Jim' (Jesus In Me) with its billboards and bus stickers and then there was March For Jesus, which saw many thousands on the streets nationally with banners saying 'Hi – We Are The Church'. With these was the model or concept of achieving critical mass through sheer numbers or spread of media as the strand, which had previously been missing. The problem with adopting franchise or cookie cut models is that they often do not allow for the diverse cultural contexts in different localities that we live in. Applying something that works in one place doesn't necessarily work in another.

What if we got the picture wrong? What if we mobilised the country and other countries to show up in public as Christians in a vitriolic song singing banner waving; 'lift up your head oh you gates, swing wide you ever lasting doors, that the king of glory may come in' (as some of the songs went), when the nudge from God was that we were to integrate, be known, be present, come with humility and join in with the others on the planet trying to make life work?

To show up fully! One is about an event, an idea, a visit; the other about permanent realignment and participating in movement.

Copy Me

When starting something new, as an arm of an existing organisation the question was, "Have you been asked to do a Franchir (which comes from the word 'Franc' meaning 'free'), or have you bought into being a Franchise?" Franchise is to repeat what already exists, in the same way with the whole game mapped out. Franchir means 'freedom within a framework', essentially marking out the lines of the soccer pitch so you know where the edges are, but you are free to play and enjoy a creative game. It's a question someone asked me while exploring how to progress working with a seemingly flexible group. If a Franchir approach, I imagine there is little ability to explore since there is too much inherited thinking as to what must happen within those lines. Does that make sense, that if we have freedom to do something new we have a lot to unlearn to break with the dominant pattern. Sometimes you think you have been given space to explore and its not until you travel out a little, that you find your are actually on a pretty strong pre determined leash/umbilical/bungee

Beats, Kicks and Sugar

An example might be how when we were working with non church youth on two housing estates, one middle class and the other, well, less so. We used mainstream Raves (think of a precursor to Coachella in California or depending on age, a mini Woodstock). Generally loud music, big sound systems, the craziest lighting effects, smoke machine overkill and heavy syncopated beats. They worked on our two areas, but then we had the clever idea to take this relationship and connection event (we used CAPS and NAPS, Created Access Points and Natural Access Points) onto another housing estate which was actually thoroughly working or underclass, separated from our turf by just one single highway. The road represented a boundary between distinct communities with our eyes set on what was deemed by police at the time to be our counties 'open prison' due to the high level of ex offenders and current crime.

The night went like this, we flyered invitations around the streets and outside schools as normal, and this was where normal ended. We had a team of around 20 people running the night in an old hut, which was probably a community centre in the Second World War years, with a huge corrugated asbestos roof. It looked like a cross between a pigpen and an aircraft hanger and had probably housed community activities for 70 years or more.

The night begins, I'm picked out to do security on the door and drug searches (R.O.A.R - right of admission reserved), which was problematic as I was in mid-flow with a bad bout of man flu (same as lady flu bit with 80% more moaning) with all the related aches and pains. Having searched several disgruntled raver lads and my female co-workers Sonia and Caroline searching the girls, I witnessed one of our 6'4" co-workers running past the door outside, with a group of angry shouty guys following behind. I went out to find myself in a 'punchy' crowd and pulled a lad off of my friend Ken with my fist raised to punch the lad on the nose, as a multiplicity of conditioned thoughts like 'I'm sure I'm not meant to do this - what about my witness' ran through my head, giving sufficient space for me to be punched by three different people. Much of the time I remained on the floor crawling, my flu filled and punched head back into the venue and receiving one final kick in the face as I did. I remained by the door, having detached a long wooden handle from a cleaners broom determined that 'none shall pass' and relieved that it was quickly over. I think we managed to run the night for less than an hour before it all kicked off. Outside, police were all around us with flashing lights asking "what the hell do you think you are doing here" whilst surveying the post conflict scene of a minor turf war.

The next morning we had to give an account of ourselves to the Anglican church team who had generally given us a long piece of rope, but not for us to hang ourselves. They were especially interested to know why several parents had spent the night in hospital A and E's with young team members who had a few broken noses and a broken wrist.

Feeling rather angry about the battering, as you tend to do when it fuels those night-time moments of 'if I had only done this, if I had only got the first punch in' etc.

I eventually, in the most un-Christian of ways, took solace in our having a new guy there, as yet unconditioned by doctrine. His name was Alky and he had removed a hammer from his pocket and had also crawled around on the floor, bashing people in the knees. Sadly, he died recently, RIP fella.

The next day I also ended up in hospital. I had a massive headache and in my blowing my nose ejected a large bright orange lump of 'glob' into the tissue. It was about the size of a boiled sweet. I couldn't remember shoving one up there and I was certain that during the previous night's fighting that no one had possessed such a unique skill of candy based violation. Determined to go and get checked out at A and E, I asked my wife to pass me a bag, any bag which would enable me to present my mucus proudly to the nurses (please remember that she is at fault as you read on).

After several concerned nurses had come in and out of the examination room, stuffing 'test' sticks up my nose deep enough to dislodge an eyeball, I asked, "what's the matter?" It's good to ask questions. She replied "there is trace sugar in the sample you brought it, which could indicate cerebral spinal fluid leaking somewhere". Feeling rather sheepish now that I had the facts, I asked quietly, "Does it matter that there had previously been a cake in the mucus sample bag!"

And that was the end of that, except for the 15 years of sinus problems, which immediately followed.

Why do I share this story, other than it being a most excellent adventure? I share it because that's the direct impact of simply taking an existing model and associated learning and trying to import it into a very different community. I'm less embarrassed these days that the whole cock up had been my idea, which to be fair was why I was there sweating and aching on door duty instead of tucked up in bed at home getting pampered.

Finally, remember my mate Ken? The tall handsome red headed fella that ran past the door fleeing the mob? As it turns out, he was the 'gasoline' which had been poured onto the 'spark'. On our own housing estate, a girl (the spark) had been coming along to our afternoon 'drop in' centre where we watched MTV, drank tea and played darts. She was actually competing in kickboxing at a national level, which was something quite brilliant for a kid from the rough side of town. Whilst dear Ken was networking at the rave and talking with a group of guys from the area, they had taunted the girl to, well, do a spinning kick on him, as you do during a chat on that estate apparently. Ken, God bless him, a secret ninja with razor sharp reflexes, had managed to catch the girl's foot mid flight and put her on her arse.

And there you go, KABOOM!!!

Again, a model is to show you that it **can** be done, it's an encouragement to explore new concepts, but it's really not about telling you how it **should** be done.

" One Size Fits One, Not All"

Not Your Story

Why do we place value on some stories and not others?

Our little group of community workers funded a local magazine for a housing estate only to find that it was mostly co-opted by the church to talk about its own in-house stories or the programmes they ran from the neighbouring community centre building.

The magazine would also have a 'the pastor speaks' section near the inside cover, a story or encouragement to the community and perhaps an invitation to the church which I'm sure they thought was a highpoint of community engagement.

There seems to be a notion that what the community needs to make it well, is stories from the church group which shows that something good is happening. The church group has little to no desire to seek out and tell the communities own stories back to itself. It's not that those stories do not exist; it is perhaps that the church isn't looking there because there is no benefit to the church. For example, I had a co-worker who was very excited about what he was modelling through his own home, having people live there and giving them positive regard, some psycho social support as a ministry narrative or to be a story to tell from the platform. All good and well, but no one would get to hear of the two families in my own street who were living in extended family conditions, as they too shared love and warmth to excluded or unsupported others. One is doing life, which it seems we are less interested in; one is a ministry story with us at the centre of it.

There was a guy who lived two doors down from our family on our housing estate; he often used to pay my kids to help him as he operated fairground games and rides at summer fairs. This was his main work and passion as he used the activity to raise funds for children with disabilities who could not afford electric wheelchairs. He had lived through such an experience when one of his own children had been disabled and immobilised.

I went into his house to help him make something once. I think I was using my welding abilities to help him make a new side show game. As I looked around his living room there were awards and pictures with celebrities thanking him for his fundraising work with children. All these acknowledgements were unknown to me and we had been neighbours for more than a decade. A few weeks later, he received an award from the Queen herself, an OBE (Order Of The British Empire) for his tireless work fundraising for children. I had a chat with him just a few days later, and he shared something profound;

"Yes, there are two OBE's in our community now, the other was awarded to a woman I had grown up with in the orphanage!" Spoken as though it were of no importance or significance. You needed to pick me up off the floor, what a wonderfully hopeful, restorative, human story and it wasn't being told by the church. Our inability to commodify the story of others for our own self affirming benefit, means we continue to tell our own stories in isolation, **out of a delusion that we are here to heal the community, instead of being participants in its healing of itself** which it is, in my view, actually quite capable of doing,

Perhaps the next story we tell, which brings hope, joy or the desire to dream is not our story, but we share it with passion and excitement regardless. Sadly we are unlikely to hear those stories if our primary orbit is around the church ghetto.

ALUN - SONIA – ME– ANDY @ NIGHT BIN RAVES

Chapter 11

Pick Any Gender As Long As It's Male

In our little hometown community, which was called Bliss, we used to be part of a network of 200 progressive churches, which were at least open to new ideas and new ways. I remember at one national gathering, we arrived at the evening meeting in a conference building and as we entered the men were separated from the women. The men were ushered into the auditorium alone, passing a warm, smiling welcoming committee on our way to the chairs. Once we were all seated, the women were allowed to enter the meeting and to stand at the back. Along with most of the men present, I had given this strange scenario about one second of my time. I settled comfortably in my seat as the male specialist began to speak very clearly to the men, probably about important man stuff but I can't remember. The formality was suddenly shattered by a woman who began shouting from the back. Subsequently shooting my adrenaline through the roof as I anticipated an embarrassing punch-up. She continued shouting and making her way to the front, with a wagging finger of accusation in the direction of the platform leader stating, "'how dare you treat women this way'". She was clearly disgusted, whereas I was clearly and deeply disrupted.

My heart was pounding and I was very unsettled by what seemed to be a genuine conflict, even when the man and the woman explained that this was a set up. It was to challenge the status quo and how easy it is to slide back into the former years of our adopted, segregated religion. I found arguments and shouty behaviour between men and women really uncomfortable, perhaps as a result of growing up in a shouty home, where my parents were often heard to argue long after I had gone to bed. I remember that it was really unhelpful to wake up in the morning and everything was okay, because I learned nothing about how to resolve a conflict. Essentially, I learned that conflict meant something was out of control and could end in something truly awful from what my older siblings had shared with me. I always anticipated violence although, I never witnessed it and here in a Christian gathering I was reacting to those same raised voices.

I would say on reflection that the woman shouting simply scared the shit out of me.

What she did through confronting the present culture was to force me to confront the inherited crap within me and it was profound in its effect. I don't think I could put into detail what was taking place, other than that I was 'woke' to gender inequality and would from that day forth find a multitude of things unacceptable. It seems strange to me now, that my mother was a housewife by definition, despite having a part time job. It was her home role as wife, mother and homemaker, which defined her primary value. My father was the provider and would take an amount from his wages each week, which was hers to manage, called 'housekeeping' money. It doesn't seem so long ago that my father would go to the pub across the street each day for a pint of beer, in an all male environment called the 'public' bar, women were meant to sit in a quiet space where swearing wasn't allowed called the 'saloon' bar. Men were managers, women were workers, men were church leaders, and women were church members and Sunday school teachers.

In that moment in the conference meeting, a stripping away began which was active instead of passive. It began with a foundational paradigm shift, that we are equal and yet I lived in a world where that continued to not be the case. I wonder if the church took its lead from the misogyny that was in society, or that society took its lead from religion? I imagine they both co-exist quite synergistically to some degree and the **church remains complicit instead of counter culture**.

#eve_wasframed

It is not an entirely fruitless task to look for Bible contexts challenging the cultural status quo and advocating against the subjugated role of women, but there simply are not enough examples and they can only give glimpses as to how believers should seek to reconfigure the position and privilege of men as the cultural default. If those counter narratives are there in the bible, and they are, they have to be viewed as very much an early embryonic challenge, which we can only hope had been built upon and progressed during the subsequent 2000 years. It is possible, and likely, that this counter narrative has progressed little or definitely insufficiently.

If you want to prop up biblical thinking from its opening gambit, you cannot start with the idea that God created man in Adam. The underlying misogyny of making woman from his rib as a mere companion then to also read that **God made mankind in his own image, both male and female**, as that would suggest he was in conflict within himself, for one half of himself to be lesser... and yet people do exactly that.

It is said that Genesis was written by Moses some 1,500 years after the concept of the 'creation' events, and if not him then by someone 6,000 years later. Somewhere he was to have written, retrospectively, the first 5 books of the Bible during the 40 year Exodus, since he never entered the promised land. The saying 'take something with a pinch of salt' is relevant here, since these are stories that are written in the Jewish tradition of creating a retrospective history. This gives context and roots to current figures in society. The Kings and Queens in the context of the British monarchs are a good example of writing current characters into a retrospective narrative with links to the divine. If you like, it's a created backstory to a character or characters and I would go as far as to state that **Genesis is a creation narrative 'mansplained' through the lens of male dominance**. If we can take anything from those creation bedtime stories it is most certainly the superiority of men in the biblical stories due to misogyny in its cultural context and not from the nature of the Godhead.

So... in 'church world', let's just say that I 'lucked out' because I was born male.

Essentially, even without trying I was born into a place of privilege, acceptance, and prominence, simply by not being female. I would have less to fight for from the outset, I would not have to justify my existence nor battle the predominantly male patriarchal community which, more than mirroring inequality in society, also had a supportive theology that women are second class citizens too. If your theology supports this, it is likely that you would have historically also used theology to validate slavery, as many did, because it's the same theological framing. You cannot get away from the fact that the Old Testament is written by men and predominantly holds a male narrative. Sadly, in all the new order ... of the new dawn ... of the New Testament, little had changed. We only see hopeful glimpses though the Jesus person interaction with women. For me, the Bible cannot be the primary context to find out what free wild women of God look like, because the Bible was written almost completely in a time where women were suppressed and such ideas remained pretty much unchallenged. Male is the biblical meta-narrative, empowered women the anomaly. Throughout church history the reality for most women has been that Jesus came to set us free, setting some of us free more than others.

If you can't look beyond seeking to empower women in a classical ministry role, then you will find a book called Carriers of the Fire - The Women Of The Welsh Revival 1904/05 encouraging. It's a good book full of personalities and characters just getting on with it largely outside of the building at least in evangelism. It doesn't really speak to society integration, but has a lot of good stories of women in mission's contexts.

So watcha gonna do?!

Baby steps towards something more enlightened has involved the church asking questions about whether women 'can' do stuff. But the question is being asked against the backdrop of an established worldview and theology that says you cannot, certainly not unless a man says you can. Based on the writings of a Holy book that was simply compiled in the wrong time and culture to be equipped to answer the question of how Jesus viewed equality. Other than the powerful lens of the passage of neither male nor female, Jew nor Greek, to be frank, if you found empowerment as a woman in the Bible, you are to be congratulated on finding the needle in the haystack.

"In terms of gender empowerment wouldn't you rather be the haystack than the needle in it?"

It seems messed up to me, to keep looking in the same place for something that is barely there, when often in society the narrative has progressed a comparatively long way. It seems that women have taken hold of who they always were, despite the axiom that religion has barely left the start line.

I mostly work in Athens these days, with the beautiful international community who have come here to work alongside people displaced by war, torture and injustice. The majority of the projects set up here attempting to address the gaping holes in care, left by the state and the NGO big boys, were founded by women and in the larger part, women make up (in my opinion) around 2/3 of the workers. I've asked a few people over the years why they think this is, and to be fair, they don't necessarily have an answer, because **there**

was no question in the first place as to whether they should or should not play a part, because that's what freedom looks like. My hunch though is probably in line with exactly that, that this is a context without established male dominance to inhibit them from being the fullness of who they are. Whilst there are still gender-based issues to deal with, being here, doing what you want to do, is not one of them, and it's bloody beautiful to see.

Let me give another example of what I consider a 'win' from my own context. In anti-trafficking speak there is something called the Swedish or Nordic law. It relates to legislation put in place around prostitution in Sweden which at the time was largely out of control and predominantly women in situations of exploitation, of trafficking. The law states that it is illegal to purchase sex. It takes stigma away from the sex worker, which is progress, but this was not the point of the law. The framework came after thirty years of progressing gender equality in the country and was implemented because the purchaser, the one with money, is in a position of power and dominance, regardless of whether the purchaser is male or female. All of this because Sweden has a feminist government which has achieved 45% representation in parliament, compared to the international average of just 15%.

The outcome of the law is difficult to measure, since traffickers will likely take their business elsewhere and it is unlikely to impact global numbers. The amazing thing is the process, and reasons for the decision, and is something to value I believe, as an indicator of a society in transformation. This stuff is happening in the world and is culture shifting. But within 'the church' we are often not particularly involved, as we are fighting for something inside a box, a reluctant patriarchy, a context, which exists aside from the progress in the world. The agenda seems micro and not macro in nature: can I speak, can I hold a position, can I serve the bread and the wine, and can I have a title in the existing construct? It's not fighting for equal pay, not especially engaged in wider issues of sexism or sex abuse. It's not engaging with politics to change the statutes of limitation, which mean that people abused in childhood struggle to bring perpetrators to justice at an age where they are confident to speak out.

What would it look like if Christian women were in active solidarity with 'all' women on these meta narratives? This would be utterly awesome, but thankfully women in society are not waiting for Christians to catch up, but catching up would be a really good thing.

I remember in my own church experiments back home, leadership was always very balanced in terms of gender mix, it was just never a question. Perhaps this was because we were given a long piece of rope to stray away from the institution and explore without following all of the models set before us. However, once gender equality became a current narrative in church groups our crew aligned with, I remember project groups forming and saying *"but we don't have a woman on the team, we need a woman!"* I am sure like others, our exploring a new world of balance was at times infantile and possibly for some, experienced as gender tokenism.

I recall on the occasion of a national 'stream' gathering, a male speaker at the front spent a considerable amount of time confessing the sins of men in respect of women - sins of privilege, of dominance and of patriarchy, in a contrite and heartfelt prostration before the women present. It was seemingly going well until he asked, *'Is there a woman present who will come onto the platform to represent the rest of those in the room?* He proceeded to apologise to her on behalf of men and said *'I now give to you that which was taken from you, I give you back your power."* It was at this point the baby steps of progress became 'shit hitting the fan' of mansplaining with limited understanding. Instead of tearful gratitude (I'm joking!) the woman said, *'How dare you give to us, that which is not yours to give!'* and then turned to the audience and said to the women, *"How dare you lay down that which was yours all along!"*

I felt privileged to have been present when some gender walls were being confronted even if it was only a beginning. This was good stuff but I felt we were miles behind changes in society since the church had largely isolated itself from remaining in step. It was indeed positive, but there would always be a highly limited ability to stretch the bungee cord of progress towards equality. I am sure that for years to come, women in those churches had to remind men of their giving up on privilege of gender bias positions since it takes more than five minutes to undo a multi-generational cultural default such as this.

In terms of perceived progress, there are some 'wins' which I am not able to celebrate due to my paradigm of church. For instance, I am not naturally able to applaud the progress of women within established religious institutions like the Anglican church or other prevalent Christian institutions. Not because it isn't progress, but women moving into a position, which perpetuates roles Jesus sought to 'finish' such as perpetuating having a mediator/priest between us and God, simply makes no sense at all in my world.

What I can celebrate is a woman becoming chief editor of a newspaper, director of a company, truly equal in her marriage, not stigmatised for singleness and all of those forerunners, initiating projects in the refugee crisis in Greece and elsewhere. It is these, which make more sense to me, and I can more readily shout about and cheer on. I guess it's a paradigm thing but I will leave it to others to cheer on progress in positions and roles in the church, which are invisible to, and of little consequence to the outside world.

One last story, before we wrap this 'topic' up along with my tiny contribution to a huge issue. I attended a weekend away with normal people, from all sectors of life and mostly spiritual people. This was me getting some time away with the Art of Hosting Community.

The focus was around enabling conversations that matter, helping group participation through various consensus tools and how to harvest the learning that had been shared. It was a strange one, as it was probably the first environment I had been in where my Christian practice was wholly affirmed and given space alongside others. After one evening meal, while people were chilling around tables, I had an unexpected conversation with one lady from another country, a community activist who was just simply lovely. I sat with the woman and we shared some small talk before I said *'Hey, I think I am meant to say something to you if that's okay?'*, *"As a man, and as someone who has been a leader in the church, I would like to apologise to you if in exploring your spirituality, you have ever been rejected, marginalised or disempowered as a woman'.* Her response was that tears began to roll down her cheeks, she took my hand, thanked me, and said *" I needed to hear that."*

In Europe the fastest growing context of spirituality for women is Wicca. Wicca actually began in my neighbouring coastal town in the UK, after the repealing of the witchcraft laws in 1950's England. Their main icon is a Christian saint called Saint Cuthburga, who was the sister of the ancient King of Wessex in southern England. She worked miracles and set up a discipleship school for women. She was later called to Europe by Saint Boniface to evangelize the Germanic pagan tribes and died in 725 very close to my home. She ended up becoming Pagan's modern day adopted 'Earth Mother'. I love this. Wicca is a relatively wholesome place of loving the creation, the seasons and some other stuff, and requires no gender inequality hoops to be jumped through for your participation and empowerment. So what is the church as a construct offering in contrast?

I encourage anyone reading this, male, female or other, to not move at the pace of an institution, but to look anywhere and everywhere for people who are 'ahead' and to go talk and walk with them. Stop waiting for permission.

"Many take the path well-worn, but they are only given a half-lived life. To those willing to brave the unknown path, the dark thicket, a remembering of love, magic, and purpose returns. There is a wild woman under our skin who wants nothing more than to dance until her feet are sore, sing her beautiful grief into the rafters, and offer the bottomless cup of her creativity as a way of life. And if you are able to sing from the very wound

that you've worked so hard to hide, not only will it give meaning to your own story, but it becomes a corroborative voice for others with a similar wounding."
From "Belonging: Remembering Ourselves Home"
Toka-pa Turner

'A paradigm shift is like a guy emerging from a metro station in a city, keen to get to his destination. He walks for hours with a map in his hand and cannot find it. He prays, lights a candle, speaks an incantation, sits in a coffee shop to meditate and still all he has progressed is nothing except the blisters on his heels. On seeing a policeman, he presents the uniformed gentleman with the map he has been using and tells him where he is trying to get to. The policeman says 'well you've been doing everything right, but you're in New York, and this is a map of Chicago.'

Again, the thing called church is not my battleground, so winning ground within that system is not my objective; it is the discovery of life beyond it. Regardless, it stings to know that there are still churches where a woman who might be a CEO of a company, can generally only hope to sing in the band and help with the Sunday school. I only hope the church world is not the only measure of worth and spirituality for such a person.

As I sit looking back through this chapter, it's protestant Easter in the UK.
I have to wait until next month for the orthodox celebration where I am in Greece. Social media has been awash with various posts concerning 'he is risen' with the classical stone rolled from the tomb entrance. A more creative one was of three men sitting on the floor in a circle chatting with someone in the background, a guy is stating, *"I know he was special but at the end of the day, dead men don't come back.... shit, he's behind me isn't he!"*
In more recent years those men aligning themselves with feminism have used Easter to share social media posts such as *'It was three women in the tomb garden that Jesus first chose to show himself to'* so as to elevate God's view of

women in the Bible, but the reality was closer to the next post I saw of a drawing of three women at the open tomb, and a large group of men saying, *"Thanks ladies, we will take it from here".*

I continue to dialogue back and forth with a pro feminist mate's posts since he is forward thinking and gets shot at a lot for daring to see the world differently. I was ranting on about how women should look far wider than the Bible for a positive mirror to reflect back an affirming self image. He pushed back saying that he was not looking to give up on the fact that even though the Bible narratives are slim pickings, that in the heat of all that cultural masculinity dominating the scene, these were small, but brave early challenges. I agree with him. We should not scorn history's attempts at cultural shifts, but **neither should we ask women to chase their spoon around the biblical soup bowl in search of the evasive 'enabling' croutons** ;-)

There will be church leaders reading this, and confidently saying, *"but women can do this, that or the other in our church"*, when the issue is not how much more they can do, but how much they still cannot. You do get some points, a smiley face in the church school report, along with some good comments at the parent teacher night, but this is not time for a pat on the back or to hesitate from going 'all in'.

Finally, just as all of the submission narratives must bow to the level playing field of 'submit to one another out of reverence for Christ' so the gender positioning must also bow to the meta narrative of 'neither Jew nor Greek, Male nor Female, Slave nor Free, because we are All One in Christ Jesus. So stop your wriggling, unless you have an agenda?

Actual conversations I have had?

Are you a leader? "*Yes I am a missionary woman, I can stand in that role and do my work for God, unless there is a man present and then he must take the lead.*"

Are you in leadership? "*No, I am an administrator, it is not okay for a woman to be in leadership, because we suffer from domination, manipulation and control.*"

I asked a friend;
"*To be honest, I've not really posed any threat to the 'powers that be' over the years as I've not had an interest in any of the church roles. I now know that very few of them have got a clue what they are doing and now that I 'could' challenge all of that, I'm not even vaguely interested.*"

Yes, that rubbish is still out there somewhere!

Chapter 12

Four Fold Ministries

And God made some to be pastors, teachers, prophets and evangelists, right?

At least that seems to be how the church functions and the roles that it is more comfortable in giving some recognition to, except it's actually the Five Fold Ministries. For some reason the role of apostolic is left out of the mix or out of roles more commonly talked about, identified and in place in the church organisation.
Lets take a brief look at our efforts to understand and outwork these roles, albeit institutionally.

I think part of the reason is a nervous distancing from such a title as it sounds too grandiose and perhaps unconsciously it sits at the top of a gift mix pyramid in a place of reverence and added importance. Perhaps you are in a context where theology suggests the apostolic is over or being the apostle is not attainable to ordinary folks, just the Pope. Where the apostolic role is adopted and the term embraced it has, in my view, often missed a critical aspect that means it would be difficult for it to be seen as more superior in position and value than the other gifts and functions.

I picked up a book called 'Five Apostles of Our Time' and gave it a little more than the usual glance as I had been in proximity to two of those written about. One had been a senior leader in a large congregation with a multitude of initiatives. The other was the founder of a growing network of churches, essentially a rather male dominated franchise. A leader of a church network once told me, that you couldn't be an apostle unless you had planted five churches, so the measure is starting four more things that shouldn't exist? Certainly one way of looking at it.

What I have observed I would personally not call apostolic, but much more teacher and prophet type gifts at work and it tends to go like this:
A person with insight determines that the church organisation should look like this or that and go in a certain direction, usually that person has to start something new as the existing church will have too many aspects of bureaucracy and hoops to jump through, perhaps it doesn't want to go in that direction. The person getting a sense of the future and what needs to be in place creates something new and soon after commencing said 'new church' (which he will call a movement), soon slips into a teaching role to manage and stabilise what has been created. It is less about the future now and more about establishing the new idea. The new is an attractive concept as it comes with the promise of greater freedom, deeper spirituality, dynamic impact, and more 'closer to God' feely experiences. So to this we add a handful of 'new' followers of the 'new' thing along with probably 80% transfer growth from other church organisations having been told of their need for *the new Dyson rollerball hoover of faith* - game On!

The most problematic thing I see in this cycle of events and processes is that it often ends up with the supposed apostolic person taking a seat at the top of the organisational pyramid or at the centre of it. Most things now emanate out from this person who generally remains the ever-present centralised founder. What I see in the Bible book is a different approach.

There is the scene where some apostles are leaving a city where they have been working and a bunch of guys bow down to them thanking them for being super awesome mega stars. They were being elevated for the work they had done in building the new thing, but instead of saying thanks and sticking around, they instead said **'don't thank us, we only helped with the foundations, you need to be thanking these guys who actually built the thing'** (paraphrased)
Maybe the apostolic is difficult to pin down, awkward to claim, a power role that is easily corrupted. I wonder what it will do with itself, how it will adjust, if the future is not to build a thing, but to simply 'be'.

Now the prophetic seems to cover all bases, affords and perpetuates position, being the vision carrier and you receive the same accolades 'dominion' as apostolic any way. In the shop of potentially toxic gifts the prophetic is king. Beware people who say 'And God Says' because they should be saying 'I think god might be saying?' It affords the listener the free will that Jesus wants all to have. The ability to use the gift of discernment and a lot less of the; 'conform to what 'I' am saying that 'God' is saying' as a statement of fact. I literally do not think anyone should be saying 'God Says', unless they are somewhat deluded, buying into the role as modelled by others, or have lost sight of their own fallibility.

I once heard the five fold stuff explained as 'tools' which help believers become well rounded individuals. The prophet enables everyone to know that God can speak to them and through them (not elevate themselves as specialist mediator in a fake old testament role) . The teacher, imparting wisdom and insights to us, in such a way that we can pass them on through oral tradition to others. The evangelist reminds us of how we got here and to not be silent, if there is something of our journey we value enough to share with others. The pastor shows us what love is, to find our love language and breathe life with it, so that we can love others from a place of having been loved.
I like the interplay in this idea, again that these roles are not positional or deemed more sacred than the janitor but that

they are present, around us, helping us to be the best version of ourselves for ourselves and in the **'life laying down loving of others'**. I long to see such gifts being used alongside those in life and work but if that's not going to happen, then people need to allow themselves a dislodging from the centralising defining nature of the church construct where these roles currently sit.

There are also some gems in the bible about elders, again paraphrasing: An apostle walks into a bar and asks where can he find an elder, the barman says, " ummm, yeah, I guess that would be Cassie, Cassie is a really cool girl, you will find her at the other end of the bar drinking a tequila", Cassie breaks from a conversation and gives the apostle a knowing nod.

I like to think they were **less appointed and more 'pointed out'** as simply being wise, older people who had caught the spirit of wanting to contribute to the welfare of a community (meaning people in a place, not a group in a building). I heard that preached once, so its not just me making it up!

I wonder what that would look like? I wonder what difference that would make to the body life of this intended social movement?

COMMENT ON THE OFFICE OF PROPHET (schmoffit)

A dear friend called Chris always used to make his own versions of words, additions or counter words. I have found that you can pretty much sing along to any song with the words spingle spangle dingle dangle dong, or dingly dangly versions of the same. Go on, try it. Chris doesn't realise it but 'spinglish' has made its way to a third generation, in that my grand kids sing along with me like that to the frozen soundtrack. In the incidence of the word prophet, Chris would have no doubt said prophet Schmoffit to indicate that the word or role was probably proudly puffing out its chest and needed slapping down to size. You're the leader? Schmeeder pfff. You're a millionaire? Schmillionaire pffff, not as cool as Snoop Dogs Shizzle My Nizzle but it's fun.

I was definitely enamoured by people with prophetic or insightful gifting. Outside the dynamism of clear, evidential physical healing or emotional healing, it is one of the more interesting gifts on display, the court juggler or jester.

Since gifts are given to us without 'repentance' so as to make clear that they are in fact **gifts** given to us, I would say that these gifts are afforded to non believers also, as displayed in other spiritually insightful people. If the sharer of insights is not a believer, it does not mean that their gift is therefore from the 'pit'. It's really not something to get all pseudo-spiritual about, it's not meant to mean you get 'out do' the other kids fathers, at the 'bring your dad' to school day.

Since we are encouraged to desire prophetic gifting, I wanted to question the role of the 'prophetic office' since I am not convinced this exists in a new testament, new world landscape, where all are afforded the ability to hear from God for themselves and to a degree, for others. The office of the prophet sounds important, like you went for an interview and God gave you an upgrade cause you'd been a good girl, but more than my ranting, I just don't understand where that came from or how it fits in the new testament world and beyond. Probably like the guys who decided if you want to be an apostle you have to have started five constructs, if you tell people what god definitely is saying on a daily basis, then you get an office.

Some years ago I was invited to a Catholic conference in Northern Ireland, which was gathering around the following of a now dead sainted lady who's name evades me but Bernadette comes to mind. It became clear to me that these 'appearances' of hallowed women for the Catholic believers is the equivalent of an Old Testament prophet. With Catholics finding themselves perpetuating the Old Testament world of having only what God has already said, unless the pope speaks, then what Mary said in a vision to Bernadette, possibly at a French or Italian lake, becomes of dynamic importance. Old Testament wise, if there was not a prophet in the land, then all people had to feed from the last thing a prophet said, since the God person had seen fit to limit himself in those stories to using prophets to share his commands, encouragement and often correction.

The weight of the moment and the message in a world where God was otherwise silent and human beings disconnected, is possibly why words were discerned, were required to be tested, evidenced and proven. If they were found to be incorrect the prophet risked being killed, somewhat like the stoning in the Life of Brian (all I said was "This halibut is good enough for Jehovah"). This was the 'office of prophet', in a place where God was silent and is a world away from the New Testament narratives that All can hear from God.

"Stop having a gift and be one"

I have been responsible for wheeling out prophetic over the years, inviting people as though I had booked a band for an evening's gig. I liken it to being a child and having the grandparents come to your house with candy, so personally I found it exhilarating at the time since someone was going to hand out goodies. On occasion, I too have been the candy distributor, but not in a Chitty Chitty Bang Bang 'Child Catcher' way, "Ice Cream, Lollypops And Allll Freeeee Todayyyy".

As I reflect, I feel we take a leap toward human invention here because it is more than a nuance when we say that one person has a prophetic gift and someone else 'is' a prophet. I think if the person self identifies as a prophet in these new testament times, or doesn't humbly shoot down the title when others afford it to them, I believe they are creating a role and position which has long since finished. I just feel that the whole idea of this smells funky and I was once a pretty big fan. The idea of prophets, like the idea around submission is just too seductive, both in terms of those who adopt positions of power, as a place of privilege as Gods mediator, messenger, and for followers, who buy wholeheartedly into the invented theatrics and messaging. Both are complicit in the fuckery of its outflow.

In the time of the Trump administration the American Christian culture had more than its fair share of people elevating themselves or allowing themselves to be platformed into a non New Testament role of prophetic office. Along with people giving far too much weight to their utterances than is healthy or responsible for people's mental health and sense of self
(I wont give more time this this as yet still 'current' debacle – I don't really want to give it any more oxygen). Equally, there are those affording themselves such heady titles for its benefits and yet, squirming away from the Old Testament consequences of death by error, when their words, dates and content are found to be wanting or even wrong (instead what I then see is the squirming of non apology, the wriggling of narcissism, unable to accept wrongdoing or error and attempts at reconfiguring their statements). So I would say that there are roles like the apostle which are rarely or awkwardly adopted which turn into position and there are those gifts like prophecy which are over adopted and at times outworked dangerously. Some of what I see at work is mental health issues being outworked destructively along with denial, which can in and of itself be an indicator of mental un-wellness.

If as a reader, you have afforded someone in leadership the office of prophet and are hanging on their every word as though it were the word of God, you may need to spend some time in the Cults section at the end of the book and get yourself untangled as best you can and as soon as you are able. Get things back in balance, back to a time where you had not pinned your hopes on the words of men.

I would add that as a person, a human onlooker I find the prophetic office confusing. When this Old Testament role was present, God spoke occasionally, without the prophet we didn't know what God was saying, and it seems he spoke less frequently than now. **Since the resurrection of this old role in new times, in these present on-going new testaments times, God seemingly just can't stop speaking special shit through special people and is suffering from verbal**

diarrhoea. It seems the prophets have a constant stream of really important stuff that God is saying, all of the time, which didn't happen when there <u>was</u> an actual office of prophet. I wonder if that's because the role requires continuity of voice, to sustain its position, more than God actually having something important to convey through them, which he could in all reality tell us all directly, yep, that's right. Also, despite Jesus being incarnate (showing up relevant to a culture of a place and culture of a certain era), God seems to still speak through some of the prophets in 1611 King James Bible speak. Perhaps in the hope that saying Hath and Doth adds authenticity, well if it's not authentic, I guess adding something that makes it sound so becomes important. This is definitely somewhere we need to 'un-divine' the humans since they seem to have gotten somewhat lost in this role. Verily I say unto thee, I doth smell bullshit. "God here, telling you that if I have something to say, it's definitely going to be in 2021 'speak', or whatever the actual year is."

"The pastoring the prophetic rules were: <u>don't</u> talk births or marriages - <u>don't</u> say god said - 'offer' an insight - don't drive a truck over someone's free will or vulnerability"

These were really private thoughts (actually most of the book has been private thoughts until now), but I thought I would include them in case it helps someone in their reframing of church world roles of spiritual gifting and the messy world of **the pseudo spiritual who had they lived 2000 years ago, would have gathered an army of followers, fought the Romans and chosen the kings throne over the cross.**

Here are the 5 fold 'thingamajiggies' in order of how we afford people power, position and authority … where leadership is at greater risk of becoming tainted.

Prophet
Pastor
Apostle (due to the rarity the term is used)
Evangelist
Teacher

Do you agree or have another perspective? There are some who have nailed down such lists as a clear hierarchy of power or position

If you have experienced control or giving too much power away, perhaps just take a minute to think about how you might re-order the above list in terms of influence in your life.

Give another moment to contemplating what these supportive tools would look like, not preparing you for life and roles in church meetings and ascending the ladder of congregational leadership, but being alongside you in the community where you live and breathe, and the workplace as calling, not suffering.

"Who Is The Fool? Those Who Saw Their Friend Executed And Said "Welcome Back - Come On In" Without Questions? Or The One Who Said " Hang On A Minute, This Seems Suspicious, Let Me See Your Wounds!"
Thomas – The Thinking Mans Disciple

'CLANDESTINA' KIDS

Chapter 13

Unconditional Love

Conscious & Unconscious Positions

It was a long time ago now. We had just come back from our first ever 'abroad' holiday to Turkey, leaving our two girls and older son with the grandparents, only taking our then baby boy Jacob with us. It was the first time I had ever been on a plane, and it turned out to be a good icebreaker for the 7 flights I would need to take in the upcoming weeks to get me to and from Guatemala via Orlando and Miami.

During this time I was fundraising by selling mirrors I used to make from recycled wood. Before my trip to Guatemala someone buying a mirror asked me "why go to Guatemala, isn't that already evangelised?" and my reply was "well yes, but with a colonial sword."

I wasn't really thinking that I was going to do anything evangelical. I had in my head that we were going to stop off in Florida to connect with the team and then take huge amounts of clothing and basic health kits for the many children left behind in villages as a result of the civil war.

I was really out of my comfort zone and travelling with a friend from my community called Zoe. We would meet up with a guy called 'Baz' in Chicago who was coming from the North of England to meet us in Florida. It was a great bunch of people and there was no real sense that we were coming from different Christian worldviews. We landed in Guatemala city and headed straight for the mountains in two 4x4's where we would work with a small community of mostly sugar cane farmers. The ascent took several hours, at the end of which was a fenced compound with several wooden structures where we would stay for the next few days. There was a clinic, an accommodation unit, and a school building where the teacher would travel 3 hours on foot to meet with the mountain children, and then there was a church. The main American missionary couple living there showed us around the place as several indigenous people flitted through the compound with heads down, moving from here to there. There was this beautiful pink flowering vine rising up the front of the wooden church building The wife of the couple explained how delighted she had been to have brought it from her mother in the U.S. and that it had managed to flower so well in its new environment.

The husband asked if any of us wanted to come for a drive to get supplies. I called shotgun for the front passenger seat where I was promptly given his handgun to hold so it didn't stick in his hip as he drove. I asked if carrying a gun was common for places like this. The story of why he carried a gun filled the silence for the remainder of the ride. Some years before they had assisted a pregnant woman whose husband had frequently been violent towards her. It was not the kind of intervention they had done before, and it was going to be risky. They conducted it under the premise that she was going to have a medical check up and only women could attend. This woman was separated from her abuser and whisked off to somewhere she and the child could begin a life safely.

The problem with participating in a local community conflict was that you opened yourself up to how the community resolved things. He told us how a man had walked into the compound one day during the monsoon with his arm hanging off at the shoulder. They bound the wound to stem the blood as best they could, but recognised that this was a life threatening injury that needed more care than they could offer on the mountain. The trouble was that outside of the compound, there was a 100 metre incline before reaching the crest, and in the monsoon the 4x4 they were driving was struggling terribly, sliding this way and that with a sheer drop on one side. Time was ticking away, and blood was still flowing from the man's injury as they sought to use the vehicle's electric winch to pull them up to the top, one tree stump at a time. Alas, the injured man died before reaching the summit from his machete wound, inflicted on him by another. In this area, conflict between men can sometimes result in the flashing of machetes, which they always have with them for cutting cane. Even small boys walk around in short wellington boots with machetes that come up just about level with their noses.

So getting back to the gun. Whilst preparing a meal in the missionary leaders cabin, the wife heard her husband calling her name with a strained voice, not really a shout, as he tried to get her attention without escalating the situation he now found himself in. The wife emerged from the cabin to see her husband confronted by the machete wielding husband of the woman they had helped escape. Fearing for the worst, his calls for his wife's attention turned simply and calmly to the words 'gun, get the gun'. Fortunately, other villagers had arrived at this point and took control of the machete man before they crossed the irreversible path of using a gun in the community. Now the gun made sense. It is easier to carry a gun than try to learn competitive sword fighting with a machete I guess. This was of course great story telling on our driver's part, but also, not at all what I was expecting. I understood the context, but a western man with a big gun just felt a very itchy to me.

It seemed that in the evening there was to be a gathering scheduled in the little wooden church building as our hosts sought to gather the villagers and their new guests together, and yes; it was for an evangelism service.

I didn't think that modern thinking people still equated helping people find faith with holding them over the fiery pit of hell, but apparently people still do that. If you knew me, you would understand just how utterly abhorrent that was to sit through with it's being counter to the story of love I had become accustomed to. As a result, I did something really stupid during the following debrief; I volunteered to do the following night's talk. It was foolish because I didn't have anything to say, evangelical rallies are not really my thing, but whatever I came up with I knew it wasn't going to be offering Hell or Jesus as their only options.

I wouldn't say I was stressed about the evening. I had given myself permission to do very little, to say very little, assuming that like me, the indigenous people of Central America also die a little inside when listening to a 40-minute sermon. I asked my friend Zoe if she would be naughty with me as we conspired to prepare for the evening's events. Quietly, and without anyone watching, we slowly began collecting the flowers from the beautiful vine, which we had been introduced to as the missionary couples 'precious thing'. We placed them gently into a hat. Feeling a little more prepared we entered the church. We walked past the concrete block, which in some churches holds the wet umbrella, but here holds the shining machetes. It was a relief that they aren't allowed in the church meeting. Looking back at this moment I guess I could have said a little more when I spoke, but working with an interpreter is like pulling your own teeth out. I felt like I was the classic Englishman abroad, speaking loudly and slowly, my face full of over articulation and expression.

The message was this:

Put your hands up if you have heard stories about this person called Jesus (hands go up). Jesus came that you might experience life, more life than you have so far. A life with more colour, life with more love. Who here is interested in this? (hands go up). Well, the good news is that this new life is free. Jesus wants you to have it as a gift, but it's good for you to invite him to come and be part of your life and to let him in. Who wants to do that? (all hands go up). Ok, so I'm going to ask you to do something. I have some flowers here; they are symbols of new life. I would like you to come and take one as a symbol of your new life, of your inviting him to walk with you because he loves you.

You would have thought I was handing out gold. I felt pretty awful asking all of the team to go out and take more flowers, further assaulting the missionaries bush, but we were running out fast. I felt that what the people needed to connect with was a simple love story. Make a simple love response, and begin life in a new, free, loving relationship. I'm smiling to myself as I reflect back on this and remember that there were no pats on the back for having been creative, or offering a counter narrative since I wasted an opportunity to mention hell.

This book does not touch on the subject matter of heaven and hell, though there are some important discussions at present about the validity/legitimacy of any of the hell or devil narratives we have been brought up to believe. A considerable one being that it is unlikely that Jesus would have referred to Hell, but to Gehenna a literal place of suffering. In all the reframing people are exploring this is an important one, so I will instead signpost you to further reading:

Andrew Perrimann - Hell and Heaven in Narrative Perspective available on Amazon.

"The question of whether the Bible teaches that the unsaved will suffer an eternity of conscious torment in the fires of hell after they die is not quite the hot topic it was a decade ago, when the first edition of this book came out, but it continues to trouble a great many people. For a growing number of disillusioned "evangelicals" it's all the reason they need finally to ditch the Bible as a compendium of antiquated, wrong-headed, and sometimes quite sinister claptrap" – Perriman

Love That Isn't Free

As I reflect on all of this, what I wanted to enact and enable was their ability to engage with the unconditional nature of the love, which emanates from the Jesus person.
This is very important. Why? Because it is quite possible that all other relationships they have with people who have taken on a role of representing Jesus to them, or to you, is going to be, consciously or otherwise, conditional. Roles and positions come into play, which, while possibly welcomed at the start, become toxic.

Relationships with people you look up to in church world do not have the up front stated clarity and safety of contractual relationship between a person and say, a counsellor. This 'knowing' where the edges are, gives healthy boundaries and realistic expectations and yet these people will, offer you advice frequently. Some of these helpers will have a defined role while others just want to be helpful to the new blood. It is wonderful to be liked, loved and affirmed but most of these people will be maxed out maintaining existing relationship circles. There will be those tasked with being your helper through forming a relationship of sorts where it expresses love and regard but rarely if ever is that nature of that relationship explained as being primarily a one way street of 'speaking into your life' as a non professional carer. The clarity of what is actually a 'task based' relationship affords us boundaries and clearly stated confidentiality and of course, a time frame **at the end of which you are meant to set sail back into life, not remain needs focused or in need of the helper**. The ability to objectively check in on ourselves, on where we end and another begins, is a critical area of self awareness. It is essential for healthy development outside of positional roles, our own projected needs and a repeating cycle of looking to the next broken thing. It is something often missed in the church world where the responsibility we assume for another's wellness and development seem to fit 'fudgingly' into the title discipleship.

What we lack in miraculous God breakthroughs in the life of an individual (which we should not and cannot take credit for), we more than make up for in our unschooled willingness to jump into deep areas of another's personal life and history. I have known those who can support others in this way with the skill of a surgeon's knife and the person centred sensitivity of an angel. Mostly though, my experience is of a therapeutic 'wannabe' who walks around with their boots on doing what they can for a person's most fragile past experiences.

A therapist trains to be able to bring a competent skill set in order to work with a person responsibly. In the church world, we permit ourselves to learn as we go along. Somewhere in the journey of learning how best to help others we compartmentalise our own screw ups as having been necessary for our learning. This idea of being discipled in every area of our inner world, does not seem to reach a conclusion, a point of arrival and of wellness, and as such the helper remains in a perpetual position and a role.

Rescue Culture

Rescue culture is something I've had to write about a few times while helping prepare volunteers from mainly western countries who are coming to work in the refugee crisis in Greece. The briefest way to describe rescue culture is that, in part, it stems from a good place. Initially, it is the desire to help others during a time of personal crisis, injustice, and displacement. It can be seen as a compassionate response to what we see and hear, which impacts us in such a way that we feel we need to get involved personally. This response is to be commended though the objective is to help people to help themselves, not perpetuate a role. Because we are all unfinished works, we carry with us aspects of ourselves, which bring complexity to the situation. **Rescuers are often those who need to be rescued themselves.** One of the main issues is that rescuing others can fulfil a need in us to be needed. Somewhere along the way our meeting the needs of others is meeting a need in us. It can be full of love, but it can also come full of positional power in the role, making the assumption that the 'other' needs more help than we do.

This can also come with the attitude of 'you should be grateful that I am here for you'.

In my personal opinion it has led to some truly dysfunctional people in positions or running projects which they build with their gifting and burn down with their inner dysfunctions, which they often confuse as being strengths.

It is interesting how difficult it can be for workers, probably myself too, when someone rejects your help or is deeply suspicious of your agenda in coming to their aid. The degree of feeling felt, be it rejection or anger, can often be an indication of where your compassion was flowing from, and the need to which it was for your own gratification or to justify the role you have taken. Rescuers often burn out after they give, give, give, only to find that no one is there to rescue them back, leaving a void filled with growing resentment

A key element of learning for all of those who are involved in counter human trafficking was the notion that rescuing can perpetuate a need to keep that person a victim. If there is indeed a rescue, it is a one off singular event and from that point forward you are merely to collaborate in that person's own **self emancipation**.

"Unconditional love is love given without conditions or expectation, but in reality, what follows is a great many conditions and expectations, some implied and some explicit."

In my experience, church culture is rife with this issue. It needs people with needs, and thrives on meeting those needs with insufficient reflection on personal motivation. In 'Christianese', rescue culture is different from simple compassion, because, in part, it is coming from personal brokenness and frequently masks the root issues in the individual who is the rescuer. Rescuers are often affirmed and given roles, which perpetuate this dysfunction without regard to where it may sustain and further fuel personal brokenness. Also, rescue culture fits well within colonial and empire approaches. In these approaches we slip into our role of superiority or psychological position of 'we are well', then inflict this upon those seen as unwell or those deemed culturally inferior (everyone else). There is insufficient exploration of where the compassion is flowing from such as your privilege, guilt, or feeling of getting involved as a form of relief from your internal world, the cycle of brokenness continues without self or external critique.

It's one of the reasons therapists remain in a support context of supervision and continue their own personal therapy. This practice keeps check on the role they are playing, the nature and source of the support, and insights they are giving. The absence of this external supervision perhaps contributes to the abuses and sex exploitation we hear about all too frequently. There are a great many other abuses taking place before the abuse of sex hits the headlines.

Again, this is coming from the context and the people who have placed such a clear expectation upon 'you' to be accountable to 'them', but they themselves are, it seems, are under no such obligation.

"On occasion it is clear that accountability and submission should be spelled... s l a v e r y."

Something, which flows freely in church culture, is a psychoanalytic term called transference. Transference is what happens when a client begins to look to the therapist with strong positive or negative feelings, associating them with being in a role, standing in for a father person or significant other. For instance, the trained therapist will be sensitised to this happening and will 'call it out' at some point. The reasons will then be explored, and root issues concerning what they have experienced, as well as the historical presence of the deficit of good things they should have had will be explored. The therapist will seek sustained neutrality, as is the healthiest role in benefiting the development of the person in front of them. I think transference goes on all the time in the church world, but instead of being addressed, it is encouraged and perpetuated.

I have met some people who understand that if there is transference, it is explored as temporary and the healthy growth and independence of the individual is always sought. But often in the church world, the parent child dynamic continues in a clouded haze of taking on parental roles and rescuing, all of which get in the way of a person's development, as much as it hinders those who flow from these roles believing them to be healthy.

You may wish to explore something called Transactional Analysis or TA. There are some great videos on you tube, which outline the interplay between Parent, Adult and Child positional relationships. It will help you identify aspects of unfinished work in your developmental years and how it still impacts family relationships today. It will also help highlight if the roles of Christian spiritual parent figures, where you have adopted the posture of a needy child, have had the capacity to adjust with time to the healthy place or relating as peer-to-peer adults. It is this non-positional relating which is the actual objective for all of us. Hopefully, we can all get to a place of relating as peers, adults, and equals.

What are the implications of so much spiritualised family language in the church world, such as spiritual mothers and fathers, brothers and sisters, brother Jesus and father God?

For me, what takes place, what I have seen, and what I have experienced is a deeply unacceptable aspect of the caring mechanism and processes of the church as a system of support and care. Whilst I have said that your faith and obedience to God is based on your proximity to, and attendance in the building at the centre, the remit of care remains within the building with its centralised 'care' people.

A good counsellor will recognise that attachments form even in their professional setting. Even though a safe space has been created, they will take time and effort to prepare the client for separation and will work to identify if the person has a support network of relationships.

Often little to no consideration is given to how someone leaves organised Christianity. There is rarely an informed process of easing yourself away from the structure, which is allegedly a person centred support framework helping you towards self-actualisation, and yet remains intensely high dependency. It's as if they don't want you to leave happy, healthy, and able to stand on your own two feet because that would say something negative about the belief system within the box. Often, and I'm sorry if this touches a sore spot for those still in the church system, the experience of those who leave can be that they are expected to fall, fail, and essentially come back apologetically because they have been more than a little foolish or even rebellious. This isn't meant to be a section on counselling, but if it were, I would say much of that shit is called projection, people seeking to leave their own issues at your door. We have one story which is used time and time again to convey that if you leave the father or the fold, you are free to do as you please but you 'will' definitely fuck up, you will break, and you will eventually come back feeling sad and pretty foolish. One story! Where are the stories of all those who cut loose, who explored and used their resilience, their resourcefulness, all that was invested in them to progress and to 'STAND'. Those who continue to make a good and meaningful life for themselves, even flourishing, because there are a lot of them out there!

MACHETE FIGHT @ THE CHRISTIAN CORRAL

Chapter 14

Love Has No Gender

"Same sex marriage isn't gay privilege, it's equal rights. Privilege would be something like gay people not paying taxes. Like churches don't."
Ricky Gervais

I won't go into any depth here but wanted to give voice to this issue concerning the churches stance on homosexuality. In previous chapters we explore how church world creates an environment where women are made to feel second rate citizens. Think for a while on how the church has responded to the LGBTQ+ community, more than inferring them as being non-citizens, a human invention born out of sin.

In recent weeks, I was watching a social media discussion between pro and anti LGBTQ+ Christians. There was a woman whose whole belief system was that being gay was a choice and therefore a sin, sin can be turned away from. I really struggle with that pro 'conversion therapy', lobotomised position. The American Psychiatric Association views the practice of conversion therapy (changing a persons sexual orientation) 'unethical'! In March 2018, a majority of 435 against 109 representatives in the European Parliament passed a resolution condemning conversion therapy. The concept that a person must be broken or giving themselves over to sin that still pervades much of Christianity does us no favours at all.

I remember back in 2004 in my hometown, there were these fundamentalist extremists called Christian Voice who came to town during the annual Pride celebrations. In press interviews they were spewing the usual damning vitriol of 'detestable practices' and "Homosexuals in particular must know that they do not have to 'stay gay' and that in Jesus there is an escape route from the lifestyle that is destroying them."

Our little posse knew they were coming and so created a small counter presence shouting 'Christian Voice, Not My Voice'. It was the usual horror show of Old Testament and Levitical hate mail, stuck onto the banners of men, seemingly wearing that one all seasons 'Sunday church, weddings and funeral' suit. These guys have also been campaigning since the 70s to erase the concept of rape inside a marriage, suggesting that a binding contract had been made in marriage giving consent to sex for all time. I find it helpful to visualise them walking down main street in Borat fluorescent green mankinis, it makes the tragedy of it a little more manageable. It's worth noting that in subsequent years the leader's wife divorced him following allegations of domestic violence. Holding anger and hate of anyone, is likely to spill out onto everyone. #fanaticfacts

As part of this Pride day, one of the guys from the local gay community was handing out chupa chups lolly pops, which I just happened to be a huge fan of, especially the strawberry cream flavour. I knew that the lolly offer from said handsome chap was his icebreaker - a bridge for an on the spot interaction. His question was leading, 'you wouldn't care if you had a son who turned out to be gay, would you?' I know I was meant to say 'no' and I wasn't trying to be problematic but I replied 'it wouldn't be my first choice'. I tried to counter his disappointed look by explaining that I wouldn't wish to bring a son into the world knowing that he was going to have a traumatic bullied childhood or to grow up in life marginalised and possibly persecuted in society. I said 'I love you, but I know that you have probably been through hell to get to this point, I would be 100% supportive but I don't wish that on anyone'.

My friend Aaron was planning his own response to some religious haters, which tickled me greatly. He was going to set up a counter web page called God Hates God Hates Gays.Com (which isn't funny at all unless you've seen the horrific God Hates Gays website). I'm not sure if he ever did it, but it's where we were all at with religious intolerance at the time and to an ever-increasing degree, all gender and sexuality discrimination.

One of the main Christian arts festivals in the UK is called Greenbelt, a gathering of younger Christians and those refusing to grow old, largely a positive experience. I have always thought of their approach as being 'open' since hearing that they ran a seminar on homosexuality, hosting speakers both pro and anti, therefore allowing the audience to form their own opinion instead of presenting a singular position as happens at many 'this is what we now believe' Christian gatherings.

In brief I have read amazing papers challenging default theology on this, which, for me, totally bulldoze the prevailing position of convenience. I'm no theologian, advancing my learning by steaming open two thousand year old letters written to someone else in another time, place and context, is not the 'well' that I am drinking from anymore, having spent 15 years doing so. If we have to go back to a book, to check if we can love and include someone, something is very wrong. Jesus himself said that the law and the commandments are all summed up in one core narrative, 'Love One Another'. In light of this, I will quote from someone I deeply respect, someone who knows good shit about how we bring bias, and pre-existing positions to our reading of those old letters, *"Our understanding of same sex loving relationships has to be 'extra' biblical (beyond its narratives), and our understanding must come through the person of Jesus because the Bible does not speak to same sex loving relationships."*

The word homosexual did not appear in the bible until the RSV in 1949. From the 1800's it would be fair to say that all texts about laying down with another man were previously, 'a man shall not lay with a boy like he would a woman'.

Gay hate got in there somewhere, someone decided that change. It would be possible to suggest that cultural exclusion and criminalisation of homosexuality influenced a biblical narrative to reinforce the societal bigotry. That's some nasty shit right there! It goes way beyond proof texting, taking what you want, to mean what you want, regardless of context, worse even, changing the wording? Dang! (Maybe you have more insight on what went wrong there)

Sod Them

Sodom and Gomorrah (Genesis) is one of the passages of choice for bigots like Christian Voice, where God was going to burn the place down because not one good person could be found there (God being like Bad Santa on a very bad December 25th). The place got flattened, but it was not burned to the ground because there were people having same sex loving relationships! Fire rained down because the community intended to rape the visitors, who also happened to be angels disguised as men. As a story, it goes out of its way to stress that every male of every age gathered with the same raping violence request, **this is not a spontaneous pride march of gay males, 'this' is a group of active heterosexual multi generational men rooted culture**

accepting of rapists and abusers. The Bible does not speak to same sex loving relationships - its narrative is to abusive relationships, often power positions from adults to minors and even incest. Let us not forget that this is a wholly fucked up place. The head of the household 'Lot', the Father of the family who took the angels in, is no exception, and why they were chosen as the 'righteous' centrepiece of the story, I just do not know. Remember that Lot first offers the jeering crowd his virgin daughters to have sex with and even after rescue from the judgement given to the City, Lot's daughters later get him drunk and have sex with him, with both becoming pregnant. This is not a 'gay' narrative; it is a 'sex as a weapon, sex as violation and an abusive sex without love' narrative. I would say that in this context, it has seemingly little to do with 'where' you stick something, but 'why'.

I think it's important to understand the difference of sex as an abuse and sex within a consensual relationship. These bible narratives speak to rape, attempted rape, cultic prostitution, male prostitution, temple prostitution, pederasty (sex with young boys) and the nature of sex within prevalent cults of the age. It was seen as a privilege of those with money and influence where having 'sex with boys' was acceptable past time.

Context is vital to our understanding. Another example of the culture of the time, for instance, is just three chapters before this story in Genesis, where Abraham is 86 years old and his barren wife Sarah makes Hagar the slave girl marry him so that he can get her pregnant. Then when the slave girl conceives Sarah gets jealous and treats her like shit, which is okay at the time apparently. By the next chapter God decides that after all he is going to let Abraham get Sarah pregnant at age 90. Go figure. And yet we pre determine that the Sodom narrative is about gays and what gays do 'isn't' okay but in the same text, offering your children to a mob to be raped is okay and earlier, raping a slave (sex against someone's will is rape and sex with a captive is rape of a trafficking victim) all remains unquestioned, seriously messed up and toxic!

Increasingly, I am aware that we no longer live in a binary world of just male and female, and it is likely that we never did. We can no longer determine who or what a person 'is' from our own perspective because that right remains their own. Just this week my wife signed up to an online course where the process asked her to click a male or female box and she commented that this is no longer inclusive. That doesn't mean we should have a list of 10 boxes to be inclusive, it means that we ask 'how do you identify?' It's not that difficult really.

I think the church organisation has only taken small steps, if any, to progressing from the gender bias that is in much of the Bible text. It struggles even more with matters of sexuality. It is my own opinion, that if the Christian faith were secure, if men were secure in their masculinity or even comfortable with the idea that they are a mix of both masculine and feminine traits (if they are whole), then we would not have to exclude everyone who makes us feel threatened. Essentially, I don't think this is a theological issue, it's a power, position and male privilege issue. We just use weak theology to back up our vulnerable position. I feel that our first feeling is of discomfort and possible threat, which causes us to back up our discomfort by ensuring it is the other person's problem. It is not that the faith cannot cope with diversity, **its not even that we aren't able to review biblical texts through the person of Jesus as we needed to do with Bible endorsed slavery**; it is that men are fearful of losing one of the last significant bastions of perceived privilege and rights... Religion!

Believe me when I say, if grown men can quote scripture to endorse hundreds of years of slavery in the name of capitalism, they can and do use the same approach to securing their position, roles and privilege in religious institutions. To my rational mind, someone who has come into church world and become 'un' gay, it is not a testimony of Gods work, but of the operant conditioning they have gone through on their way to their own inclusion in the church world, which is deeply saddening. Since church operated a conditional process of Behave, Believe, Belong in one order or another, which means you do what you need to in order to be accepted

"Why are there so many gays and gender 'this and that's' all of a sudden? Because where religion and Christianity decline as the dominant culture - the real, the actual, can surface without threat of rejection, torture, imprisonment or murder".
Because that's what we brought!

If you, as a reader have been rejected or condemned within the context of this subject matter and you're waiting for an apology or some kind of restitution, (which means that we not only apologise but go some considerable way to address the imbalance of opportunity and loss of inclusion which has been created) don't hold your breath. If the Black Lives Matters movement is any indication of how slowly a cultural shift can be made in society, a committed and cohesive response from communities of faith to the gay community is likely to be a long time coming. There will be those who will resist at all cost any acceptance of their role in wrongdoing.
Again, as with all gender discrimination, do not look to a broken misguided, institution (dealing with thousands of years of inherited bigotry and misogyny) for inclusion, equality, equity, acceptance or significant change. Look somewhere else. To quote from one of my favourite movies 'Stigmata', *"The Kingdom of God is inside you, and all around you, not in mansions of wood and stone. Split a piece of wood and I am there, lift a stone and you will find me."*

Get Tae Fook *(urban)*

I once swore at a roomful of young hardened estate kids, because I felt the J person told me to. Yep - I did that!
We had gathered a bundle of wonderfully mouthy teenagers from two housing estates into a room because we had this big, wide, hardened traveller (who was respected in the Gypsy community) called Eamon coming to talk 'earthy real

thug life type shit' to them. He was a truly unique individual, a good old salty dog. He used to come to our house for a cup of tea and would ask for two teabags in a cup and 'leave them in', it looked like brown soup and stained the cups. I believe he had been a bouncer or doorman and was full of colourful pre Jesus stories, about his past shenanigans, which he would tell with slightly too much enthusiasm. Anyways... this guy with a huge personality, who was perhaps wider than he was tall, did not show up. Since it was guys from my estate, I was told that I would need to step in to do the talk. I had an idea what I would say but checked in with my team saying, *'Okay, I will do it, but I'm going to say what I feel I should say, and you won't like it. Do you still want me to do it?'* - Yep!
It went like this:
40 teens in a room, me standing there at the front like a school teacher patiently waiting for all the laughing and jeering to calm down... pausing for far too long before saying to this guy at the top of my voice 'Leon.... Fuck You!!!' (insert people mouthing at me and being angry), then again 'Heather... Fuck You!!! (cue more growling at me and people definitely 'up for it'). Then another over long pause followed by me saying in a quiet voice "Leon, Heather - God will never, ever say that to you!"

So if you're reading this and you're gay, trans, queer, bi, non binary from another group which finds voice and freedom long after I've written this, well then; Fuck You!!! And in the same vein as my talking to the teens, know that the God person would never, ever say that to any of you... quite the opposite in fact.

The Art Of Un-Gaying

Please allow me a moment of confession, an outing of myself. I used to play drums in the obligatory mood emoting band in the Church of England. We arrived as an almost ready-made band from the Baptists down the road where upbeat and happy clappy was not as tolerated. The friend who fronted the group was gay.

I remember after one of the song singing sessions, meeting with the church leader/vicar who edged up to me and whispered in my ear, *"Could you have a quiet word with the band leader about wearing more appropriate clothing for worship, I found it was a distraction from my worship today".* He was telling me that his eye had been drawn to some Aztec style embroidery over the zipper of an otherwise perfectly normal pair of jeans. It was the late 80s and this was a fashion norm, so this clearly wasn't about what the guy was wearing, it was about his own insecurities. As well as feeling cornered, I remember giggling internally that he was really just telling me, *'Gaz, I spent my morning staring at his crotch'.*

I found that amusing and also an utter load of bollox, since I know he knew my friend was gay and seemingly didn't want anyone else to find out. Insecure 'church world' leaders are often quite adept at whispering, getting you to do their dirty work and seeking that you align with them in the most basic and often used manipulation.

After on-going intimidation and ridicule causing my friend to feel isolated and excluded, he turned up at our door one day, tearful and essentially asking us to 'pray away the gay'. It was not something I had a concept of though I know the ideology was prevalent in 'church world', heck they even have retreat centres for it. Since I had not sufficiently developed my own counter church world understanding of same sex relationships... I'm sorry to say that I obliged and used all of the magic mantras I could conjure. Yes, I'm that guy who tried to un-gay his friend.

It is with some relief and much celebration, that because I was participating in bullshit, it of course didn't work, and my very gay, very wonderful friend has been in a same sex loving partnership for close to 25 years, actively pushing back the hateful clouds of bigotry.
I feel pretty emotional about this as I write, because this does actually feel like offloading something pretty ugly.

Please do not waste energy on trying to educate or challenge people stuck in doctrinal positions of convenience. As I have met with same sex orientated people over the years, the most damning thing is not their same sex attraction, but the abuse of being seen as born into sin. What I mean by this can be drawn from a recent comment on a discussion group from an ex Lesbian now Christian woman. ' God loves Gay people, I was Gay once, God can heal us of that sin'. Indicating that a same sex orientation means you were born broken and need fixing and to remain gay is to remain broken and in sin. Worse still is the psychobabble position that all gays were victims of abuse or as gay men, simply crave the embrace in a man that they never found in a father. Nobody, especially a therapist, starts from a position waiting for it to be proven, they work with the person valuing their choices. That's part of the problem of organised Christianity, it frequently has a position, which you will fit, conform to, or not.
I will tell you what's a sin, bloody conversion therapy.

I heard an American comedian talking about his country 'red neck' father who was 85, who had voted in his state to allow same sex marriage (going against everything he had been brought up to believe). Some time later the comedian mentioned that his father was struggling with the concept of transgender people and the comedian's friend said, 'wow your dad's such a bigot'. The comedian said "hold your bloody horses, he's 85, he voted pro gay marriage having been born in an era where being gay was a crime, a mental issue to be solved by prison and lobotomy, so cut him some slack."

I think being progressive is also about becoming unconditioned by cultural messages, **embracing change, moving beyond what we were culturally born into and not forcing change upon others for how they were simply born.**

You may not know the actor and entertainer John Barrowman or have heard of Torchwood, the Dr Who spin off series, but he is a wonderful gay man who supported our anti trafficking work. I watched him participate in a documentary where he was in a scientific centre, which studies same sex attraction. He participated in some of the experiments, which were created to identify natural attractions as either heterosexual or homosexual. Having undergone the test, the scientist came to him with his findings and said, "the results speak for themselves, you are clearly heterosexual". Barrowman's face dropped to the floor, and after a painful pause, "Na, I'm only kidding, your as gay as they come". John then wept tears of relief, which seemed to express shaking off years of the questioning and demeaning voices of others, eradicating further need to justify himself to anyone.

I would hate, deeply hate, for any human being to need to go through some form of test to finally find peace and rest in who they really are. Please scrap and stop hiding arrogantly behind the invented phrase 'Love the sinner and hate the sin'! It is terribly offensive and wounding when you tell a person that who they are, at their core, is a sin. **It is a statement in which there is actually zero love present.**

"Nowhere in the bible does it say - Jesus accepts you as you are but loves you too much to leave you that way. If it had been there, it still wouldn't have been put there for gay people!"

To end this chapter:
As someone who was a leader of a Christian church construct, what I can do is apologise to you, the reader, if you have been rejected, bruised or made to be critical of yourself because of religious people. I am deeply sorry that you were not loved in the way that you should have been, accepted in the way that you deserve, and enabled to explore faith without feeling your gender identity or your gender orientation was a sin or that you are broken. In truth our gender, our sexual orientation and our relationships all come under the same measure, the same plumb line of goodness, known as the 'fruit of the holy spirit'. I think it's a pretty decent universal filter of what underpins healthy relating. It is not a list of rules and behaviours to obey, but is a way of identifying that we are hanging out with the God person,

walking with the Jesus person, and have this supernatural internal deposit of the Spirit person as our 'voice within'. There's nothing shit about that.

What defines our love and our relating is that these things are present:

Galatians 5

The Chapter begins with this;

"It is for freedom that Christ has set us free. Stand firm, then, and do not let yourselves be burdened again by a yoke of slavery."

The Fruit

'The fruit of the Spirit is LOVE, JOY, PEACE, PATIENCE, KINDNESS, GOODNESS, FAITHFULNESS, GENTLENESS and SELF-CONTROL. Against such things there is no law.'

I believe that in the simplest and best terms, the T-shirts and banners at Pride marches sum up the Jesus person's sentiments pretty well.

'Love Wins' and **'How Can Love Be Wrong?'**

Check Yourself, Stay Savvy People, Don't Be A Muppet.

I've opened a can of worms.

They just sit there, the worms. Hardly the chaos that's been advertised.

Chapter Break

TAKE A KNEE

(breathe)

It's important to take a break, a breather if you will.

If I picked up a book like this it is likely that I would have been drawn to it in the hope of finding a way to change it or myself. As I've said, I read very few books. It would have to have a stunning title. This book was initially called CHURCH - Its A Bit Shit, but I listened to friends and changed it, although with that title, I would have definitely picked it up.

I am writing from a point of view that the church as we have known it is irreversibly impaired/broken, and to varying degrees, should be disposed of (more politely - moved on from as the 'go to' methodology for the Christian faith). It perhaps didn't break; in so much as it was formed with inherent flaws. I think I'm going to be unpopular for that view (as much as I place considerable value on people taking forward steps, this isn't a place I want to play that. As I said at

start, I am not looking to be my normal mediating gently
...en self).

The church system as we know it isn't going anywhere. It is likely incapable of letting go of the shape, form, and order of what it has in place, a leap is beyond its capability, it does not have the ability to put to death something willingly or strategically which it sees as critical for its perpetuation. It will remain in a cycle of reinvention, but not in a cool way like Madonna did. I speak in the extreme because in my experience, others who are going through deconstruction have often spent considerable chunks of our lives trying to produce change from within. If I had any hopes for the readers of this book, that's you, it would be that if you are post construct, post building as the centre, then **please hold space**. Take time to journey and deprogram inherited thinking. It's ok, freedom doesn't bite, but it does have responsibilities. Just don't repeat the cycle, because I'll tell you, it's there waiting for you somewhere, perhaps hiding around the next corner pretending to be all cuddly and warm.

This is a very different moment because we are not building something new. We won't be able to say, "hey there old construct, come and look at this new thing" to reassure you that there is another boat in place and waiting before you leave the one you are in. It is possible, hopeful even, that there will not be another 'thing' to look at. **I think this is the redemptive nature of the term 'the way'. It will be the story of an individual, a deeply personalised sharing of their experience of recovery, discovery, joy, life, and well, stories. Just that, people's stories, welcome to the land of stories.**

I heard this little story once which I think is relevant. You've also probably heard a version of this somewhere. It was three generations of women in the kitchen preparing for Christmas dinner. The youngest saw her mother with a huge chicken, which she proceeded to cut the bum off of. This is something called the 'parsons nose' and my parents used to tell me it was the best of the chicken.

The daughter thought this was odd and inquired of her mother who replied, "I've always done this, it's what you are meant to do when you cook a chicken in the oven."

Not satisfied with the mother's explanation, she asked, " who told you that?" To which the mother replied, "no one, it's what my mother always did". So the daughter called her grandmother in and explained the situation. The grandmother simply explained that the only reason she did that was because she only ever had a small baking tin and it was the only way to make a chicken fit!

Nothing I am writing in this book is about restructuring what 'is'. It's about trying to give people the confidence and a counter narrative to journey outwards and deeply explore, to know deep in their insides, that its okay. I want to make clear that you can do this, and it doesn't need anyone's permission to be explored.

I don't know if in your spiritual journey or church container that you heard of, or passed through, what was called the Toronto Blessing or Outpouring. It happened in the 90's, seemingly flowing out from patient zero, the Toronto Airport Vineyard church. I personally have vivid memories of swimming in its waters whenever the opportunity arose. Why? Because it was bloody good fun, a fizzing Alka Seltzer to the mind numbing monotony of the one trick pony of the churches 'feelings' conjuring apparatus. It was said to have an underlying ability to challenge controlled, rigid behaviours and fear. It was said to be no respecter of religious conservatism as it challenged the created inherited order. One Anglican pastor told me he was in a healing meeting with the bearded wonder John Wimber Vineyards leader (didn't he sing Islands in the Stream with Dolly Parton?). He said that when it came to the time of healing, people were crying and wailing all over the place. He remembers stating strongly in his mind that 'God is a God of order not of chaos, so this can't be God'. To which the God voice replied, **'it might look like chaos to you, but I know what I'm doing with each person here'**. Great punch line.

Continuing with the Toronto reflection, the observation was that this myriad wave of tangible experiences and healing, which impacted many churches in a viral person-to-person way, was to shake things. Some of the conversations at the time were that it had the potential to throw all the bricks of order and restraint up in the air. What it lacked was the ability to overwrite free will and the powerful pull of the familiar. It is the warmth of even this dysfunctional norm, which would cause most to rebuild those bricks back into the same structure and the same order, or to have undertaken a mere shuffling of the cultural furniture.

"Think long and hard before following anyone who says they know where we are going. This is not that moment and may not be for quite some time, if ever."

My hope for this book is somewhat similar to the church sign I mention at the start of the book, 'A church without Walls' (balls), except a different aspiration coming from a personal perspective that **the church should <u>never</u> have had walls**. I want to explore outside the immovable object of such human construction. It is, after all, the sacred rule, the law of 'two feet' that you can actually simply walk away. It will still be there in ten years if it doesn't work out, as is the nature of an institution (but do wait a decade). I think you might perhaps find something so intriguing that it will ruin you for the 'ordinary'.
The people I talk with could never go back to the old; they don't even know what it is anymore.

I think this is a helpful comment from blogger and filmmaker Nora Bateson on systems, in rich wording just on the edge of being too deep for me:
"This is why when responding to complex emergent situations, the problem is not the problem, even though it may look like it is, some try to multi-solution the complexity. The itch to pull apart complex systems and list all their components is an impulse informed by old mechanistic thinking, leading to more of the same kinds of problems. You cannot merely fix the parts and reassemble.

That methodology is not going to shift the submergent issues. They will keep reconfiguring. The tending must be to the relation-shipping between the parts. And this is messy. It requires perceiving in the <u>second or third order</u>, which most people assume is impossible... it's not"

In all honesty I had to ask friends Ellie and Ioanna what that last bit means. Ellie has been a friend since childhood who I consider to be insightful and outspoken concerning any systems, which are failing people. She helped me understand that the second **order** is the leaders who formed the model or inherited the model, determining the changes to the way of things, essentially top down. **Third order** is opening up the back of the church constructed clock, allowing everyone to see its mechanical workings and methodologies, which in turn, enables people to self determine any necessary changes.

Ioanna, an Athens born anarchist and wonderfully engaged thinker concerning social constructs says, "the process between **second and third order** is deconstruction. This is more complex than simply pulling a system apart since it has been held in place by multi generational historical thinking (we are the conduits for repeating these systems so the challenge is also a deeply personal one). We need to look at the relation-shipping between different parts, but also between ourselves and these parts, as well as ourselves and others and ourselves with ourselves (paraphrased).

Personal deconstruction is a considerable undertaking where people are finding greater gains and more holistic living. But, to deconstruct a system full of inherited culture and practices, it requires such multiple levels of change both human and structural. What currently exists cannot, in my view, evolve.

Whilst some people in the system give genuine consideration to change, (whilst others are largely consumers, wondering what the fuck I'm moaning about) the concept of change is actually a perpetual part of its own ideology, but it is unlikely within our reach or grasp. **It is likely that those who leave to explore alternative economies, different ways, and an earthed connectedness, will be the ones who determine**

the future. The construct can observe, learn or reject accordingly, likely the latter.

"Comfort the disturbed, disturb the comfortable"

The objective is not to fix what is broken, nor is it to break that which considers itself to be whole. It is to bypass this all together and explore the potential of a different life, a faith life, beyond created systems. This is a concept that will scare the crap out of some of us, make some of us angry, force others of us into child-like insecurities, and maybe even make us want to protect, well ... our doctrine. Why? It's possibly because we have become 'churched' and it is now our inherited created culture that has assigned the role of perpetuating it, making it sparkle and shine as best we can. We might think we are being dynamic but are likely still historians guarding our museums. I used to joke that it only takes 10 minutes to go from being un-churched to being churched, which is an exaggeration, but does honestly highlight our ability to absorb like a dry sponge the construct's internal culture, with very little questioning, which is shocking.

Again from Nora
"Out of the old scripts and assumptions, entrenched linear thinking habits will seek cause and effect both backwards and forwards in time. Who is to blame? What is the goal?
These questions push the possible actions back into the patterns that birthed the problems in the first place. Fixing the symptoms begets more consequences – and around we go."

It is often the case that those in conflict with the life and outcomes limiting nature of organised Christianity are the ones required to give an account of themselves and of their reasoning for the decision to vote with their feet and leave. It's actually an incredible indicator of the distorted behaviour within 'the upside down'.
It's an accountability often expected by those who are themselves, so often accountable to no one. It has long been accepted that pastors are themselves the least pastored,

lacking almost anyone to be vulnerable and truly known by. Hear what I'm saying there since it contains empathy mixed with disdain. There are those who, due to some jaded idea of power, feel that sharing deeply is beneath them. Then there are those who are trapped in a context where being deeply known is likely to lose them a job and a reputation, and is unlikely to result in care or healing. They are also the first to experience conditioning and control as they are trained in colleges to perpetuate what 'is'. They are then employed by pre-existing groups, to do their bidding, to sustain their interest and sense of progress, without ruffling too many feathers, To sustain, and build upon, the pre existing narratives.

Current news media is full of failing Christian leaders and dysfunctional behaviours, plagued by ineffective accountability. We know about the older institution's deep failures such as Catholicism, but it is also within prominent church streams, Hillsong being one of them.

My wife immediately asked why I single out Hillsong in the above issues, to which I replied, " because they have long since been on trend as the ones who have created the most dynamic, wow and now relevant contexts. They portray themselves as the best of the best of the best, and right now, they are on trend for poor leadership accountability. Hillsong is simply the most current example of how the system, however shiny it may seem it is still institutionally broken.

Perhaps one reality for this book is that readers, people who are wonderfully unique individuals, will seek to make free will choices about how they wish to continue exploring their relationship with the Jesus person, or to not do so. It is not these people, or you, who should be required to give an account of themselves. It is those trusted with responsibility, the leaders and organisations carrying the name church that need to answer.

PAUSE:
Take some time before moving onto the next chapter to reflect on all that you have read so far.

e days where I might have prayed for someone or
n over them in more familiar Christian ways, I would
always end those moments with a simple prayer to try and re
earth and humanise things practically I will type it over you,
in the same spooky hopes in a simplified version:
"Jesus, if its useful, help it do its work, if its bullshit, burn it
up"'

Now don't go book burning, but do ask what things are
sticking for you in a positive way?
What's gotten under your skin and into your spirit?
What's given language or words to thoughts or dis-ease you
may have had for some time?
What's been a positive challenge for you towards change?
What's been offensive and why?
What has pushed you to protect a position, and what is that
position?

Is there a next step, which requires movement, or perhaps
self-acceptance, and settling into who you are now, in these
days, and those to come?

PARKER

Chapter 15

Collective Connective Trauma

An Exploration Of Unnecessary Vicarious Suffering.

I have some genuine concerns about how we relate to the Jesus person. I think these concerns require some thoughtful consideration, beginning with the question, do we, as Christians, unwittingly choose to live in a state of collective trauma?

The exploration in this chapter is meant to stimulate thinking and questions regarding the narrative of our Christian culture and its orbit around the cross as the death place. The reason that this is particularly of interest to me is because I am frequently supporting people through their recovery from trauma, whether it's their own experiences or a taking on of that which belongs to others around them. As such, I view trauma as something we should want to understand and acknowledge, but ultimately move away from after visiting it in a healing context as a way to express emotions as part of a pathway forward into recovery. **I want to make this very clear. All forms of trauma are to be viewed as something to recover from, not something to continually re immerse in.**

In recent years there have seen high profile happenings, and a bogus interference within politics, which has soiled anything about the 'prophetic' quite considerably (yes Trump). You can take the below story as a parable on trauma if you wish, reading it literally or metaphorically. This is the story of a speaker whose life had been somewhat disrupted by being 'drunk in the spirit', which is not such an alien concept unless, like him, it is almost a semi permanent state with varying degrees of intoxication. Yet, even more unusual, was how his situation became worse as he drank water, he even lost his job as pastor. Having heard him speak in person, the oddity of his disposition takes nothing away from just how insightful this person was, and how the healing words he spoke brought transformation to others. Fruitful transformation is ultimately the test of such things.

One story I heard concerning this gentleman took place when he was invited to speak in a church in Germany in a city, which was almost levelled by successive British and American bombing raids in WW2. These raids on both sides marked a horrific turning point in the Second World War when targets were no longer buildings of strategic importance, people no longer collateral damage, but deliberate civilian targets. Entire cities and their inhabitants were now the objective. For instance, over a three day period one February during WW2, 800 bombers dropped 2,700 tons of explosives and incendiaries designed to create city levelling fire storms on the city of Dresden. I actually met an English airman who had been part of those bombing raids. He had been shot down and spent the remainder of the war living as a prisoner. He told me, through tangible, still present emotion, that he was taken into the city as forced labour to help with the clean up. He said, "I got out of the vehicle and climbed up on a pile of rubble and I swear I was the tallest thing standing in the city"!

Anyway, back to our slightly spirit pissed protagonist. He arrived as a guest in the German city and was ill prepared for the cold weather. His host kindly took him to the store he owned, and the man chose a brown sheepskin jacket with exposed woollen cuffs and collar.

At the evening meeting, wearing said jacket and in a growing state of water induced drunkenness, he felt the need to depict his insights for those who had come. I am told that he made two 'okay' signs with his hands, twisting them upside down onto his eyes to become, what we called as children, 'Biggles' the fighter pilots' goggles. It was not lost on the people there that the jacket he was wearing was essentially a 'bomber' pilots jacket. He then began to walk about the platform emitting a droning monotone hum from his lips 'BRRRRRVVVVVVVVVV', and then said, " you can still hear them can't you? You can still hear them and you are still waiting for them to come again."

My mother used to say 'the proof is in the pudding.' This meant that we would judge something by its outcomes to understand if it's true or useful. Upon speaking those words to this German community, while also pastorally encouraging people to let go and receive peace, asking them to embrace that the Second World War bombers were not coming again. Many were said to be tearful while others howled in travail as they released long held emotions, and yes, releasing their trauma.

Some of those present were carrying the historical trauma of something which had devastated their community, an experience in their living memory known as an individual *first person trauma*. They also carried a collective trauma or shared experience. They all heard the sirens, fled for cover, hoped and prayed for the best amidst the smell of burnt cordite from explosives and the hot smoke clouds which laid heavy in the air from burning buildings.

This is individual trauma and that of a shared collective experience.

There were also those present born after the event, able to identify with the trauma through stories they had heard and through identifying with something that has happened to their people, their nation, and tribe. This is *secondary trauma*, (since it was something they did not live through) but it was also *collective trauma* by proximity, birth-right, and identification. *All* of these levels of trauma bring an emotional experience and connection to the story/happenings.

I share the above as an illustration with the hope that you are still tracking with the theme. A shorter version might be;

At school I am a bully. If I punched you in the stomach you would experience first person trauma, the pain of which you will feel for days, and the active memory of which remains for a lifetime if unaddressed. When you go home and retell the story to your Dad and he turns red in the face, laying awake that night thinking about justice and retaliation, Dad is experiencing secondary trauma. He is taking on something, which happened to another. Some years later you have a family and share the story with your own children who learn that the world is not a safe place, that bad people are out there, and those bad people did something to a member of your family in years gone by. The children will then experience, and perhaps be affected for some years by a trauma, which happened to their family or tribe. This is trans-generational trauma, or trauma through identification with those afflicted in their tribe, their collective.

The nature of personal, secondary, and collective trauma is a theme, which is very much on trend at the moment in terms of restoration for individuals and communities. It is good and right that we also explore it for ourselves in the context of religious belief and practices.

We are not looking at trauma for the sake of academic exploration or research, but instead it is a way for us all to have the opportunity to understand what we may ourselves be carrying with us and from which can hopefully recover. Also, we want to understand that we have the ability to pick up and take on the trauma of others, which often leads us to burn out. Again, I hope that you catch that the purpose of identifying trauma is to have the opportunity to recover from it.

It is a relatively recent understanding and approach that allows us to value secondary trauma. This is the trauma that has been taken on through the hearing or observing of another person's story or experiences (nurses both hear and see another's trauma). In the hearing, the listener has their own unique experience, feelings, and yes, trauma. It is prevalent in healthcare for counsellors and for listeners to experience trauma as another's experiences pass through them, leaving its mark. In the context of working with refugees I think some of those most impacted by this in Athens, are the legal teams and their translators. Especially the translators, as in some way, a victim's story has to pass through them, go through a process of internal re-interpretation and then final re-utterance. Many of those who find themselves in Athens as refugees seeking asylum are escaping war, torture, injustice and frequently carry the loss of many family members. The toll this takes on the listener can be an accumulative burden with hearing about trauma up close and personal on a daily basis.

It is the order of things, we want to help people identify where this secondary trauma has taken place and to enable them to process what needs to be felt and to put down that which was not theirs to carry. If they don't learn how to put this down as a self-discipline they risk going 'pop'! These things become destructive, corrosive, emotionally draining, and the listener becomes, with unfortunate regularity, burned out.

It is a reality taking place all the time in Greece with workers and volunteers who are frequently exposed to the painful experiences of the refugee community. This leads to withdrawal, depression, anger, guilt, and other complex emotions. It can result in workers leaving prematurely, often requiring an extended recovery time alongside family and friends who have little understanding of what they are dealing with.

Stretching The Concept Of Identificational Trauma

What of the horrors of our distant histories? I have personally been interested over the years in the Armenian

206

genocide which happened at the hands of the Ottomans, modern day Turks, and an event that the Turkish Government still denies. I know that this is something deeply felt today by Serj Tankian of the band System Of A Down because of his generational proximity through his grandparents who lived it as it happened a little over 100 years ago.

But what of events and characters, dated so far back that we would have to conjure, evoke, or even create feelings or attachments, perhaps through the power of suggestion, to gain some kind of experience of the trauma? Maybe even back to events that happened more than 2000 years ago? I believe it is possible to reflect on history, remaining somewhat detached, and to have some feelings and thoughts concerning them while learning **from the 'remembering' without taking on an emotional connection to the narrative of the trauma**. Remembering historical events is a positive, and at times, important process 'lest history repeat itself.' I believe that whilst we might feel sad, or moved, that this is very different to trauma and the taking on of trauma to form an unnecessary open, active wound.

Collective memory is important. We are all part of a wider story of a family, of a community, or a nation context, as we work out who we are in the context of others, and not just as an individual, this is all part of what makes you the person you are.

This next bit mentions torture and may be triggering:
My mother worked in a bomb factory near her village polishing shell casings ahead of the D-day landings of WW2. My father fought in Burma against the Japanese, witnessing things like men having been crucified with their genitals in their mouths. My grandfather lost fingers having been blown up on the Somme in WW1. These are the things I want to remember. I have feelings about war as a result of their experiences. I am generationally close to the narrative, but I do not wish to share in my father or grandfather's trauma nor the PTSD that they lived with. In reality I have done, due to my proximity to the stories, needing my own recovery and

from trans generational and identificational trauma.

:rience of walking this through would suggest that I carried something deep and painful on my insides. Things like my fears, superstitious rituals, my anxiety, and a very strong aversion to torture themes in films. I have written down many nightmares over the years concerning war, fleeing, decapitations and torture. Once when I was at a conference a man tapped me on the shoulder and asked if I had a father in the Second World War, and if, as a result of that, I had adopted strong behaviours around superstitious acts, believing in them to keep me safe. I could only nod yes as he offered a hand on my shoulder and said a very simple prayer that produced in me the deepest, most gut wrenching howls and tears for around one minute. An equally deep feeling of warmth followed this moment, something I would equate to 'sunshine' breaking into my insides.

We will get to the Jesus death place in a moment.

For me, exploring trauma some years after these events has been part of my walk seeking to understand some of the moments in my faith journey which cause me to hold onto the Jesus person as a source of my spirituality.

I would suggest that addressing trauma, regardless of its nature or source, is important in becoming a healthy individual. To walk through our own experiences, to identify with our roots, and experience the shared story of a collective or community is part of our humanity.

What your people have been through will be part of how we associate ourselves with others. For instance, New Yorkers or indeed Americans as a whole will have some association with collective loss, even if they were not directly involved with 9/11. I have an English friend who was living in New York at the time of 9/11. Whilst she was not at the site during the devastation, being present in the city she shared in the collective experience, and through friends who were impacted, took on their trauma as a secondary experience. I am aware of her working through several stages of recovery many years later. I anticipate that the effects of ripples emanating from that day are still felt.

In short, this shit is real. But don't worry; we don't have to drown in it.

Collective memory helps build identity, which, if you were the winners in history, your collective memory will build a group identity, which is different to that of the perceived losers. One perspective can potentially carry a historical resentment to other groups or nations as you adopt the posture of victim. Another might be a vitriolic elitist superiority as history's winners. This can perpetuate an unhealthy arrogance, as we perceive our cultural identity as 'better' than others.

So, let's move on and literally get to the **crux** of the issue.

Dangerous Over Identification With Death And Torture

My question here is this; is our perpetually and emotionally placing Jesus back on the cross a necessary part of the Christian heritage? Or is it something of our own making? Did Jesus say of his murder place "come hang out with me here often and get a taste of what I went through?" If he didn't then why was it necessary for me to hear as a young believer that Jesus was whipped with straps containing Metal spikes, which would have torn his flesh away exposing his organs? Literally, I was told 'his kidneys would have been visible due to the amount of flesh that would have been removed'. The obsession with whether the nails went through the palms and the top of the foot, or through the wrists and ankles, otherwise the nails would shred muscle and skin and not support his weight is perhaps less historical discord and more unhelpful visualisation.

We even have a dramatic 'walk along' play with the 'stations of the cross', often with actors conveying all of his humiliation and suffering, allowing us to more than visualise the cross and his last words. Can you see the difference between useful 'remembering' and having our emotions played upon by re-enactment, or a repeated graphic retelling to force us to feel?

Lets just say that, being a person who feels deeply, watching the Passion Of The Christ's over indulgent, graphic torture murder movie was a one off. Thanks Mel, I really dug the suffering in Aramaic as it made it more authentic says Gaz sarcastically. Pastors going to see it first to advise their congregants if it was safe viewing, like they could say no!

Now that I am aware of the complex nature of trauma I consider this to be contributing to a perpetual state of **collective trauma** and not, as perhaps it should be, contributing to a **necessary remembering**. It would not be remiss of me to suggest that this may even form a type of 'survivors' guilt in the listener.

" Relive The Cross Often In Remembrance Of Me."
#thingsjesusdidntsay

If the idea that I am presenting has any merit, then what are the implications of having married ourselves to a collective memory centred on traumatic events? One we are constantly revisiting, taking upon ourselves an emotional connection to trauma which we did not witness, experience, or conceive of in our lifetime.

Most collective trauma, like war, means both parties have sacrificed and experienced loss. Our revisiting of trauma like this is to solidify the mantra 'never again'. In this context there is a sense of normalisation. That the revisiting of past events and drawing them back into the collective consciousness is preventative, of value, and positively influencing the present and our frames of reference. The revisiting of the trauma of the cross is to embrace the suffering at an emotional level, the ready willingness to endure, and that we may be called upon to undertake our own cross and suffering. In fact, that concept is more than implied in the actual, then and there, new testament context.

Paul said, 'for me to live is Christ and to die is gain'. This is referencing his own trauma and suffering in the context of his journey in an obvious volatile confrontational context. He is actively addressing powers and systems in an anti

Christian culture where death was likely or imminent. It sows into us the notion that suffering is partly an anticipated necessity of following Jesus and doing his work. However, in this decade, if your work for him is managing a business, that would be an unnecessary perspective, though I do know a lovely Christian couple who up until a few years ago were running a restorative integrated business in Kabul, Afghanistan who needed to exit and drop everything or face imminent likelihood of death at the hands of the Taliban, so who am I to say.

Again, identificational trauma is often due to national identity, (it happened to your country or it happened to the people where you live) or trans generational trauma (it happened to previous or present generations of your family). I think perhaps psychologists need to explore an additional category around how religion frequently asks us to over identify with historical deaths of their main geezer or subsequent martyrs. I believe it causes us to take on truly unhealthy ideas, feelings, and also a posture as we enter the world of anticipating death or pain and the willingness to do so. As a Christian I never questioned this because it seemed a necessary aspect of whipping our flesh and controlling our will, but since I am no longer in the church world, it has been a growing concern as being something pretty messed up.

Trauma Through Adoption

What happens in Christianity is often a willing adoption of a trauma. In identifying as part of the Christian community, you are brought into a context of taking on the trauma that community has chosen to identify with and reinforce in its collective, immersive, emotive remembering, which is a constant.

How does this compare to secondary trauma? Having your own experience of someone else's story and experiences, the normal process of detachment and recovery, over choosing to adopt another trauma and relive it, daily?

I guess there is a question here regarding how we might visit a historical event and acknowledge the sacrifice without trying to form an emotional or experiential connection to it. For the victims of trauma, the objective is to recover and to come through the feelings attached to the events, able to visit memories of such things with ever decreasing emotional pain. It becomes a remembering without diving back into the suffering.

The problem with suffering because of our faith, or persecution due to our beliefs, is that an incredibly large percentage of us will do no such thing. **The vast majority of our suffering and endurance is with life in general, particularly in the West. It is not the suffering of the New Testament.** Suffering because life is tough is not the narrative here. The narrative I'm describing is one of suffering specifically due to your faith and perhaps strong persecution. It is something worth reflecting upon. Look back over the last few years and equate our own personal difficulties with that which gospel writers speak. We are not literal soldiers who have to be able to contemplate or anticipate their possible or likely deaths, this is not our experience on Monday morning, however much you 'don't like Mondays'. Their narrative on suffering was deeply related to the task they were engaged with in the day to day, the communicating of Jesus, often to a hostile audience or environment at a time where death was likely. It is plain to see that their commitment to speak about Jesus was to risk a share in his suffering. Each writer felt certain that the end was imminent and that Jesus' return was perhaps even to happen in their lifetime. It could be said that they endured suffering and frequent death based on a misplaced expectation.

If we must take up our cross and carry it, then there is the sense that we are not living for ourselves but for him. If we can successfully unchain all the shackles added by the Church into a simple following of the 'freedom' person, living for him can still be seen as a dynamic alignment of value and worth in the real world. Who of us are expecting to die as a result of the gospel? I don't mean getting sick from a bug bite in the jungles of Borneo or being spat at for annoying people on a street corner shouting "if I could hold you over the pit of hell, then you would all choose Jesus" (please don't do that you silly bugger).

For some, to be a Christian, and to be known as such, is clearly risking your life and may result in death as a direct result. This is not our norm, as such, absorption of the suffering narratives is, I believe, misplaced and unhealthily life affecting. It could even be a contributing factor to mental health issues, actually, almost certainly so for some.

There were many social media posts about Jesus and the cross over Easter, and I am choosing this less extreme one for the context on how we keep revisiting the cross;

"I believe that the only way to truly understand Jesus's love for us is to sit at the foot of the cross for a while, to experience His suffering, to look into His face and to hear Him whisper in his dying breath...'I did this for you'. Only there do I start to grasp the craziness of His love for me, the Creator of all that is, the most powerful being in the Universe, who died for 'the worst of all sinners'...me!"

To understand Jesus' love we must look at the multiple stories of where he showed his love. When we are asked to absorb that the primary symbol of his love is that he died for you personally, and that it was your sin, along with the sin you are yet to commit which caused him to be there, then it also means that we view ourselves as pretty awful people elevating the meaning of the sacrifice. He is big and able while I am small and perpetually a bit shit. I understand the notion of the martyr, and perhaps on numerous occasions in the history of all nations, there is someone worthy of remembrance. It is appropriate to visit such a noble or valiant sacrifice without having to measure our own worth. I think there is a need for reframing the cross as a place we visit and the way we revisit it. To not see it as a measure of our life's worth and also not seek to live there, or visit to only evoke an emotion. The actual Jesus person showed us what love is, long before the cross so to make that the central theme of his love, is of our choosing but for what reason?

Jesus said 'It Is Finished' and perhaps that is the same sentiment that needs to come to the fore. Jesus is not in victim mode, craving our attention as we sit around the campfire with him graphically explaining his torture. He is not trying to guilt us into a response.

Food For Thought

The cross was rarely used as a symbol during the first three centuries of Christianity since it was an on-going literal death place. In the second century its use was minor, even becoming a source of mockery with Christians being called 'worshippers of the gibbet' (gallows/guillotine/cross). **During this time the cross was primarily viewed as the place criminals receive punishment, so it was at best an ambiguous symbol.**

When Emperor Constantine became 'leader' of the faith it is possible that the cross grew as a symbol after he abolished crucifixion in the Empire (stopped murdering Christians). It perhaps became a symbol of historical suffering and not an on-going living threat as it had been until then. During the 16th Century some chose to reject the cross, believing it to be a focus of idol worship.

Even religious sects like the Latter Day Saints have reviewed the use of the cross as being the symbol of the dying Christ, conflicting with their primary message of declaring that there is a living Christ.

The main concern here is the glorification of the death place, and that we, as believers, are led to anticipate a future of possibly having to go through our own test of obedience, condemned to our own 'death place'. Recognising the nature of Jesus through valuing his words and following him is a different perspective than frequently revisiting trauma, anticipating trauma, taking on trauma, and idolising trauma.

I'm repeating myself here in the hope that we can take a bite of what I'm suggesting and digest it. The taking up your cross and suffering narratives all exist in a context of extreme violent opposition and persecution. Death was not only possible, if you were discovered as a Jesus follower, it was also likely.

If you live in that context it bears some meaning, but for the most part, the majority of us absolutely do not live in that place. As such, visiting the narrative becomes an unpleasant, potentially sado masochistic fantasy, if one chose to do so solely to evoke feeling.

I have been present at several Christ resurrections in Greece. It was interesting this last covid year since Jesus rose earlier in the evening this year due to Churches needing to be closed in time for curfew. I have witnessed what I can only view as an outsider as 'elation/ecstasy' mixed with tears of relief and joy of several old people at the stroke of midnight when Jesus is again resurrected, as though a literal rising has occurred and the mourning since Friday has been experienced as literal loss.

Having a bad day, experiencing difficulties with the boss at work, struggling with mental health or physical illness are all difficulties, but they are not persecution. They are not your cross and they are not suffering for the gospel.

As such, we should question the focus on the death place and our potential 'willingness' to go there.

Having said all of this, the real question is what is the impact of all this on your self-perception, your worldview, and your psyche, having in all likelihood participated in a community or organisation which has made the cross and suffering central themes? Is it likely that you carry a trauma, which does not belong to you, and yet, you accepted the invitation to participate. I think this needs some exploration and consideration. This is a conversation that I had some years ago that I feel is related to how this impacts our thinking. A friend of mine in Seattle called me with a kind of epiphany he had experienced from recent conversations of his own.

It went like this: "I'm worried that we have a messed up view of God! I have spoken with far too many people recently who believe that God only moves us on from something that we are 'in' by going through crisis and suffering. From the people e spoken to, it seems they struggle greatly with ring change as a choice. They seem unable to transition to a place where God says to them 'what do you want?' It can't possibly be that easy, and **the idea of making a free will choice, trusted by God, is viewed as a work of the flesh.** Sadly, this says something really shitty about God. That all change comes with pain and there is always a lesson to learn through suffering".

Part of actually growing up within a Christian worldview is knowing God is interested in our choices and asks us what we would like to do and when. (If your concept of God is now another divine personality from those available in the spectrum of beliefs, I hope that He/She also affirms your free will choices) I think such ways of thinking are impacted by our understanding of going through the cross and suffering. Such thinking is tainted by adopting trauma, which is not ours. In the same way, we may consider aspects of the Christian tradition to repeatedly 'infantise' the adult Jesus to remain the baby Jesus (Ricky Bobby's favourite version of Jesus in Talladega Nights). Perhaps we are guilty of repeatedly 'victimising' the Jesus person in the same way that some infantilize him, when in truth, **he neither places himself as infant nor victim.**
#evangelicalsaresmorecatholicthantheyrealise

Take a moment.
How has exposure to the above themes impacted you? To what end?
Is there a re-alignment needed if it has been or has become an unhealthy perspective and life framework?

Lets just bring this concept back into the land of the real;
In what other context would you visualise the brutal torture and execution of a loved one, or have it re enacted in front of you, repeatedly, and to what end? Does the Jesus person want us to come to his death place repeatedly or does he wish us to simply remember

THE HOLY LAND EXPERIENCE ORLANDO
'Full Colour Entertainment For All Ages'

Gaz Kishere

Chapter 16

Collaboration

Collaboration is not meant to be a gathering of people around what you are in. It is not about sending people invites to come to your party, after you have put everything in place. It is not committing to others your surplus of time and energy, the small amount that you have left after your own agendas.

I remember in my own town there was a considerably hierarchical charismatic church caught in the trend of running stadium events, believing these the be the magical missing component having watched videos on happenings in Brazil and other places. It was probably after booking the stadium, deciding whose name was going to be at the top of the flyer, and selecting the programme of speakers and preferred worship 'most professional' singers, that it was finally taken into pastors networks under the guise of 'we would love you guys to partner us in this' (code for 'we need numbers'). I like the party invite concept, but people tend not to come and play, especially when they have parties of their own. It's too late to ask for partners when you realise you

218

and your five mates just ain't going to 'kick it'. Regardless, it would have fallen apart once an honest conversation was had about 'who' gets to keep the converts.

Collaboration has been on trend over recent years as one of those progressive ideas that we bolt onto our schedule without addressing what we already have going on, feeding it with the crumbs of the attention we have left over from other things. But everyone wants to be collaborative right?

In the NGO world it has been really pushed by big funders like the EU as one of those commodified ideas, stolen from the grass roots, with none of the values of thinking.
The majority of funding applications today require you to deliver a partnership programme and go in for the funding bid with multiple organisations, but when the funding dries up, so does the collaboration. It's meant to stimulate a spirit of working with others, but the core of collaboration should flow from an attitude of solidarity and being 'in' something together for the sake of others. In reality organisations, like churches, operate in what people call 'Silos.' They are independent, self-reliant entities with their own focus, agendas, and methodologies. So when a funding body says
'you can have 100,000 pounds if you work with five other groups in the project delivery,' it's all about the money and like churches, the majority of it funds administration and not helping the needs. Believe me, as soon as the money is gone, it's back to the silos with an eye on new funding streams.

Some collaboration is an invitation to others as a way to build up what they are in, not to work in a different way because that would diminish the organisational DNA and pre existing workload. I once asked a pastor of a forward thinking vineyard church if he had thought of coming along to some of the pastors networks and he said 'what's the point? We all have our own vision and if they get on and do theirs, and we do ours, it will all work out." I think he missed the point, or perhaps had a more realistic angle on the inevitability of all such ventures, having to eventually bow to the superior independent visions of the individual groups. Other groups simply ask ' what's in it for me, for us, for my crew? Profile? Income? No, Then what's the point?'

Collaboration faces the same issues as those working towards unity across a diverse congregational landscape. As soon as you build and define, you are knowingly or unknowingly separating yourself off from others who are not exactly like you. The sheer dynamics of having your own machinery to keep oiled, and a programme to run, means you have very little capacity for anything else, except at a token level of being able to say 'we are doing unity, we arc collaborating'.

One famous modern church movement wanted to have a brand of their church within 15 minutes of every community, essentially doing a sales pitch to existing groups and re-branding them as part of the franchise (see Star Trek 'Borg'). Working with others around what energy and resources you have left over is not collaboration, and growing your group through rebranding is simply mergers and acquisitions. In the movie Hook, Maggie Smith plays 'Granny Wendy,' and when she hears Robin Williams, playing 'Peter Pan,' describe his work in mergers and acquisitions, she says with concern, 'Oh Peter, You've Become A Pirate!'

"Unity is not the icing to your pre existing congregational cake. If anything it is the missing ingredient demanding you re-mix and bake again"
But nobody is going to do that!

I'm not really carrying the unity thing anymore. I don't see any significant change to the big picture by making one dysfunctional thing awkwardly try working with another dysfunctional thing. I think that's part of accommodating potentially dynamic concepts into a strongly immovable dysfunctional Christian landscape. When I look back at things I used to celebrate as significant, like a catholic priest having a coffee with a protestant minister or a project, which contains workers from more than one congregation or denominational stream, I find it lacking. I think I probably shrug my shoulders a little more and say 'so what' because it is an anomaly, a token gesture or really not that significant against the backdrop of deep and widespread counter Christian structures values and behaviours.

Let me try and explain that better;

Most of us will know about how on Christmas Eve 1914, British and German forces managed to put down their guns during a momentary truce and have a game of football. It is a beautiful and romantic story about our humanity, our being people and not just enemies. 9.7 million military personnel died in that war along with 10 million civilians. There were hundreds of thousands of soldiers taking a break from killing just metres away from each other and only one game of soccer that we know of. This small drop of hope changed nothing, even those present at the game went back to the business of killing one another the next day. It is a great story, but is great because it sits against a huge inhuman canvas of nations seeking to dominate one another through attrition. The light shining bright in the darkness is wonderful, but it is still a sea of darkness, which dominates in that often used analogy.

What am I saying?

Let's move away from tokenism, let's acknowledge momentary glimpses of light but see them for what they are, simply moments before normality, the meta narrative of a sectarian landscape and life and outcomes limiting structures resume. The glimpses, the anomalies no longer invigorate me, they sadden me because unless they can catalyse actual change, I feel, for now, they are a distraction or worse, are a false indication that something of substance is truly happening.

This person talking to that other person is 'great', this group doing something with that group is 'amazing' - But Why Is It? What Truly Madly Deeply has actually happened which is worthy of note?

One last grumble, not for the book, just for the chapter, is concerning buddy leaders, the guys we ask to visit and share the platform like we are all mates from the wider ministry world. We show our congregation that we are connected; we can deliver on big names. Lets face it, the chances that we buddy up with or invite onto our platform anyone we don't already agree with, who wont strengthen our existing narrative is, well, pretty darned slim.

This is called self-referencing, you invite people to contribute, build up your group, and strengthen your ideas based on your criteria. It's a love fest', you say they are great, they say they are great. There is no space for a counter narrative here.

Got a little dark there, so, let's move on.

A LOVE LIKE BLOOD

Chapter 17

The Others

A brief thought on how organised Christianity often involves separation from other versions and groups, creating diversity without unity.

A Conversation Starter For The Coffee Table

Territorialism?

I remember as a child growing up in a council house with a main traffic-strewn road at the front and at the rear of our gardens a small access lane blocked at one end. It was just wide enough to fit a single car with a turning space at one end. On one side were our gardens and on the other a 12-foot high wooden fence, blocking our view of the new ... old people's homes.

Once mother had barked at us to get out of bed with shouts of 'it's sunny outside' and various coercions, we finally obliged when we reached the threat level of 'the milk is on your cornflakes and they're getting soggy'. This backstreet was our world growing up, and I mean OUR world. It belonged to the several kids whose gardens opened up onto our 'back lane', *"Are you coming out in the back lane later?" "See you in the back lane!"*

This tarmac strip was ours. Somehow even as a child I very clearly had a primal concept of demarcation of territory. I already knew that this came from the alleged indwelling lion, pissing and squirting invisible self-created lines of territory. We determined who was invited or welcomed into our lane, even as kids we would be more than happy to throw stones, swing sticks or even fists if we needed to.

I wonder if this primal idea of pissing and marking our territory is a foundational source of racism, sectarianism, tribalism, nationalism and denomi-'nationalism' (for that is what it is). This idea that by simply marking imaginary lines between geographies, peoples and religions, flowing from something so seemingly inherent or indoctrinated that by saying something is now ours, it is! By creating the 'me', the 'us' and the 'we' along with, the 'mine' and the 'ours', with complete synchronicity we create the 'they', the others, the 'them'. This comes with exclusion, rejection and eventually the toxic, threatening 'other', which is to be hated, feared and fought. In our world, in that back lane, that poor lad's name was Danny.

Whilst fear and hate are the outcomes at one end of the spectrum, is it possibly the inherited actions of children pissing out fictitious lines at the other? Justifying it aside from love and logic, because it is a primal right, not only of an animal, but of humans? Or should it have remained with the animals without being adopted by us? If so, it is not to be celebrated, nor perpetuated since we are only animals, by our own choice.

If any of this is around for you, where do you think you picked it up? Is it doing any damage to anyone? If so, how are you going to put it down?

A little nudge maybe:
There were a few routes on and off our housing estate where we worked with the Anglican church, the most natural being the one which led to the main highway where all the stores were. This involved a drive down a slope and up another one with many a twist and turn enjoyed by less careful drivers. The councils/ municipalities solution was to create a chicane, additional curves which forced you to only be able to pass one car at a time. Since you could see this trafficking calming scheme from either end of the road, people would then race to get there first so they didn't have to wait for someone. Also people would at times go head to head trying to state through brute force that both had got there first and had right of way. This was not a trafficking calming scheme; it was a traffic-angering scheme resulting in arguments and road rage. Such is the nature of our inherent competitiveness, and a seeming need to mark our territory. Do you think anyone cared that there were arrows making it clear who had priority?

What is it that we carry inside of us which makes us feel the need to be dominant, to master others and to personally go to war over an infringement of what we deem to be our rights as an outworking of what we consider an acceptable behaviour or response.
One place we really need to understand such responses or reactions is critical race theory (CRT) especially in the USA, a truly divisive reaction to Black Lives Matter. It is perhaps explained best through a news station I saw reporting how everyone is apparently pro black rights, all the lovely white people. It went on to state as an absolute re writing of history, that all the America's constitutional founding fathers were against slavery. Reality? 41 people out of the 56 who signed the declaration were slaveholders. White pride and Black rights arriving at the chicane in the road together

Sectarianism is defined as conflict between two different political, cultural or religious groups. Dependent on the different beliefs or ideas and how strongly they are held it can lead to conflict, hatred, discrimination or prejudice.

Elitism is defined as the belief of a group of people who think that they have superior intellect and/or greater insight. It can denote a group of people with a higher degree of training or wisdom in a given field. It can also be present where privilege is granted or succession given from senior family members in a hierarchy or system and wealth. In reality you view yourself as better than or above others.

Both of these aspects can seep into the thinking of church organisations. Rarely in these days does one form of church express prejudice or hatred to other groups in the same street or the same town, not in the way they might have, in say, Northern Ireland during 'the troubles'. This is to say, there is rarely outworking of animosity in a visible way. How it is expressed is in distance, fear of losing a congregant to another church, a fear of contamination or being duped by an inferior or suspicious teaching or doctrine. People might suggest this is not the case, generally as they view themselves on the top table of what's on offer out there, but just wait until the next new thing moves into town, just a little way down the road.

I was once in a Pastors gathering where I communicated that I was working with others present to deliver a course to young people, about integrating meaningfully in society. I was abruptly cut off by another pastor, arrogantly ranting: *"Gaz, the last time I heard you speak, you said you were post charismatic and post evangelical, when I am proudly both of those things. I won't be letting any young people on that course, I don't know its theology nor its doctrine"*, I think this was perhaps coming from the angry fecker end of the religious/anarchist spectrum (see chaordic anarchist chapter). But ultimately what he said and how it was said 'proudly', indicated far more of a concern to me than any potential heresy I could be peddling. By the way, congregation's talk about people running off and being heretical, but to my knowledge, heresies mostly come 'top down' from leaders or organisations.

Elitism is not based on a concept or feeling that you have greater insight or that you have truer truth or in Christianese, a more palatable or more conservative imagery afforded to Jesus, depending on your taste or political learning. It is something that sneaks in where you feel that your truer truth, your righter 'righteous' right causes you to demonise and discriminate against the other, viewing them as 'less than'. At which point you might think you're on solid ground when in fact you're simply fucked, excuse my French.

A biblical truth remains (if you still feel there are such things) and that is this; God has one church, one body, one bride. He does not see as we do, nor build as we have built. In fact he tells you not to build, stating *"I will build my church,"* and so, as my Dad would say, *"Stick that in your pipe and smoke it!"*

"Beware the sectarian elitist ideology, that different, is wrong"

If you have never read Church Beyond The Congregation, its author James Thwaites is a fascinating fellow from Australia. He has an amazing mind and from the 90's onwards did so much to give people confidence to journey beyond our constructs. Some were able to go further as a result of his insight and challenges, some others came along for the popularity ride and just pulled a little on their organisational bungee cord before it pulled them back to the familiar and a need to quickly rebuild what was.

He would on occasion use humour to counter some of the religious thinking which we all considered ourselves to have been free from. On a number of occasions he would do something spontaneous like pretend to lose his train of thought the further he moved away from the anointed lectern or pulpit.

Some of the folks from our 'Bliss' gang travelled a couple of hours along the UK coast to Bogner Regis. It was a rare chance to sit in a room with James and see which way the wind would blow, and what might be blown away. I guess there were perhaps 30 people and 15 groups present. I have fabricated some of the group names to make a point here. James asked us to go around the room and state who we were by way of introduction:

"I'm Gaz from Bliss in Bournemouth", "I'm Chris from Revelation Church Bognor", "I'm Lucy from Gateway Church Portsmouth", "I'm Simon from New Life Church in Chichester," etc. This took around 15 minutes with each saying who they were in the context of their group identity. There was a pause at the end of our contributions, where James was looking at the floor, perhaps even staring evasively at his feet before it became clear that he was giggling to himself. This then grew into a laugh as he spluttered out the words; ***"This is brilliant, you identify yourself with these group names, like they are real, like they actually exist and are not just constructs of your own imaginations".***

Taking the piss can be good therapy at times, though not everyone had the ability to laugh at themselves. His point was this; 'Do you think God really cares about what you call yourself, how you define yourself, particularly when it only serves to fragment the body?'

Isn't this just more children pretending to be lions and pissing their lines of demarcation, albeit with apologetics, a smile and perhaps misinformed good intent. I wonder just how counterproductive all of this is in reality?

I have to own that I was one of them, churched after 10 minutes into my faith journey, swallowing all the Jesus plus, finding things inflexible and experiencing that taking a step forward in our experimentation with the church construct seemed like another world, but was simply a step, okay, maybe two, give us some credit.

"Don't let the safe pull of the familiar, distract you for one second, from the deep joys of your glorious re wilding"

She Is Safe In The Squat Busy
Building A Community With 90 Others
Empty Buildings Were Re Tasked Because Camps Are Full

Armed Police Commence
Systematic Squat Evictions
Athens Greece April 2019

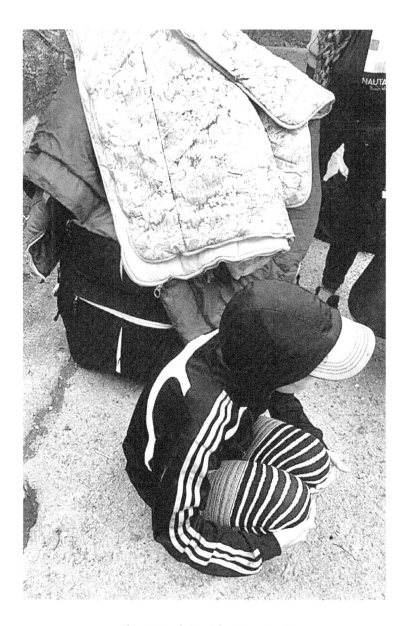

She Is Back On The Streets As
More That 1,000 Asylum Seekers Are Evicted

'NASIR'
Part Of The Clandestina Family
Died Aug 21, 2021 In A Greek Refugee Camp
(A Few Days From Being Reunited With His Wife And Child)

Chapter 18

Newbies

What do we do with new Jesus people?

Do you even want there to be newbies?

Well, for a start, you don't keep doing 'church' as is, just in case it's needed for newbie care. You can't perpetuate a false need of church just in case we have some new believers. Church as an organisation is not the opportunity to opt out of relationships and actual shared journeys. The presence of the building is not to be perpetuated simply because we don't know what else we can do (and that's likely the case). One of my most long-standing aversions has been the concept of a revival; I just never really caught the buzz. I'm not sure that this concept is even in the Bible. It is something I have never prayed for or sought to bring about, unlike some others I know who have for what I'm sure are noble reasons. Regardless of any ideas about heaven and being saved, I would not desire for anyone to find themselves in a local church, though there are those newbies I can't hang out with because of geography who are going to one, for now. I am not sure I would be benefiting them to involve them in my complex theories for now, when currently they are looking at the construct as support, so maybe later. I think it would be selling them short to signpost folks there, giving them half a blessing, feeding them both the bitter and the sweet. At the moment it is seemingly all that there is to offer. I recognise that we are in between times. Truly alternative ideas and contexts have not yet landed and this is the problem of being between the 'already' and the 'not yet', a new way and an old 'one-stop' shop. For example, an Afghan family who are part of our extended family came with their own questions about Christianity, had their own deeply personal affirming encounters and have now found themselves making home in another country. I would not wish to poop on the support they are getting from the construct 'centre' there, since it is actually, to some degree, functioning as a support centre. It would seem pointless for me to have moved on from construct 'cans and cannots', to simply perpetuate that voice for others. I will though, be more than happy to shout 'Stop – Watch Out' if I think they are in a place where they will put their hand in the fire and get burned.

"Of The Many Thousands Who Responded At Billy Graham's English Crusades, Just One Year Later, Less Than 20 % Could Be Found In Church Attendance. Where Was The Disconnect?"

A wonderfully bearded guy who worked with YWAM had the job of linking people's desire for missions to a global setting. I was told that if you can see it or dream it he was the guy to help you make it happen. .

In a passing conversation we shared, he told this tale with the tone of a bad 'dad' joke:

"Gaz, I was talking to this guy the other day who had seen more than 40 young people come to faith, but now they are all back in the world," he paused and then pumped an animated fist into the air and switched to a more cheerful tone " Great", He said, "That's where they are meant to be." And that, my friends, is the whole lesson. I have fond memories of Mr Sullivan (aka Mr. Beardy) taking time to talk and share kindness with checkout assistants, to leave them feeling a sense of worth and value. This transformed my shopping experiences for decades to come.

As in the other chapters I highlighted that I joined a church, which largely served to take me out of my cultural group and tribe, consequently I have spent several years enjoying the delight of reconnecting with it. My frustration has always been centred on why people can't come alongside you in what you are in, to support you without taking you out of it. Generally, it's because the practices of their beliefs, the care and support are carried out in another world called church. That's the simplest answer, and has been the experience of many. As I have mentioned elsewhere in this book, as long as we have this concept of the church of elsewhere, and not of where we are, this is unlikely to change. What does it mean to have someone start a journey of faith and remain in their life, work, and cultural context? How would we support that? Could you dare to come alongside someone without passing them onto the machine? Is that where we should be heading? One thing that's clear, its not us, or other people such folks would be following, it remains the 'one' that they are walking with, the primary 'idea' of the Christian faith, but it will be hard for them, just as it is us, not to follow people.

Disciple
noun
1. a personal follower of Christ during his life, especially one of the twelve Apostles.
2. a follower or pupil of a teacher, leader, or philosopher.

If, like me, you have found yourself moving away from some or all of the formulaic ideas about this, then what does this discipleship thing mean moving forwards? If you have a model, and if it involves the number 12, then you probably have little to contribute creatively here, other than the idea that we can only relate to so many people meaningfully at one time.

It is one of the more current conversations for the post-construct explorers who are also trying to work out if we want to help anyone at all find their way into Christianity. I guess in a much simpler world discipleship looks like friendship and sharing life. Like Jesus, you're limited in how many people you can be that close to. You don't have to panic. You don't need a model to reach or to disciple 10 or 20 people. The reality is likely that when you were in church world you may have brought one new person along every 5 years, if that. Perhaps a meaningful journey is less of a project or even hill to climb, if your not trying to introduce people to a new culture and world instead of new ways of being.

If the backbone of helping someone begin such a walk remains a relationship, then perhaps alongside the riches of the informal there could be a limited period for formal development. People exploring spirituality and practices do courses all the time, without any need of forming a commune in the woods.

As I mentioned earlier, instead of the church programme being the current place of learning, a place, which even Jesus, could not have graduated from. Perhaps it should look more like school. A place to spend a concise period of time to help get people going, where you actually get to graduate. A specific focused period and then you're off, getting on with the rest of your life without the instilled doubt that you will leak, needing a weekly meeting to be built back up.

I have long been an advocate of the concept of **'information is retained in the place of application'** by which I mean, you absorb that which is relevant to living, you become those things. I'm not in a place in my own journey where I could say with any confidence that I am advocating for some new formal faith based contexts of learning, but I still want to explore alternatives which could undermine or subvert current church organisation practices and inherited assumptions.

"If something is of value we should inwardly digest so that it can become muscle on our bones through action"

The bottom line for me is this; those gathered at the mount to hear the Jesus person speak to the presiding culture, heard it just once and then buggered off like the rest of us. They retained some of what resonated and felt personal to them or important for their slice of society, the outworking of which could be deemed transformative, as they began to live out of those new insights. If I have been talking some poor guy's legs off with what I foolishly deem to be useful, I always say "take that 10% which we all just about manage to retain and don't worry about the rest". Nothing much has changed in terms of human nature. We are not going to shrivel and die if Sunday meetings stopped, or if you no longer have the means to zoom in to the new pandemic birthed online services. Surely, you/ we, have enough to be going on with and numerous wisdoms to share, probably for a very long time.

What would it look like though if there were some helpful, basic teaching modules, and therapeutic support to help get us underway? Would that be a solution to the problem of 'what happens when Sundays stop?' If the church as it is cannot make the shift, then the on-going cycle of enculturation will cause us to be increasingly irrelevant and 'otherworldly' to the real community and society. Whilst I have said previously that Church was never meant to occupy its own sphere but be present, living out life and work in all the actual spheres, it is a present reality that Church occupies its own pseudo sphere with its own language, behaviours and thinking. This remains an active daily problem in how we will ultimately screw up newbies for the mainstream, their proximity to and relevance within the 'norm', our own human incarnate place. I will say it again and again, 'All creation groans and yearns, waiting for us to show up', as the embodiment of his values, transformational thinking and wisdom, not with words alone, if at all, but through who we have become. This is the 'only' authentic Christianity.

"If Anyone Causes One Of These Little Ones—Those Who Believe In Me—To Stumble, It Would Be Better For Them To

*Have A Large Millstone Hung Around Their Neck And To Be
Drowned In The Depths Of The Sea."*
It is said of this verse that it does not relate to children, but to
the childlikeness of new believers. He rebukes those who
could manipulate or mislead them - Yep!

Being swamped by numbers of believers isn't a
current problem we have to juggle since the church in the
West is in terminal decline (even if your own super dooper
shiny pop concert is pulling in the crowds, it has little impact
nationally). I think futurist George Barna refers to terminal
decline as the time when the practicing Christians represent
less than 10% of the general population, so yeah, pretty
much now.
My friend Kent refers to this as being, in part, a problem with
our R rate. He uses this empirical measurement of Covid 19's
spread from one to another as the tool. In terms of faith, he
suggests that most of us have an R rate of less than 1, that's
certainly true in my experience. Yeah, so no sudden panic of
convert juggling to worry about, but we do need to rethink
things.

For the first 1000 years after Christ it was forbidden for
ordinary people to have access to the Bible text. Even
without being forbidden it certainly would not have been in a
language that you or I would have understood. By 1382,
Wycliff had created a handwritten translation of the Bible
into English. Then, Martin Luther translated it into German
by 1522. Tyndale was the first to bring the English Bible to
print in the 1500's, translating from Hebrew and Greek,
something that he was later executed for. The drive of all
these efforts was that 'ordinary' people should have access to
the book in their own language and be able to read it for
themselves (perhaps to undermine the newly appointed
hierarchical priestly cast). Though a copy of said text would
have only been affordable to the rich.

It's interesting to know that this process of translation and
making it available to people was strictly forbidden under
Rome, the intention was that only priests would have access

to the texts. There is something here about elevating a specialist's knowledge or access to the Bible texts to centralise the power and governance of the church as an institution. Yet, how has access to the Bible stopped the pull towards those priests, ministers, and power bases, I don't see that their fears of loss of power were realised?

How central to faith is the Bible? Considering that we as people had little or no access to it for the first 1,500 years of Christianity. How critical is it to become a scholar of its texts? By 1820, only 12% of the world could read and write. Today 25% of the world's population remains illiterate.

"The bible is a collection of books, of stories. It is not, as some behave, the fourth person of the trinity, the tetrad!"

I used to think it highly suspicious when a book's own text told me it was true and must be believed. You can include in this suspicion the spurious self-elevating text of 'all of this book is useful for teaching' that whilst written into singular stories, seems to get spread as a notion throughout our approach to the library. When movies are made now, they have to state that likenesses to real people are incidental or that the story has been dramatized for TV. If I could find such realistic statements in the Bible it would be more authentic and probably inline with what the Jewish writers meant. Is the 'just because it says so' enough to prove that all of the written word is God-breathed and good for teaching? Apparently not all of it was good enough to make the grade, I imagine the council of Nicea, working out what the main storyline was, what was out and what was in, was quite a debate. Please remember that people like you and me decided what text was more useful than the others and what the core narrative would be. Humans wrote it, humans read it, and humans decided what was divine. Does that raise any concerns for you?

What makes the writers in those contexts more tuned in and superhuman than the writers of now? They blathered on, rather like I am, and for sure included their bias, personal life issues, cultural framework and working through the filter of their own personality. Perhaps we make too divine the humanity of the authors and too literal the story they tell. Is it about reciting doctrines or sharing stories which convey values and wisdom alongside other sources?

Isn't it questionable that at the very inception of our faith, we are informed that 'all scripture is god breathed', and that yes, men wrote it, but god gave them the words. I would be suspicious of why we have to accept this as foundational to all that follows. I don't think adopting this idea is helpful to keeping our brain's desire for inquiry intact.

"The Definition Of Mixed Messaging Is When Those Who Tie Your Ropes Safely To The Shore Are Those Also Saying 'Sail And Explore"
#imgoingtocopywritethisone

People continue to experiment with helping new believers in their journey of discovery. I know some people who are helping refugees and migrants find connection, faith, and stability. In reality some of those arriving at Europe's shores fleeing one dominating harmful religious construct, are keen to explore one which says it is freeing and full of love, so I think there is a degree of assisting another's genuine inquiry more than evangelical mission. Those leading it are very much holding space, by which I mean they have created a context for these new believers to explore the Bible without being told everything prescriptively. They are being given the space to have their own experiences, revelations, and understandings of the text. Actually, they had to lose a translator who kept telling everyone their own learned/taught understanding of the text as they translated and defeated the object of the protected space. It seems ordinary people can gain enough to help them on their way without intervention and over parenting. You know what? They are doing okay!

How much do we need to know? How much is enough? And is that okay since our teacher is still alive, and through his spirit reminds us of all that he has said and all that he and the father continue to talk about?

I write these things as questions, not statements or facts. We have far too many people making statements of facts and giving answers before they even knew what the question was.

"Are You Coming Sunday? You Missed Last Week And We Don't Want To Let The Devil In!"

#scaryshitiveheard

Take a moment. Imagine that the text that follows was the only fragment of scripture that made it through the last 2000 years and into your hands. Would it be transformative enough? Would it give you a sufficient sense of the dynamic nature of the Jesus person? Would it be enough to be able to live more meaningfully for yourself and others and while being thankful for the divine he/she   as narrator of such wisdoms?

If I give everything I own to the poor and even go to the stake to be burned as a martyr, but I don't love, I've gotten nowhere. So, no matter what I say, what I believe, and what I do, I'm bankrupt without love. Love never gives up. Love cares more for others than for self. Love doesn't want what it doesn't have. Love doesn't strut, Doesn't have a swelled head, Doesn't force itself on others, Isn't always "me first," Doesn't fly off the handle, Doesn't keep score of the wrongs of others, Doesn't revel when others grovel, Takes pleasure in the flowering of truth, Puts up with anything, Trusts God always, Always looks for the best, Never looks back, But keeps going to the end.

1 Corinthians 13:3-7 MSG (*I don't 'put up with anything' because I'm counselling people all the time for sacrifices of self that they shouldn't be making*)

I think in just this passage there is enough for a lifetime of working out, digesting, absorbing, seeking to 'become'. It resonates and shows that its author is worthy of gratitude.

Instead we are overwhelmed with information and narratives, our sense of belonging gravitates around the gathering, the church, church as a building, church as a programme   a centralised organisation and some very confusing aspects of created family. What if this was not there, had never been there? If we start decentralising things, coming alongside people in society, bringing our gifts of leadership and support into the life and work spheres then what are we going to do in the building? What happens to the programmes? What will we do with the salaries and tithes? What if we grow up? I imagine we'll have fun and be creative.

"I have heard it said that church as a construct, is masturbatory, it is concerned primarily with self love and not being an agent of Love in the world"
What are we going to do with texts like this one here:
"Do not forsake the gathering as some have done... instead keep exhorting one another" - Should read:
"Don't stop hanging out with other people who are into Jesus (but not only them), keep building one another up, pulling and pushing with one another towards better things".

It's nuanced, but if you look back at a verse like this one in Hebrews you are going to see 'do not forsake the gathering,' or as some stretch it to mean, 'do not forsake the meeting'. The Church at that time had no building; it had no programme in the diary or geographical fixed context except the occasional home for a shindig. It was and still remains about our relating and not giving up on one another or we will miss out on one another's encouragement. The trouble is we accept church as it is, as it has been for a long time, reading Bible passages though a Church as building lense, to retrospectively affirm that. For example, some reasonably well off people host a get-together in their house. Like with kings, the servants take on the faith of their housemasters. Then we start doing maths around how many people, owners and workers would be part of a household and then say 'see this is an early congregation', but no, not actually. We seek out mirrors to reflect back to us our own image regardless of what was actually taking place. I'm betting that's not how most of us readers were taught about that 'forsaking' verse and forsaking the gathering because we are churched, and therefore conditioned to view scripture in a way that endorses what we have in place already, instead we could easily use it to uproot and render 'the structures we have' as meaningless.

Yep, I can go along with that; **don't stop hanging out with other people who share your faith, hang out with a lot more people who don't share your faith and in all things, love one another.**

In truth, having the Christian badge is not going to make me want to hang out with you but I will tip my hat and smile. Being a believer doesn't make you someone I want to chill out with because it's not a cure all. You can still be a control freak, an arsehole narcissist or have a pile of vested interests in position and power. I am sure I will find love for you, but I won't like you. We just aren't going to be drinking buddies because we could be riding very different horses and probably, in reality, have considerably different ideas about the Jesus person and what is referred to as His body - church. But if there is a sense of shared journey, a mutual respect, a regard for dialogue, and encouraging one another forwards then I'm up for that. Though to be fair, I also find all of those fabulous values with a great many people who don't have any badge at all and find the 'I'm a this or that' defining stuff to be counter productive in almost every respect.

Encouraging 'one another' is not what takes place in a Sunday gathering. It is a systemised context of the specialist teaching you the passive listener. You are there to be informed, taught and lead inline with a fixed denominational narrative. You might get to hang out for a few moments before or after, but whatever that meeting is, there isn't a lot of exhorting 'one another' going on, apart from some relational maintenance over the coffee and donuts (if you caught that wave of the spirit in the 90's).

Don't stop hanging out with people who 'get' you, people who see what you are seeing, who will cheer you on and speak the truth with love. Don't stop loving and encouraging others, and along the way, some might even wish to explore 'the way' alongside you. Don't reject their insight, wisdom and journey tales because it does not fit your narrative. Gaz 1: 10

So Be Courageous In Your Search Of The Real - Dig Till You Hit Rock, Only To Find That It's As Fluid As Water

A friend of mine called Malc suggested in passing that **"church is becoming much more individualistic, but in a good way."** Instead of constructs and containers it is becoming much more about a 'line of sight'. In my line of sight I will have some people I love and share life with, those of faith and those of none. You may share some of the same people in your line of sight but will also have your own people you feel called to walk with in life. Perhaps instead of just being a throw away comment, there is a deep freeing revelation here. We will have a growing ability to lay with our head on our pillow at night and see in our minds eye those we are drawn to in love, those we share 'practice' with, those who invest more into us, and those we perhaps more readily pour ourselves into but never from position. Don't forget those wonderful people we can talk crap with over a beer/gin or two.

It has to get simpler doesn't it? My wife Victoria has a low threshold for people being 'up' themselves with inhouse church speak. I remember we had some friends over for dinner and she had gone into the other room for a few minutes. I asked her out loud what she thought of the conversation we continued to have and she replied, **"What you are talking about sounds like a cult, and how you are talking about it sounds like you have mental health issues!"** Best answer ever.

Alongside the on going un-muddling of thoughts I asked a friend many years ago, "if you could strip everything back, what would still need to be in place for you to say that church is happening?"

He replied that there are probably just 3 things:

- A sense of on-going journey and of movement (yours)
- An on-going revealing of who the Jesus person is for you
- An on-going sense of meaningful relationships with others

Encourage each other!
Nuff Said

See chapter 22: The Chaordic Path for encouragement that deconstruction is a search for substance, trusting that such will arrive without pushing.

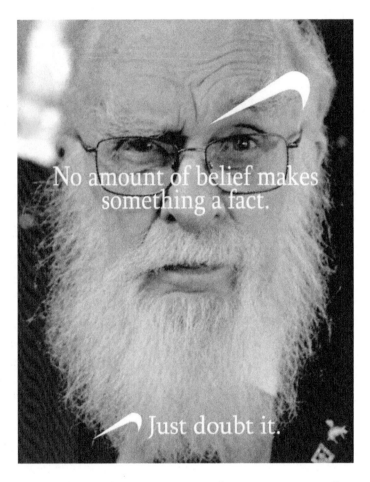

'It Is Not Doubt But Certainty That Drives You Mad'

Chapter 19

Realignment and Recovery

The Other Side Of Pain

How we experience things is unique to the make-up of a given individual. I remember that often in the ministry time, (I don't have another way to refer to that stuff yet) I would be a recipient of some kind of healing release where tears and snot were far too frequent a companion. I began to resent being prayed for, possibly since I was an easy target (lol). People insecure about their ministry usefulness got their money's worth out of responses from me. I am a sensitive fellow, and a sponge for picking up other people's stuff. I now readily refer to what I am as being an intuitive empath, a description I got from the wider world for personality types like me. It's a really good fit.

A leader from another congregation tried to explain to me that because my co-worker and I were wired differently, a baseball bat could hit my mate and just go 'ugh!' Whereas someone could fart near me and I'd pick up a demon, apparently but I think that's a largely discriminating view of empath's by the insecure headstrong. Not sure what I think about all the stuff I experienced along the way, all of which had its own frames of reference and terminology. I am of course still re-framing those things. The bottom line is that we are all different and of course will experience things differently. Some can ride along on the wave of manipulation and control for quite some time before it erodes the core of who they are. Others might be sent into a deep downward spiral at having been undermined just once, trust in the 'trustworthy' is broken in an instant, replaced by an overwhelming deluge of betrayal feelings.

While I was training to be a mainstream counsellor I was obligated to receive counselling myself. This is standard practice so you can operate with integrity as a recipient of what you yourself are offering others. Also, because in client work, you can be triggered by what you hear and you are likely to stumble across yet more unfinished business of your own. This is a normal practice, which is often entirely absent in most church contexts. During one series of sessions as a recipient, I kept talking about a feeling rising from my stomach to my chest, but never quite surfacing. This went on for a few sessions. I would repeatedly find myself at this point. Eventually my counsellor said, "it seems important for you to understand what is making its way to the surface, trying to express itself. It is possibly about control for you, needing to understand what it is before you can let it out, to know if you will be safe?" She was spot on. We were working through matters relating to my relationship with my father and along with the conflicts I had witnessed between my parents. These had been further reinforced by the tales of more horrific outbursts of violence, which my older siblings had witnessed long before my arrival. I had disclosed, with a degree of humour, that when angering my father I could outrun him up the stairs and jump into bed, covering myself with blankets. He in turn would come past the stair landing, opening up the lid on our clothes airer called a 'Flatley.' He would reach in and remove one of the flat bamboo rods that the clothing would hang from, and proceed to beat me through the blankets to little avail. It's interesting how at times we tell old stories with a degree of humour, not realising it is masking pain. Despite the reality that I would purposefully provoke him to anger, since any response was better than none from an emotionally absent father, this game of too and fro seemed to have left me with an emotional mark in a way that it was not possible to physically do, through the multiple bed blankets. Having the counsellor establish with me that I was safe, that I was in control, and that she was there with me if for any reason I was unable to 'gather myself back to myself', I slowly allowed this unknown feeling to come to the surface. I did not intellectualise, I did not seek to control or understand it, since I knew it was simply something needing to be expressed, when out of my mouth came the words " my father abused me", quickly followed by deep body shaking sobs and tears.

"Once you know who you really are, being is enough. You are neither superior to anyone nor inferior to anyone and you have no need for approval because you have awakened to your own infinite worth."
Deepak Chopra

The reason I share this story is that I would never have called what my father did an 'abuse', and well, certainly not when I look back as an adult. However that isn't how I experienced it as a vulnerable young boy living as all kids do 'in feeling', aka feeling everything all of the time. For some reason it was important for me to call it what it was, as it had been experienced at that time. Framing things favourably for those who wound us, or taking the blame ourselves, is a common coping mechanism to help us manage difficult memories as we try to keep control and manage those complex feelings. Sometimes part of our coping mechanism is to let the abuser, the 'wounder', and the usurper of our power 'off of the hook' by viewing it through a selective lense. Instead, we just need to call it what it was. Part of the reason we do this is that in letting them off the hook, lessening the deed that was done to us, we unconsciously seek to get ourselves off the hook by not having to deal with being the victim of abuse. So much better to call our abuse something less than it was or is it better to actually call something what it actually was, without making excuses or justifying it.

There are many games we play in order to deal with difficult things, but also the system plays its own games by suggesting that our disclosure or exposing the abuse would cause damage to the Church or God's people.

I have had experience of this myself when once, as a pastor, we adopted a whole bunch of lovely people from another collapsing congregation where good rational people had become drawn into partner swapping along with the leaders. I was told that the national leader of the network had told all concerned to, "keep a lid on it", since it would be, "damaging to the kingdom of God if it ever got out". Dealing with abuses or damaging behaviours needs to be dealt with sensitively, but silence is never a kingdom strategy, it's an avoidance of honesty and accountability, the compliance by participant, an indication of submission to authoritarianism. It took several years of cautious pastoring to allow people to finally disclose to their friends their own involvement in the previous church's mess, to finally be known and to put it down. The national leader, in my view, extended people's suffering.

We are often in recovery from our childhoods and the power that parents or significant others were afforded to build us up or tear us down. I believe that in the same way power is also afforded to church leaders. I don't think it has so much to do with them having inherent power to shape us for good or ill, though there may be some truth in that. I feel it has more to do with the degree to which we open ourselves to those people and give them permission to become involved in our deepest inner workings, either by invitation or imposition.

"You need to learn to get up from the table, when love is no longer being served"
Nina Simone

Words As Violence

I have on occasion worked with a lady in town who used to work, mostly alone, in counter trafficking education. Even as I use that term, I hear echoes from the church world of voices that would describe her as 'uncooperative' or 'independent'. However, none of this is true since several of those working on anti trafficking here are faith-based groups. She simply could not move at their pace or jump through their religious constraints to get where she was going. This is something I understand and applaud. She did an incredible job of mobilising those in youth culture, encouraging them to be advocates of anti trafficking awareness campaigns in the most insightful and creative of ways. Someone should write a book about her. One day she messaged me to say that she had been badly 'trolled' on social media by anonymous people from fake accounts, attacking her personally and her work. A friend doing similar work in Cambodia used to tell me, *"if you're not getting death threats, you're not doing your job very well"*. Well, she wasn't getting death threats, but the messages and posts she received were abusive, in fact, they were violent. It was at this moment, in this situation, talking to her over the phone that this concept really hit home to me. Verbal abuse is no different than physical violence, except the marks that verbal abuse leaves are internal. **The worst cultural messaging I grew up with as a child, other than 'boys don't cry,' was "sticks and stones may break my bones but words will never hurt me."** A destructive untruth if ever there was one. I hoped to get her to hear this, so that she didn't underestimate the impact of what was coming at her, so that it was not minimalised. Verbal abuse, control, manipulation, undermining, disempowering, are all simply acts of violence!

You remember what I said earlier, how sometimes our pain needs to express itself in words as well as emotions? I have found that on numerous occasions it has been healing for someone to acknowledge and name something for what it actually was and is. We just need to keep feeling our way through this stuff, towards recovery, which is more than a sentiment it is a strategy.

Getting Mind F$cked

Covid has been 'Zoom group' land for many of us. I have found myself in a couple of 'whats app' groups, which have ebbed and flowed over the last year. They are mostly just about sharing stories, and as such have been a form of mutual encouragement and continued growth during tough times.
Due to the limited nature of such communication, we can at times be triggered in an unconstructive way. Or, at times, people just say shit without any desire for conversation like with most social media platforms. I have limited capacity for such things (though my wife points out that I put quite a bit of my own crap on face book) and tend to just drop those conversations like a lead balloon, especially if they seem more about statements, learned behaviours, and positions that seem unlikely to change.

In recent months I have been triggered by, and reacting to, people who are shouting out methodologies or formulaic thinking based on 'working harder' like this;
"Having Doubts? All you have to do is go deeper into God. You have to have a stronger faith spelled 'RISK'. You need to dwell in the courts of the Almighty, sing of his praises and have a mind-set of being triumphant over death and all things. Set your face like a flint and keep going, even if people fall to your left and your right." These 'get up and go and go and go' folks, I guess, have their time and place but it's not a universal narrative. For some it's an encouragement, for others a critical parent voice placing in your subconscious the idea that, "you're a failure, you're simply not trying hard enough'.

Another 'moment' was a friend's media post calling for all pastors to, *"press in, and don't give up, even if you feel you have to give up, even if you're tired or burning out, the church needs you more than ever in these days".* I countered this with the suggestion that 'stopping' or 'resting' was <u>not giving up</u>, so why frame it as such, **why do we use such strong 'failure and letting down God' terminology**? Isn't that just manipulation?

Some people need to step down, step back, re orientate, stop, or even do something totally different for their mental health. They need to do it simply because they can, and that's ok, that's called free will. You can choose to take or reject other people's advice.

In general, Christian narratives have strong elements of:
Go Deeper, Try Harder, Be More Disciplined, Don't Give Up, Keep Going, Pray More, Don't Be Ashamed Of The Gospel, Take More Quiet Times, Keep Reading The Word. The reason I point these themes out is to highlight how unhelpful they can be for people's mental health, self management, healthy self expectations, and along with avoiding guilt from others expectations. Remember to apply the relevant tone to these words; **Some people knowing shit can be a real gift and help, while some people knowing shit, is simply shit.** I think part of our recovery is in growing a resistance to these formulas of behaviour, the internal and external expectations that are often a heavy burden and devoid of reality. Some are keen to say this stuff is the heart of the gospel message, but to me, that sounds more like your good inner Catholic telling you the benefits of kneeling at the altar and whipping the flesh into submission. We need to embrace that less is more, and understand that more in itself can be a self inflicted pain and frequently not a 'God called for' suffering.

In contrast to this is the story of a prisoner's last minutes on death row. Having refused all spiritual counsel, the chaplain still pleads with him as he makes his way to the gallows. The prisoner turns and says, 'if this Jesus were truly who you say that he is, then I would walk barefoot across broken glass to meet him.' On occasion, whether for the Jesus person or simply a person who we love deeply or have compassion for, we would all be willing to make personal sacrifices and endure suffering. But that is a choice, a deeply personal choice.

The Pathway Through

The concept of the power of forgiveness extends far beyond Christianity as a necessary aspect of healing, in relationships, of our past and even towards our inner self. By the time we move away from contexts, which have wounded us or caused us to lose sight of ourselves as an individual, the journey towards wellness is as likely to take as long as the wounds would have been deep. It is a process, as you move forward, healing will rise up to meet you.

"Healthy People Do Not Stay In Connection With Unhealthy Things. So If Someone Tries To Tell You, **"You Just Left Because You Got Hurt,"** reply with **"Hell Yeah I Left Because I Got Hurt**." Don't Let Someone Shame You For Any Choices That Improve Your Quality Of Life"
PJEC

There is an element of the chicken and the egg here in our recovery. It becomes easier to forgive once we have distanced ourselves from those who have hurt or betrayed us, along with the passing of time and working with ourselves so that 'those others' are no longer afforded position or power in our lives. Forgiveness can be the end of a journey of inner wrestling and moving on, or can be what begins such an inner work. We can forgive if we want, but we may not want. We can forgive a little more easily after some time has passed because those who wronged us are of much less concern and do not cause the same anxiety because we choose to no longer associate with them. The Bible says 'forgive others so you yourself may also be forgiven', but that's not the reason why I'm saying this. Firstly, in this instance, the forgiving of a perpetrator is for you. It will allow you to move forwards as your insides tend to remain in knots until we let go of these people. There is an element of forgiveness, which is rightly selfish and about you, looking after you, and pulling the hooks out of your skin, hooks inserted by others. Holding onto others in a state of un-forgiveness, sadly in my view, allows on-going abuse. What do you think?

"Forgive others, not because they deserve forgiveness, but because you deserve peace."

Rumi says that 'the wound is where the light comes in', but I would adjust that slightly to say that the concept of forgiveness is where we allow that light to come in and begin to do its work on the wound.

I became increasingly used to helping people understand that forgiving someone is usually not the end of things, but more often the beginning of healing and recovery. I guess it's opening the box for those things to be accessible for recovery, more than kept close and held onto. I think forgiveness holds spiritual power, which goes beyond mere cerebral, therapeutic, and logical help. In speaking ' I forgive' or a meaningful variant of those words, we step across a line in the sand, where the universe and the sacred are waiting there to embrace and hold us in wide, warm, open arms. If you're not ready, then you're not ready but there is another layer I'm going to talk about in a while, so stay open.

Don't Rake Over Old Coals

def: to revisit, to drag up, not let go, get stuck in a loop, unnecessary dwelling on the past.

My experience of recovery from childhood, work life, or church based aspects of unhappiness is that there may be multiple offences or situations where you were wronged in some way. I tend to view these things as having been the *absence of things you should have had and the presence of things you should not,* their presence tends to have the same impact upon us as adults journeying out into life as they did on our childhood where such foundations were laid. I have been relieved to discover the concept of 'representative wounds'. In short, it means that the pathway to recovery need not mean raking over every single wrong that was ever done to me.

I remember watching a T.V. documentary where previous residents in a healing retreat were raising significant concerns about the methodologies used. One of these was the re-sanctification of the genitals. This involved the pouring of communion wine down your undies if you had been in sexual sin or sexually abused (no, I don't know if they warmed it up first). Another was the story of a man undergoing deliverance from something called soul ties. The suggestion was that as he had sex with any women in prostitution that he was subject to all the idols they had bowed down to, as well as all of those idols previous 'jons' had bowed down to, like some incredibly freakish accumulative disease. You would be right in thinking of this as highly contrived and also brutalising as a healing process.

My experience has told me such rigid, tool driven list ticking is not how healing and recovery takes place. You are not a car coming in for an annual road safety test with 70 points for scrutiny.

More often than not, there is an area of pain or experience, and what comes to the surface is a situation where there is 'symbolic' or 'representative' memory, perhaps a singular example of the multiple things, which took place. It can be a constant or triggered memory which acts as a key into the previously closed box, which when turned, allows the light in to do its work on several or many other similar occurrences.

"Recovery from past trauma is selective. It is not swinging a stick at a 'memory pinata' so that everything that has ever hurt you, comes flying out!"

(for some, there may be a greater need to work through each significant trauma or memory, but this is not frequent)

An example of this might be a situation I found myself in as we settled in for Covid Lockdown #1 in early 2020, along with our youngest son Jacob aged 24, who came for two weeks and ended up stuck with us for three months. My son Jacob had bought me the book *Scattered Minds* by Gabor Mate for the previous Christmas, inscribed with the idea that it was given in humour, but not really. *Scattered Minds* is the perfect book for unpacking what it is to suffer from ADD (attention deficit disorder), which is kind of an oxymoron since people with ADD, like me, have an aversion to reading books. I would normally wait for an audio version. To show willingness, a year on from getting the book, I skateboarded to the beach, which is a slow two mile sloping of roads to the coast from where we live. You are allowed to go there during lockdown, but you are not allowed to swim or otherwise enjoy yourself, and so I set about the task of beginning *Scattered Minds*, with my scattered mind. #covidrestrictionssuck

In writing this now I am still in touch with the emotion, which I felt then as I began to read about an ADD sufferer (the author) the same age as me who basically maps out much of my experiences and problems. From issues with my ability to concentrate to how I learn. It caused me to recognise my wife and kids resilience at having walked alongside my numerous dysfunctional default settings. Not to mention, I finally understood why my father used to say that 'when' you were a kid, you were an absolute bastard (PTSD speak for a son who won't sit still). The first two chapters took me ages to read because I wanted to take notes. This was, in part, to prove to my wife and son that I had finally begun to read the book they were so 'un-subtly' pushing me to begin. Besides that, I wanted to note down every parallel universe he described which had mirrored my own.

A few days later I felt pretty unsettled during one of our morning daily 'team covid' check-ins, which included questions like 'how are you?' or 'how is your inner world?' Then we would meditate and make dinner plans to keep us sane. On this specific occasion I felt I was being hassled on a number of fronts, 'read more, watch less TV, drink less booze.' I would wake for breakfast to my son Jacob, standing at dingly dangly eye level dressed only in his boxers, pointing out the next thing I needed to do, to be well. To be fair, I was unlikely to change any of my habits from such an approach. The focus on what I wasn't doing well just pushed me over the edge. I had to push back or I'd fall off, and so stated how utterly unfair their estimations of me were. There was little acknowledgement of what I was doing well, such as projects, accomplishments, aspects of change. From nowhere I suddenly said, 'you're just like the bloody teachers in my old school reports making statements totally focused on the negative, which makes me want to do jack shit (cultural English for zero).'

For some divine, but also deeply human reason, I found myself unable to choke back the tears. I sobbed very deeply for perhaps three minutes, followed by a warm wave of freedom and healing. This wave is something, which has become very tangible to me. It's that 'wow, what's this?' Followed by,' and gosh it's over now ' feeling.

For a number of years I had used my school reports as an aspect of comedy. My mother found them again when I was an adult in my thirties and passed them along to me. Middle school teacher comments such as 'Garry has excelled this year...(pause for effect) in avoiding every kind of work.' It's amazing how many different and creative ways non-life affirming educators can write 'could try harder'. I thought such comments were funny, so I laughed them off, and as a result I utilised the unconscious masking coping mechanism of humour. In doing so, I failed to notice that I had been either top student, or in the top three students, in English throughout my time at that school. It was an abusive environment where the smart people got ahead and those who lagged behind were ridiculed with scathing comments in school reports. There were canings on hands and butt cheeks, teachers saying horrible things, slaps across the face, lets not forget the slipper for poor results in the oral English spelling test which was given by an incomprehensible Glaswegian, Scotsman.

Why am I taking you on this trip down memory lane?
My moment of healing was not of my choosing, and there was no raking over the coals of every disheartening or harming thing that happened to me at school. A moment, a trigger, and a period of my life, when many shitty things were moved on

from. The symbol of the school report shifted from a symbol of self-deprecation to me finally being able to see I had also been good at some things.

The Power We Give Away

A critical moment of 'moving on' from wounds is often forgiveness. It is an act of no longer sitting in judgement over someone or several someone's, but handing it over to God or the universe. It is said, "holding on to anger is like grasping a hot coal with the intent of harming another; you end up getting burned." The other part is letting go of the coal. Doing such a thing is not simple. It is often an act of will, more than something you ever want to do, but we need, if we are able, to let go. There is the Christian idea of letting go and letting God, handing the responsibility over, but if you were sexually abused you might one day forgive, but may also rightly want someone to be brought to justice.

I know personally how emotionally consuming it can be to hold someone to account for choices or decisions they made in a role of responsibility. It is not something you do for the sake of it. It brings no pleasure since it utterly robs you of peace in the ever-playing courtroom of your mind.

I remember putting into place some monthly meetings of accountability that involved external mediators to help leaders, past and present, to resolve, and perhaps, hopefully take responsibility for things, which were not okay. I believe we were in this process for around 12 months before the person under much of the scrutiny apologised. Much to a colleague's amazement, he asked, 'But why say sorry now? Why couldn't you have just done that months ago?" To which he replied, "the mediator told me I should apologise so that you guys can all move on." After hearing that answer my colleague walked out of the room, astounded at the ignorance and lack of genuine remorse. As he walked out of the room, I'm pretty sure I heard him say, 'oh for fucks sake!' You can't invent repentance and remorse because it requires recognition of wrongdoing. It is accompanied by a feeling, which is either present, or it isn't.

If it isn't? Then they're probably broke, not woke.

'How are you?' 'I'm **FINE***', 'Oh, so you're Fucked Up, Insecure, Neurotic and Emotional?'*
Baz

Our personal desire to hold people to account can, if we are not careful, lock us into an abuse that we continue to relive. We keep it in a box of our own making without realising that its keeping an active doorway wedged open to the abuser. If you've been through this, or are in this stuff even now, you know what I am talking about. Ask yourself if you are stuck holding a wound in a place where it cannot recover until such times as the perpetrator is brought to justice or held to account? The reality is we could be waiting many winters until that day, if that day comes at all. Some of those people will undoubtedly be a narcissist who will rarely, if ever, apologise unless it is for personal gain. While we are waiting, isn't it a good idea to cut yourself fully off from that energy sapping umbilical? A practical note here is that of the physiology of our brain/mind because some of our recovery will require a measure of re wiring, and of forming new synapsis.

If we, almost as a ritual, speak out that 'I forgive' whoever, for whatever, it means we lay down a marker and hammer a stake into our minds of 'knowing' we have done so. When the green monster wants to make you relive the shit again in the night hours, seething with animosity, we pull on that stake and say 'but I've forgiven them'. It's not a cure all, but it tames the wild horses, which want to cause our mind to run into dark corridors, seemingly at will. It gives us a bridle to pull on and say 'no, I've put that down'. This knowing and halting can begin to literally rewire the brain. Little neural pathways will form from the sparking of synapsis enabling us to not be subject to a losers loop like a scratched record which just wont stop playing. But, forgiving, not forgiving, whatever that concept is for you, it is your private business, nobody else's and I am certainly not telling anybody what they should do, only highlighting the nature of such a process.

I am just touching the surface of this subject here, but it would be unfair of me to leave you with only the aspect of forgiving those who wrong us without exploring what is perhaps an even more powerful aspect of forgiveness. I have met people many times over the years that have walked through the fire of letting go, of no longer holding onto people who have hurt or abused them. Too many times I have found that they forgave others, but have not yet forgiven themselves. 'For what?' I can hear you ask.

An important aspect of recovering from spiritual abuse is to get to the final layer in forgiving ourselves, which is to cease punishing ourselves for the power we gave to others over our lives (or that we were not strong enough to resist power taken from us). I state specifically spiritual abuse, as often other aspects of abuse are forced upon us, and the nature of spiritual abuse is that we may have been complicit in it happening by permissioning people or systems to have that power over us through obediently following false ideas of submission. It is really important that we, as the person that we are today, older and wiser, knowing what we now know, find a way to forgive ourselves for things that happened when we knew far less about what was going on. **Knowledge, self awareness, and a growing healthy independence affords us the universal 'power of two feet', the ability to walk away or forwards.**

'Toxic people will make you feel like you are holding a grudge. **No dude, that's not a grudge, that's a boundary.'**

I don't want to over spookify this stuff, but I do think there is a different aspect of power at play when we submit into spiritual stuff. At its core, this spiritual submission is a submitting to people. A good friend once told me that because he was in a prominent role of Christian leadership, he was told that his kids were likely to be targeted by witchcraft and the demonic. He said he was far less worried about such things and much more concerned about his role and authority as a father. He said that a coven could chuck as many curses at his kids as they like, to slow them down or destabilize them, but if his son comes home with a painting or drawing from school, and he doesn't acknowledge and affirm the work that has been done, he would be tearing the kids heart out.

Just think of your own parents and parental figures, and how they had incredible influence in the role they had, power or authority over your self-perception and worth. I believe it is the same with leaders in the church construct. There is a significant authority there with the power to build us up or tear us down. Perhaps it's not spooky at all, not a spiritual authority we are wounded by, but instead the power dynamic of the child-like role we take upon ourselves and the parental role we place upon them or that they adopt. As I've mentioned in a different chapter, church is a high dependency culture where it is not geared to helping you become a full 'self actualised' adult. Part of this is the church's on-going need to parent, and our taking on the role of submissive children. As such, we afford those people all the power they need to affect our happiness or oppression, to cheer us onwards and outwards, or keep us locked inside. I've personally heard pastors grieve the fact that their congregants are still immature and yet, they do not know that they, and the system they perpetuate, will likely always result in such.

Breathe

The good news is it does get better. You do move on and you do recover. **This rarely happens though when you remain in the context of abuse, in proximity to the toxic, or in anything that does not meet you eye to eye, equal to equal, and adult to adult.**

"What doesn't kill you gives you a lot of unhealthy coping mechanisms and a very dark sense of humour."

I don't consider my own church journey to have been especially abusive, though there were some moments, which left significant marks and required recovery. Mostly the abuse I experienced was one of buying into a life-limiting culture, wearing its t-shirt, losing that t-shirt, and then buying another one in a repeating cycle until I could no longer be part of what is an incredibly small world with an ever-decreasing orbit.
I simply prefer life unbounded and 'unbranded'.

The church construct is a mess. Some people cannot continue their journey towards wellness and fullness by continuing to participate there. The church and its leadership will see itself as having the answers to your internal world, and it will have multiple methodologies for shaping your self-perception and worth. All of this is about your mental health, the church is apparently 'all about that' with minimal, if any, qualification to do so.

"Putting someone against the ropes is not a therapeutic strategy, It's abusive bullying."

If you have a physical sickness or broken body they will pray for you to receive divine healing. If it occurs, they acknowledge that it doesn't come from them. In matters of the mind they seem more than happy to walk around inside your head with their boots on, displaying very little understanding of the complexity of mental health and emotional healing. They will pray for your kidneys, then send you back to the doctor you just came from if there is no miracle recovery. If you have depression, they are now the experts, continually willing to keep 'having a go' and yet they rarely refer you to external specialists. Why do you think that is?

The reality is there are many good things to be found in the faith community, along with opportunities to grow. There

ꞁ be many words of affirmation and encouragement, but
⸺ ᴉing from people afforded position and power, it only
takes a single wound to turn septic and place us in a situation
of needing to become well again.
Christians refer to their church community as family, but this
in no way means that it is functional because, well, it is not.

You are moving on when:

- *You are able to 'respond' to things you once only 'reacted' to (less triggers).*
- *The space in your head is not full of guilt for things you did or didn't do.*
- *You think of those who hurt or controlled you with less anger.*
- *You have boundaries and only those who respect you are allowed in.*
- *You understand that what you saw as power and strength was limited and mixed with dysfunction.*
- *You regain objectivity and you can review things from 'above' experiencing those things subjectively, full of feeling.*
- *You can be misunderstood without having to try to justify yourself.*
- *You are letting go of the wrong people, even if they don't want to let go of you.*
- *You feel no obligation to be in a relationship with people you would rather not be, you begin to make friends more than maintain acquaintances.*
- *You are removing the hooks that other people and experiences have put in you.*
- *You have cut the umbilical, that once may have given you sustenance, but began to flow back the other way, giving your energy to the parent or system.*
- *You can hear advice and exercise your right to reject people's well-meant intentions.*
- *Unlike a victim, we do not leave one toxic environment and seek out another.*
- *Anxiety is occasional and manageable, not constant and overwhelming*

- *You can confidently reject false criticism as being untrue*
- *You can own your part in things, and not punish yourself.*

Any of these things can be an indication that you are moving forwards and recovering. If you are experiencing them, then you are to be applauded. Well Done!

As part of checking in with 'ourselves' and as part of our recovering from encounters with toxic people, here's a short mystical story:
An elderly Buddhist teacher and his young disciple are making the long journey to the next town, when the come to the edge of a wide river. The water is deep but they plan to cross and as they do, they see a woman contemplating her own journey to the other side. The young disciple offers to help, but it is the old man who agrees to carry the woman safely across to the other side. Some miles further on, the young disciple enquires as to the appropriateness of the old mans contact with the woman, and so he replies, "Yes, I carried the woman to the other side, but the difference between you and I is that where I put her down on the riverbank, it is you, that carries her still."
In our reflections, remembering's and perhaps re-ordering of thoughts, it is a good thing to ask ourselves if we still carry certain people on our insides, where it may be time for us to put them down.

The Power Of Voice - Permission To Feel And Express

In supporting individuals over the years in various forms of recovery and psychological healing, I have found one thing to be consistently true: feelings need to be expressed. If you have been in abusive or traumatic events, or starved of love and affection, or lived in harm's way, that pain or yearning often has a voice still asking for space to express itself.
As a practical illustration, I tend to view this as another person inside of us, another us, another you, which has not

been able to catch up and join with the rest of you because of being stuck in unexpressed 'feelings'. We have incredible resilience, and I am ever grateful for coping mechanisms that have gotten us here. However, as adults, they may not get us to where we are going. They often leave us ill equipped to deal with the abuse or control you might experience in the here and now. Some old friends have simply served their purpose and can now be in the way of our growth.

I often tell people that whilst some things need to be intellectually acknowledged, named, and voiced, there are aspects of our mind and memory that relate more to the emotional self. It is almost as though an aspect of ourselves gets left behind, holding those unexpressed emotions waiting to re-join us in our journey to make us more complete. The 'left behind' self also has something to say, but it is rarely words. It is travail, deep sobs, streaming tears and more than your fair share of snotty noses.

I think I mentioned in an earlier chapter that I swear. I have, in my own recovery, found that particular means of articulation helpful in expressing myself and externalising feelings, instead of storing them in my limited capacity 'emotional cup'. I don't mean swearing at people, though my early endeavours of driving in Greece involved a whole bunch of this. I mean I swear with myself, I say it to the wind, to the walls, maybe even to the God fella, in order to say what needs to be expressed in the strongest of terms. A friend tells me from time to time, when my F bomb is getting over used and losing its impact and he is usually correct.

I have a dear and long-term friend called Shannon in Savannah, Georgia, who naturally introduced me to the concept, along with an incredible capacity to burp after drinking cola and playing the armpit fart game at dinner tables. (This is where you blow into a straw tucked under your armpit, try this, it's a must). I would, on occasion, vent in her direction and she would use this phrase for me, until such times as I began to say it for myself. You have to imagine the southern accent and tone, but essentially, when people screw you over, you say "FUCKERRRZZZZZZZ !!!!"

There is a friend I have worked with in counter trafficking, and she is the sweetest Christian woman you could ever meet, pouring her life into the recovery of trafficking victims. She had sadly been subject to misogyny in toxic church environments, passive non-support, and active undermining. I could tell that this one instance had wounded her. She is the last person I know who would ever swear, so it was with great delight that I toyed with her about the notion of externalising feelings with the occasional swear word. I expressed with all the authenticity that I could the uber expletive "FUCKER! FUCKERSSSS, AND FUCKERRRRRZZZ" of my Georgian friend's vocabulary.

I didn't really anticipate that she would repeat this at all, but it was fun walking her through the idea. I loved her enough to go further, feeling that she needed to hear the authentic version, and have the best hope of 'fully expleting.' I voice messaged my friend in Savannah and asked if she could please express in voice messages these verbal talents. I received three or four short messages with her giggling at the idea of 'spreading the word,' but she complied. The best part was that she went through all versions, lengths, and tones in that amazing accent.

I dutifully forwarded them. Later in the day, the 'orator' messaged me to say that she had been waiting in a bank, or some other such public place, trying to fulfil this strange request in earshot of others. Simply brilliant!

But seriously, like a mother says whilst holding back the hair of her daughter as she vomits into a toilet, "better out than in."

Your Internal World

On numerous occasions in therapeutic conversations I have used the term 'gathering yourself back to yourself', and perhaps I have mentioned it in other chapters. It is something that I have actually drawn into my frames of reference from Buddhism. Along with peoples growing interest in mindfulness and other practices, other useful terms are being 'centred' or 'grounded'. I have found these terms to be of huge importance since Christianity might only lean towards our being anchored in Jesus and not place sufficient importance on your being centred. Not on who we are in the context of a divine being, not on who we are in the context of others, but critically upon 'who we are in the context of ourselves'. Perhaps it's like slipping our feet into comfortable slippers, with our own name on, or just feeling truly comfortable in our own skin. I believe these to be important but absent ideas, ideas which we can learn so much from. They are really helpful ideas /tools as we begin to rediscover ourselves in a new 'centred' way.

Since Christians carry the message that God gives us grace sufficient for today, it is perhaps helpful that we explore and take on as a practice, the ability to be fully present in the here and now. Please consider exploring some of these ideas, they won't bite!

This was my phone screensaver for a number of years:
'Unfuck yourself, be the person you were before all that stuff happened that dimmed your fucking shine.'

Fact: The gift of counselling is anonymity, a detached relationship that creates a safe space to be unsafe in, by which I mean to truly let go. For many, church should not be this, and cannot be this. It is especially toxic if you are being offered help in the same context as abuse, fear, or control.

You can find my mentoring, coaching and support page here, where I seek to come alongside people through their transitions:
www.facebook.com/movingthewalls

Chapter 20

The Marriage - The Divorce

& The Ever After

I find myself in a difficult position as I acknowledge that I have conflicting values. For a long time I have tried to place value on anyone taking a step forward, but at the same time, I believe that people need to lean in and take a leap. I don't say this to add to the already pressurising voice of the church, "do more, go deeper, work harder". I say this in terms of your own emancipation from things, which may be inhibiting your free will or progress. When I was doing 'cool' bar church I used to get requests from students of a local Bible college to comment on emerging church stuff. I think they thought emerging church was people leaving the old and doing something new. There was a desire for me to convey a concrete 'this is it' and 'this is how you do it.' In reality, my comment was more along the lines of 'the whole of the church is emerging and taking the next step for them' though I think I was trying to be mediating. It is not about the actions of one group. These steps generally come at a cost for people.

Previous beliefs and practices are so deeply embedded that to embrace new ideas requires a leap of faith, or a sermon from the visionary pastor stating 'now we are going in this direction'. Due to church structure remaining the same, there can only be micro steps. I value these steps, but they also do my head in and I'm done with waiting for them. All this makes me question what is the likely cost of a leap, versus a manageable step?

Recently I had a rather lovely but unusual call with a journey friend from way back when we were exploring the church world together. Like me, he had also transitioned from the normal world, and into the church world while he was still young. What was unusual about the call is that in his part of the world, it was two in the morning, and work stress had kept him up. I, however, was having a midday bath during lockdown to try and kill an hour or two from the long days. We talked as the bathwater cooled around me, and as it turned out, we were both in a reflective mood concerning our exit from organised Christianity. Whilst I had managed to sustain some sense of the Jesus person in my exit (if only due to his commitment to seemingly 'stick' around as an opportunist), my friend would describe himself as agnostic. In some way I guess that he, like many others, had left the concept or experience of God back in the building, and perhaps even back in the adventures of his youth. He said, "I think I'm probably agnostic" since he hadn't ruled out God showing back up at some point, but the onus was upon God to do so. What really moved me was his description of moving away from the church world and the 'true believerism' we had all adopted. He described the feeling like a divorce. He went on to describe the sense of having lost a part of what had once been an all consuming world, which I feel is telling, because it is not just the sense of God that many leave behind, but the culturally immersive trappings of church as a sphere and the relational benefits of a ready made members club.

I remember that small group of friends I had around me, while also exiting that world. We all had to go through some kind of loss. A loss of programme and diary, a loss of alters, icons and provoked 'feelings' whether they were the voice and words of a preacher, or the seductive song singing experience I like others, remember feeling pretty naked and exposed. To this feeling I know some of my critics would say 'see, we told you so', but **this was not the nakedness of humiliation from being cast from the warm log cabin into the winter snows. It was the nakedness, the stripped back-ness of it being simply you... and simply Him**. I like the sentiment of that. It feels warm and fuzzy and for the most part true. Although, it does not express the vulnerability of asking, 'will the real Jesus please step forward?' Not knowing if he will once you have dropped any and all counterfeit versions you may have been presented with or had adopted.

" When people are talking about church, I do not assume, I ask what it is that they mean. Equally when they are talking about Jesus I ask the same, as we may mean very different things, some peoples Jesus leads them into conformity and rule abiding while the one I know leads to freedom and exploration"
AH

I felt rather protective of the people who were going through this. I know full well that each of them have people in the background who are waiting for them to fall and fail, legitimising their own position or their own fear that 'out there' is unsafe whilst 'in here' is safe. Also they have people with genuine love, hoping and praying that they come back to their senses (from their own loving reference point) from within the fold. I do want to acknowledge that some of the love and concern from others was/is genuine, just misplaced and limiting. People's beliefs and conditioning can make them genuinely fearful of what might happen to you if you re-join the world with all those other people in it.

Some of us got into a mess, some of us screwed up, some of us hurt people we cared about, but it wasn't that anyone had gone backsliding into 'sin,' whatever that word means. It was that all the shit that was always there, hidden by performing, masked in the culture of 'behaving to belong', suddenly had nowhere to hide. People were real and yes, naked, but people were growing up too. **They were holding onto one an‹ as they passed through the loss, into reality, from ᴜ.ᴜ world of the upside down into the here and now.**

Each had their own walk, for some it was a new experience of a faith based journey and reliance on the holy spirit person, while others, once they had put down what had been handed to them in pre 'worked out' packages, were left with little of substance. I applaud the bravery and the pursuit of the uncertain over the absolutes. Any decision to embark on the path less trodden, the road less travelled (seemingly un-trodden /un-travelled) is an admirable choice to make.

A friend stood in a line outside a certain church in Brownsville, Pensacola where he had flown because God was doing shit. People were having experiences, even as the line drew closer to the doors of the meeting, people were feeling what he described as 'the weight of God' - there was an anticipation yes, but the experiences were without hype. However, he said that the culture inside the building remained the same. Someone spoke repeatedly about sin and the only thing missing was a stick to beat people with. My friend said *"It was really very annoying, all the guy said was Sin Sin Sin, so people left heads down focusing on sin... if only he had spoken about Jesus Jesus Jesus, the people would have left thinking about Jesus, and the sin would have taken care of itself."*

This won't be popular but it's a fact, I would say that the sum total of all that is left after my evangelical grooming, of evangelical 'go convert people' is to offer simply this 'If you have a question, if you have intrigue, if you have enquiry, that's a really good start. It's God's responsibility to show up in ways that are personal to you, and make himself known... it always was'.

What is it that you have left? What still makes sense and has substance for you?

"It messes with your head when you realise that Christians do not have the monopoly on love and are all too often late to the party."

I found it funny that after a childhood where my parents would have described me as being a 'little shit', that my becoming a Christian would be less threatening to them and perhaps even encouraged. The idea that others might step in and take some responsibility for my personal development and 're alignment' towards having my ducks more in a row, I thought would have enticed and delighted them. Instead, when I was baptised at the age of 18, they declined to attend. My father warned me that doing such a thing was like "getting married to the church" despite his own rather Catholic upbringing. My mother and father grew up in an age where identifying as Christian was probably still following whatever the king or queen did, as generally people became what the royals at the time decreed. My father said he was a Christian because he fought in the war for King and Country, and my mother because she sang in the church choir of the small country village where she grew up.

I felt my father was partly responsible for beginning my interest in such things as the Jesus person, since it was he who watched all the 'filmed in Cinemascope and Technicolor' Hollywood Bible tales. Looking back at his words now from my age of 55, his warning of marital obligation to the church was pretty close to the bone and accurate concerning the years that followed.

My father actually had a dynamic encounter in his last days, which seemed to be in stark contrast to the ideas of faith he had been brought up with. For what seemed like a couple of years, my father fought leukaemia and was in and out of remission. My father was not known for being emotional, except when he was watching movies. Instead of allowing him his moments of emotion, on cue, at the right moment in the movie his eyes would leak and eventually he would dare to look and see if we had noticed, only to find us ready to jeer and take the piss. He would always say something like 'what's the matter with you, it's a real man who can cry'. Perhaps, if we had not chosen to turn his emotion into our own moment of comedy, he would have felt safer to express emotion over his years of torment. His own father had abandoned the family, going to work one day but actually leaving the UK returning to Australia where he re married.

On his returning to the UK again some years later, his new wife followed him and turned up at my grandmothers house asking where her husband Mr Kishere was, only to hear my grandmothers say 'What? No - he's my husband!' My Grandfather subsequently spent 2 years in prison for bigamy. My father could, possibly, have resolved some of his PTSD from WW2, leaving more of those war years behind than he did, but I think that generation had little idea of emotional development. In the end, we largely put his repeated remissions from leukaemia down to a resilient desire to march one last time with his Burma conflict comrades, in what was to be to be the 50th anniversary of victory over Japan and march once more, he did!

It was meant to be just another session of his going to the hospital to receive his next treatment, hoping for another remission. He was in a private room with glass windows. I could see him sitting on the side of the bed as I approached, the nurse had her hand on his shoulder, and I could tell that this was a 'moment' I needed to allow to happen un-interrupted. When the nurse left she held the door open, as if to usher me in, and I came alongside my father whose tear strewn face was doing its best version of that British stiff upper lip that he had been conditioned to control. But he was failing. He simply said, 'well that's it, it hasn't worked, and, well, that's just it, nothing more to do'. Which is his way of not saying, 'I'm buggered, I'm going to die very soon.'

Some important things happened in the few days he had left. I think the course of those days were different to all that preceded it because of the ridiculous things which happened next, just after the nurse had left and I had entered the room.

Please know that I am not into most, if not all expressions of evangelical conversion processes or thinking, but, at this moment I did want my father to know comfort, and perhaps spiritual connectivity to whom I felt could be a constant companion in these days. I tentatively asked my dad what he thought about faith and he simply said "I'm doing alright', to which I got somewhat 'arsy' and annoyed and said, "Dad, stop being a stubborn bastard, now is not the time to continue to be stubborn'. He allowed me to pray for him, but before I could reach the end of whatever it was that I was making up, there was a knock at the door. A man stuck his head round the door and said 'Hello Mr Kishere, I understand that you have had some bad news?' It was the Baptist minister from my sister's Church. I stepped out of the room so he could speak with my dad. I saw through the glass that it was a solemn conversation, my father showing his usual discomfort with tactility, the pastor's hand on his shoulder. He probably stayed less than five minutes before we swapped places. I had just begun to sit on the bed next to my dad when there was another knock on the door. Another head appeared, around the corner and said, 'Mr Kishere, how are you doing? I have heard that you're not having a very good day, I'm the hospital chaplain!'

My father let out a somewhat loud expression with the words **'What the bloody hells going on here?'** I thought this was hilarious. It was good to see my dad getting cornered in a seemingly divine moment, at his point of need. I think at this point, he probably said 'fukkit, what have I got to lose?' and chose to identify as Christian, not culturally, but instead because of a personal encounter. I feel for my brother as he was the one who was present as my dad had a rather uncomfortable... either complete full stop to his life, depending on beliefs, with the lights turning forever off, or transition through the C.S Lewis 'doorway' to another place (again something I am in my own process of reframing).

My mother was also not an emotional woman. I mean, she could show emotion, but not deal with anything other than the superficial. She could swear and shout like an absolute trooper watching Saturday afternoon wrestling but otherwise kept her internal world private. I remember once saying to my mother that I felt there was a bottle cork in the middle of her forehead and if I pulled it out, she would cry for a month. After hearing that she cried, not for a month, but just long enough to allow some of that backlog to trickle out for a moment. She was relieved not to be present at my fathers passing and I understood why.

What is it with these last days' encounters?

I remember asking my dad in hospital some weeks after the barrage of clergy, what it was that he most regretted in life. It is perhaps an insensitive question, but in the days before he passed, he had been doing what I can only describe as 'self work' (I love that this was all spontaneous, nobody had told him anything about how he should be as a believer). He told me in previous years that, after fighting the Japanese in Burma, he thought that the Hiroshima and Nagasaki bombs were a justifiable evil since he felt that many millions more would have died should the war have continued. In response to my question he said two things. First, "That was a terrible thing to do to people." I replied by asking 'what was?' He said, "dropping that bomb and killing all those people, what a horrible way to die." This was said with genuine emotion and remorse. The next thing he said he regretted was, 'This", I asked "what's this?" He said, 'This.' This Christian thing, I regret that I won't have more time to enjoy it."

My mother found herself in the hospital because of a heart attack, and then had a stroke on the operating table while having bypass surgery. To this day I don't know if she actually had the surgery. I just remember her slow recovery back to only partial normality. When it was her time to die, I left the room where I had been at her bedside with my sister. I had been triggered by a sound, which was all too memorable from my father's eventual passing, the noise of the automatic morphine injector, which was essentially permissible euthanization, a merciful application of pain meds, which would cause a less traumatic death. I knew the sound from having been at my fathers bed the night before he died, so when I heard this familiar buzzzzzzt of the next injection, I knew my mother close to passing and I needed to find a private place, 'not' to have to keep my shit together. On the night of my fathers passing, I had been in the room earlier as my father shouted from his sedated state, "I want to go, but they won't let me!" I don't know who 'they' were in his mind, but both my sister and I whispered in his ear that he had permission to go, that his work was over and we were all going to be ok.

Each time I crossed paths with my sister at my mum's bedside she was keenly speaking comforting bible passages to my mum. I watched, as my deeply sedated mother would pat her hand around on the bed before eventually finding my sister's hand, holding it until her calm was restored. It was strange since she seemed to do this often over several days. Similar to my father, during the evening where we were encouraged to say our goodbyes, my mother did her usual pat around the bed for my sister's hand as she quoted Bible passages and gently told my mum that it was ok to 'go'. My mother patted around, found my sister's hand, but on this occasion it did not satisfy. She patted some more then lifted up her hand and reached for the sky. My sister said, 'that's right, you don't need my hand anymore, take his.' And that, as the saying goes, was that!

I am glad that there seemed to be some passageway that my parents passed through, not for me to find some religious solace (though it does give me some) but for them.

With my fathers fears that my baptism was some form of marriage to the organisation of church, I'm glad that my parents didn't have to get married to the church. I don't think it would have suited them well, and I think they would have bought into the cultural trapping of behaving and performing more than it being truly transformative. I'm happier that they, from my perspective, got to experience the Jesus person without the complexity of the church, or what may have been a messy divorce. Nope, they escaped that. You see, I still believe that the Jesus person, the idea of him, the thinking on some stuff that he may have said, led to the beginning of change internally. Their passing, gave me some hint as to their being a 'what's next', again, theology aside and just simple human seeking, it remains a nice idea. That shit still works for me. But unlike many, I managed to bring some of that with me after my own divorce from the constructed Bride, while others may feel that it is forever broken and lost.

As an aside, I used to write poetry and do performance poetry from a stage. For some reason, I intuitively like that

I've written 'bride' in two places in the book, firstly my pursuit of a <u>prettier one</u>, and my own divorce from the <u>constructed one</u>. It feels poetic to me and perhaps in Christian 'speak', in terms of this descriptive word for the body of believers, I am perhaps inwardly anticipating new romance. My friend Kent beat me in a combative prayer time once, you know the one where you're in a circle thinking of something dynamic to speak which will be world shaking. I had declared out loud and confidently that I had just about had enough of being 'post' things, to which he brought out his dagger of being a smartass in our dual of words and counter prayed **" I feel full of anticipation and intrigue, that I am, as yet 'pre' something"**. I concede that he won that one.

Free Child And Conforming Child

It is worth looking at these psychological positions/defaults as it sheds some light on how we can lean towards early adoption of ideas and behaviours. Perhaps even how we can find ourselves leaning into believerism, instead of towards resistance and questioning. The conforming child is more open to suggestion, to explicit, and implicit forms of communication, and carries a stronger desire to fit in and belong, to succeed, and be affirmed. They will more readily adopt a culture with little to no critique.

I like to think of myself as a free child, but I am not. If I were, I would not have been so irritated by a member of my counselling class many moons ago. She was a single mum who would disappear abroad in the term breaks to some rainbow mountain festival with her daughter, oddly enough up an actual mountain in France. This got under my skin. When the course lecturer was affirming her, my trigger reaction was that she was a waster. This was as clear an indicator as there could be that I am, in part, a conforming child. I simply did not like that she got to be 'in' and affirmed when I was doing everything I could to show people I was worthy of being there. I got affirmed for effort and conformity; she got affirmed for her ability to move with the wind. If you have had any exploration of Celtic saints, and the word Peregrinate (the wild goose), you will know that even in our early faith roots there was a pure dynamism of being able to flow with the wind of the spirit. I have personally had to address *my default to conformity and the reasons for it because I was finding myself as the performing monkey in my work world, and then also in my church world.* I think in the context of this book, the downfall of the conforming child type is that we can buy into the church world and go deep into its beliefs, rituals and practices with little restraint, and as mentioned, little critique. We know little of what it is that we are now actually immersed in, and yet, we can be very excited about it as though it is all 'absolute'. We believe what we are told, adapt to behaviours, and adopt beliefs pretty much without question. Literally, we are like everyone who has ever joined a cult so, never say never.

Watch out when the conforming child becomes balanced and discovers the lightness and liberty of the free child. I think this is part of what happens when people begin to exit organised Christianity. They become free to ask questions, free to make decisions for themselves, and are likely to have a strong and growing aversion towards anything that might limit their desire to fly. It is also the reason for some of the animosity, which is often very vocal in the directions of those who leave, a resentment of their freedom, and their not respecting or remaining in the camp of the conformed. Free child types make conforming child types 'real itchy'.

Epiphany Moments

On reflection, there are some seminal moments and changes in how you see things. I didn't want to quote the matrix, as so many others have already, but the 'take the red pill to see things as they truly are, or take the blue pill to remain blissfully ignorant' moment fits the situation. Seemingly, I began to see things as they truly were, and it felt painful. I literally hurt inside, going way beyond mere discomfort. I see these moments now as my glimpse into how God feels about the bullshit or at least that's how I have chosen to frame it. A tiny insight into how the free child and the Jesus person can thrive together as one.

An encounter with a side's person (usher) one Sunday morning was the tipping point for me. A side's person is an invented semi sacred role in the Anglican church for people who put out the chairs and pass the collection plate around. You could tell that some folks felt 'elevated' when they passed the plate around in their polished shoes and Sunday suits.

On this occasion I just couldn't remain in the meeting. I was angry to the point of feeling sick, and I just couldn't hear the same old 'work harder pray more' stuff. Hiding in the foyer, which is like the waiting room before entering the holy of holies, decorated with pictures of missionaries working in the Sudan, Peru and elsewhere, a side's person came up to me. He was generally a decent chap, though I sensed some degree of a stick up his butt for he was, indeed, a true believer. Without any awareness of my having a moment, he came up to me and asked, "Why are you wearing earrings?" He asked with a patriarchal superior tone and followed it up with, "you are meant to bring the young people up to your standard, not go down to theirs." I had not yet rediscovered my pre-Christian virtue of being able to tell someone to go F themselves, that came a few years later. This incident confirmed that the church of elsewhere would not be the ending point for any of the young people I was working with, nor eventually, even myself. I have found that in such encounters it is not simply a personal internal groaning, since one voice is reflective of a generational, patriarchal control, and my reaction is also that of those I represent, a generation fighting for air and for change.

Can you imagine the young lad who has recently discovered the Jesus person, a lad whose mother used to lock him in the wardrobe, before his father returned home from work, to protect him from a beating. A young guy in distress, who I once found cutting a cross into his arm with a razor, desperately trying to get a handle on the next wave of mental anguish he was going through. Never ever would I bring such a beautiful traumatised human being anywhere near such a judgemental positional . On the flipside, outside of the suit, tie, and church role, the middle aged 'sides person' had some kudos in my personal view. He was an ex soldier who owned a cleaning company and was awoken one night by guys breaking into his van and stealing his mechanical equipment. Without thinking, he jumped out of bed and gave chase through the housing estate before making the sobering walk of shame back to his house, the neighbours twitching their curtains and viewing his fully naked manhood. Seems the dude doesn't do pyjamas. To rub salt in the wound of this 'tipping point', a minute or two after said sides-person declared his out of touch comments on youth culture, a previously very normal woman from the church arrived late, looking more than a little flustered. She looked at me and said, "Oops, they are already praying, I had better not forget to cover my head," and proceeded into the inner sanctum, hat in hand. Sadly, she had been subject to the then vicars wife's mentoring, who was ultimately preferring the control of 'submission' to husbands and to the law over modern freedoms in those days, other normal people began wearing hats all over the place, having been indoctrinated into some resurrected 'Laws' (read oppression). The lady who was late to the meeting, who was brilliant in all actuality, was not just a lovely person, but because of her refusal to do things by half, her chosen head covering was the praying woman's equivalent of the Queen's royal guard with the tall black bearskin hat. She rocked it!

Even though I would remain in the church world for a further six years, I was undeniably on my way out. **I could not un-see what I was seeing, nor un-feel what I was feeling.**

It's kind of a joke in the counselling world that when a couple comes to you for help and the guy says, "I want to leave her," and you ask why, he says, "she baked me peach pie and I hate peach pie." It is never just about the peach pie. You may be able to articulate very little about why you want to step away from organised Christianity, but I am certain there is always a lot more to it than the fragments we are able to bring to mind, or the symbols we state as if to say, "this happened, now leave me alone". Whether it results in separation, moving on mutually, or the ripping experience of broken relationship and divorce, it is always an accumulation of things, which erode us and finally become unacceptable.

In the sentence 'I'm moving on because I have had enough', we often mask that we have had to experience and endure considerably more than simply enough.

In going through an actual divorce there is much to recover from, some of this recovery comes in the context of the new marriage/partnership. In the divorce from fixed beliefs it is not a foregone conclusion that you will be married to a new 'thing' to cushion the blow, soften the discomfort. This isn't necessarily about comfortable transition from one thing to another, it's about an ending. It means you have to come to terms with the gap it may leave if you do not discover new relational contexts or fuel for your spiritual self. Continue instead to explore, perhaps boldly with new understanding and boundaries, it is an important part of filling the void left by extraction from the old. It's okay, its just something called life where we have to be more in tune with the season, embrace Fall and enjoy Spring, perhaps after enduring Winter.

Please tell me if I am wrong but our attendance in the church organisation is voluntary? Isn't it? So why do we need to find a way to say why we are leaving, to excuse ourselves? It is a separation, a shift, a move in your self desire, where there should be no requirement of a divorce lawyer to help you build a case and yet it feels like there is this need for many. That's an indication of a bad marriage right there.

'If You Want Change, You Have To Stop Accepting What You Are Used To. Growth Is In The Unknown'

Maybe you're not healing, because you're trying to be who you were before the trauma. That person doesn't exist anymore, because there's a new you, trying to be born. Breathe life into that person.

Unknown

church - a counter narrative

Chapter 21

Reframing – Reimagining - Reconstructing

I have a friend called Ruth. She is an inspiration to me since she was always emerging towards something with more meaning and relevance for us. Whenever something came up in conversation concerning change and old language, she used to make an L with her thumb and index finger on both hands, invert one L on top of the other into a rectangle picture frame, look through it and say 'reframing'. It's a silly thing but it's stayed with me. Just like the time someone else suggested wearing Jesus tinted pink glasses. They said we have to come at all of it, all of it, through the person and perspective of Jesus. Like wearing pink-lensed glasses, our perspective would change and more would glow. It's not the best example, but we have those Bible verses that are heavy with authority, rules, and order. For instance: Mathew 18 v14 onwards can be paraphrased as;
'If a brother does something harmful to himself or others, go to him and point out the problem. If he does not listen, go with another one or two people as witnesses to this inability to turn around. If that does not work, bring it before the

...ole church. If he is still unwilling to turn it around, treat him as you would a pagan or a tax collector.'
How did you read that? What was the tone in which it played out in your mind?
I wonder, in what context, or again tone, have you heard it said or taught?
Would you describe it as legalistic? Or maybe full of grace?
Let's try it with these grace enhancing, Jesus pink coloured glasses:
'If a brother is messing up, go to him and try to win him over, find out what's going on, what's behind it. If he can't hear it from you, take some mates, people he may also listen to so you know without doubt that you have all tried your best. If this does not work, heck, let the whole community try to bring him back to his senses, back to health, back to balance. If even this fails to work then folks, treat him as you would the pagan, go back to the beginning and start with love. Nurture and believe in him, treat him as you would the tax collector, call him down from his tree and have dinner with him in front of those who reject him. Show him honour. Don't give up, leave the door of your home always open.'

Personally, I have never heard that communicated from a grace position, because generally it's used when you failed to force conformity on someone followed by cutting them off, rejecting them, and finally casting them out. It's sickening to say, but I have heard people who have messed up being forced to say what they did wrong in front of the church before being asked to leave. Honestly, for no other reason than to save the pastor's skin, protect the organisations reputation and to make the issue wholly someone else's problem, and then like Pontius Pilot, the church wash their hands of it. This is a passage about remaining in a relationship with people, not them keeping or losing membership to an elite club. It is about someone possibly causing harm to themselves or others. It is not about you projecting your fear or control when someone no longer wants to play the game or to accept conformity. On the flipside, this passage isn't about people who choose to be rude or are arrogant arseholes who are hurting people. This is more likely used to keep people in line, following the organisational narrative and paying their tithes to keep the staff and building costs paid.

RESENTMENT OF DECONSTRUCTION SPEAK

Lets try the Law/ Grace game (oppression) with another context, which is current. I have heard that there is rising venom against young people who are using the word DECONSTRUCTION during that profound of all life phases, the teenage years. The years where you question everything, and are at your most resistant to inherited thinking which doesn't stand up to scrutiny. Church leaders are using language like this to undermine deconstruction exploration; *'Deconstruction is rebellion masking itself in trendy language which hides a dangerous condition of the heart. People who are deconstructing are talking poisonous stuff and looking to recruit converts from those amongst us who are also rejecting God and the love of the community. These people must be resisted. Nothing good can come from pulling at the long established foundations of the church since they are divine and everlasting. We should not readily take such people back into the fold without asking them to repent and to lay down their false teachings. They are deceived and as such are wolves in sheep's clothing. They will eventually come to their senses.'*

There are quite a few people out there who are looking out of the church world and seeing that deconstruction (which has been more prevalent over the last 20 years or more) has FAILED, based on a 'construct ' position. The new has not arrived on the landscape as another slightly better construct, or there hasn't been a book written on how to do it. I think that's a terribly loaded set of scales and for those with this view, I would suggest that you are colluding with the system, casting armchair judgement which purposefully or otherwise discourages others off of setting sail, considering a journey outward. It perpetuates the largely patriarchal narrative that you are obligated to work with what is and change 'it' from within. People will say, 'If you feel the church is imperfect, have a responsibility to fix it' "Nope". Ultimately, it is a more subtle but contrived form of systemic control.

If you push me on it, I honour those who remain in the church world. Those who have been brave and have undertaken what they identify to have been some aspects of personal deconstruction. This is not to be confused with having been deconstructed. I would liken it to making out behind the school bike sheds, maybe some first or second base fumblings, but never truly dating or moving onto that 'next stage' of the actual relationship and journey. Beware those who would say, 'I deconstructed once, both my legs fell off'.

Deconstruction is a word given to those who are exploring possibly the last un-reformed aspect of church life, the structure, the centralising, and gravitational pull of the building as a church. I read somewhere that aside from different songs, visual aids, and other new attributes, we are all still largely Catholic in nature. We are a passive audience listening to a specialist, treating the building as holy, the priest as intermediary, and the sacraments (the rituals) as sacred.

Whilst many of us may feel uneasy in the early days of a new journey, it is to be affirmed and celebrated. All changes in structures and systems came from such brave souls as these and their venturing outward. It is possible that they may discover the as yet 'undiscovered' or long lost riches and freedoms in finding the Jesus person in the creation, the world and the real.

Let us stay in a relationship, sharing our journeys, and our findings. Let us not reject but instead inquire of those who are exploring different journeys and put away our own toxic fears of contamination by new thinking. Let us never cease in our willingness to hear and be transformed by 'The Way,' whatever your way might be.

'Everything you hear - is an opinion - not a fact
Everything you see - is a perspective - not the truth'
Marcus Aurelius

Now back to picking a new name for reconstruction...
Perhaps reforming is a more useful term to use as it sounds
like it has shape and rhythm, but not a structure, so it
remains a little fluid, flexible, and able to embrace new
learning. I have adopted rhythm, shape, and form terms as
being less fixed and coming from a more Chaordic approach
(see chapter 22)

Reforming is largely about the self, the internal not the
external, who you are as separated or separating from the
old, who you are in the context of the ever emerging new,
who you are in the context of others, earthy relationship
building, and not to forget, who you are now in the context of
the divine which feeds your spiritual self. We are perhaps
entering into the world of the non-badge wearing global
community.

- How are you reforming at the moment and how is it
  going?
- In terms of the old and the familiar, have you
  journeyed outward enough to sufficiently say that
  you are further into the ocean than those shores you
  have left?
- What things cause you to feel a tug at your insides,
  pulling you back towards the old as a way to sustain
  some of your ideas about the divine or your spiritual
  needs? Perhaps emotion?
- Is there anything pulling you back? Can you identify
  what it is and where it came from?
- What do you want to do about it? Do you even want
  to break the cycle?

Be transformed by the renewing of your minds? A bible
principle I believe as is holding our thoughts up to the light of
heaven to check them out, which in reality is what
mindfulness practices are about. We will have internal voices
to hold captive, which are black and white, enforcing
concepts such as; in/out, biblical/ unbiblical - safe/unsafe -
belonging/rebellion. These voices remain in our mental
'merry go round' for quite some time, but slowly the voice

which beckons us into the field of dreams, into the creation, towards more, will come to the fore, and along with your own voice, they will hold hands and walk together with ever increasing confidence into the new.

It is undeniable that church as a construct has landed Christianity here. Well, it's got some of us here. It's also lost a whole big bunch of folks along the way, continues to bleed young people like a cultural haemophilia and is now meaningless to 99% of the people in your street. Where is the reflection, where is the critique as to our growing disconnection from everyday people? However as with childhood coping mechanisms, perhaps it has more than reached the limits of its ability to get us where we are going, lacking the ability to fuel our forward momentum and movement.

Reframing Is A Critical Part Of Our Reforming

When what you know seems unstable, uncertain, questionable, no longer an alleged substantive fact, or is something taken out of context to prove a point (proof texting), fixing it may not be a simple case of taking out a single broken brick and putting a new one in. For some, doing this would make the whole damn building collapse. Somewhat like my friend who expressed feelings of 'divorce' from what was once adopted as certain, some of those crumbling bricks were foundational, and so slowly but surely, it will all collapse. Reframing will determine what it is you are able to pick back up and bring with you. What aspects will have a meaningful place in your reforming, either alongside or in tandem with your deconstruction, or sometime after the fact as you hold space, as you explore once more from the grass roots up. A friend encouraged me to not just dump everything without due consideration. He has a more gracious relationship with church as an organisation than I do, depending on the day and the situation. He is often there for people in the system whom he helps guide through the next religious injustice or abuse. He protects them as best he can from the church constructs bite and reach. Yet has remained able to cheer the church on in a way, which values each seemingly courageous step. In reality he does something I have not been unable to do. There was a period of months where he reminding me to not to throw everything out, by which he meant my understanding of church, my connection to the saints, and who I was as a Jesus follower. The English phrase he used at the time was "**don't throw the baby out with the bathwater**," to which he added "since some of those babies are intrinsically who you are."

For me, one of the things I had thrown out was something we called being 'prophetic' and in reframing, there were some elements I felt I could revisit. I spent a good few years praying with people and getting insight into what was going on for them, good or bad, past, present, or future. It may have been learned behaviour, but I would on occasion have my hand out in front of me in a gentle 'towards the person' motioning. I recognised this as being in response to all of my insides saying to me 'this person really needs to hear this, to get this!'

I had stopped doing this after I left the organization.

My mate 'groovy' Dave from Cornwall is to blame for a lot of my reforming of 'gift' type things. I shared with him how I felt like I'd lost my ability to speak to people in meaningful ways, just sharing insights or ideas. I told him how so much of it had been positional or in a context which gave you a platform, which I now felt uncomfortable with. I reflected how I didn't know how to do it, without fear of it being tainted from my experience of 'gifts' in the church world. You would all love Dave. He is a 6 feet something gentle giant who continually feels like he is not dynamic enough, because he is often around people with projects, who have ministry roles which are classically Christian and deemed sacred or useful. Of all the people I have ever met, Dave is the one who knows how to love and give of himself to others the most. We were on a boat in the middle of the Mediterranean when he said 'well that's not great, you shouldn't feel you can't speak'. As he said it, he put his hand on my shoulder. I suddenly slipped to the floor, overwhelmed and sobbing. There was no hype, no magic show, no Jesus conjuring, no songs sung and I was definitely not in the mood for any funny business. It was one of those times my familiar Jesus person slipped through the few cracks I had left open to the spiritual. Dave said, as I was sobbing on the ground, "Having things to say to people, offering wisdom into peoples stuff, which may help them continue to become who they are, that's HUGE! Gaz, mate, you gotta open your mouth again."

Everyone needs a Dave. Someone who thinks they have nothing to bring, and yet, everything they bring is precious and healing. I hope that I can be a gift to him in return and continue to be a mirror reflecting back just how 'HUGE' he is.

I use a different language to describe myself when I do that weird stuff these days. I use the language of a wider, more palatable world. I simply say that I am an empath who inevitably finds himself able to read people and situations in a way that I hope is helpful to them.

My wife Victoria, aka Vic or Vicki, takes the piss out of me all the time for how these chance encounters happen. *I say chance encounters because I want to make it clear that, in detoxing, I no longer seek to 'act upon others,' nor do I spend my day walking around with a psychological precept that 'I am well and they are unwell'. I feel it is very difficult to separate colonial elitism and superiority from those perspectives, or in simpler terms, the assumption and arrogance.*

Vic has also asked me to stop making eye contact with people, since the people who I would really prefer not to have an encounter with seem to view it as an open invitation to come and download all that's wrong with the world. It's true, I don't have a t-shirt stating 'available' on it, but it happens all the time and is a real pain in the arse if it's date night (my wife read this and said 'what date night?!).

We were lazing on a beach one afternoon and there was an American couple behind us who were trying to visit lots of places in Europe for a couple of days at a time, what we call a whistle stop tour! We had not connected at all, though I was very aware of them being there. I had seen a Roma boy come along the beach begging and he asked them for some food or money and the woman said, "no, I'm sorry". But, by the time the boy walked past again, she had taken some snacks from her bag and gestured to him to come and take them. At this point I'm sitting on pins and needles because I've got something I want to say to her. I wrestle with it for another 10 minutes before saying to my wife, "well shit, I've got to say something to them." Vic rolled her eyes, smiled, and said, "oh well, if you absolutely must". I took her sarcasm as the permission I needed and went over. "Hey, I realise this is a bit weird, but I'm stuck with the annoying ability to read people and with your permission, I'd like to share something". They were both totally cool about it, though I'm aware that he was a giant of a man and it made me a little nervous to be saying this stuff to him. I told her, "I saw what you did with the boy and wanted to say that generosity and regard for others is a big part of who you are, but it isn't out of guilt, pity, or reaction. It's an informed kindness. You may at times say no to someone, but then you hold it and check with yourself to see if it was the right decision, and that shows real maturity". Turning to the guy I said, "shit, you're a big fella, but you don't have to carry everything. I feel you have inherited a male role of being the problem solver and protector, and you feel it all rests upon you. But this is a partnership. You have this woman alongside you, and you don't have to carry it all". I smiled and walked back to my spot.

On another occasion, there was a guy and a hippy chick in the checkout queue in one of those supermarkets where the food is cheap, but you'll grow a beard and become malnourished waiting at the checkout. The guy and girl I spotted shopping were a few people in front of me, very normal looking, but looking at her as we waited, my heart was beginning to race. I was picking up this incredible energy from her. But you know what? I totally bottled it, left the store, and then thought I'd been such a cowardly dick in not speaking to them. When I saw them again as I was driving out of the car park I passed them by, bottled it again and then kicked myself. Like a stalker, I drove around the car park in a circle, determined not to miss the chance a third time, and pulled alongside them saying, "hey mate, I'm not trying to hit on your girlfriend" and turning to her I said, "I just wanted to tell you

that you shine. You exude energy and light and it's powerful and beautiful." Wow, you should have seen her face. She was undone and replied in shock with things like "oh my goodness, thank you, that's such a wonderful thing to say."
In another chapter, I ask a question concerning teachers who have a Christian faith position, "am I a Christian teacher, or a teacher who is a Christian?" Your identity is firstly as a person who has located their purpose as being an educator. Your role will flow both from your expertise as a teacher and from your faith. Your identity is in the integration of faith/spirituality into your work and your being. This then followed by the fact that the kid who wrote something, which you said was excellent and showed real ability, probably doesn't give a shit where it came from. All he cares about is that it was spoken and did its work on his self worth. Also, his restoration doesn't care if the words of hope, nurture, and growth come from a believer or non-believer since the purpose is another's growth and self regard.

I don't Christianise what I say to people. The message is what's important. They will have their own inquiry as to the source, just as it should be. Actually, even to this degree, I'm not sure whether I want to say 'I Love You' or 'God Loves You' because most folks really just want to know that they matter to another human being, that they exist, that they have value, and that someone is celebrating their birth into the human race. On occasion I inquire of my inner self if this is a moment of them exploring faith, and if it is, I'm more than happy to bring that into the conversation as a free unconditional offering. A Christian doctor does not feel it necessary to state that the author of his abilities and guide to his surgical ability could possibly be afforded to a supernatural being.
I guess those are some of the things that I'm reframing as I go along, perhaps you are too.

'Slowly slowly, siga siga' as they say in Greece. Reforming has been necessarily slow, and I feel that's important since this is about moving from a point of arrival, and stepping back into a 'rest of life' holistic, on-going journey with questions. I still have genuine compassion for people who struggle with knowing how far they can journey forwards whilst still trying to keep a foot in both camps. I find it difficult to see people remaining in close proximity to a place of high dependency, toxic personalities, and addictions (or simply nice stuff), seeing it as anything other than an over complex juggling of masters. My favourite line from the movie Sweet Home Alabama comes when Reece Witherspoon's character realizes she's in love with two men, her previous husband and the man she intends to marry. Her father says, **'honey, you can't ride two horses with only one ass, sugar bean'**.

If proximity to the old, and continued participation in the construct limits your forward movement, then it's a problem. But this is something for each individual to work through. Having said this, I am mindful that in my hometown there is a massive 'in recovery community' of ex addicts and alcoholics which the state services place there, moving many of them from England's north to its southernmost edge to be as far away as possible from their dealers and addiction feeders as possible (I'm sure the South's addicts head north for the same reason). This is to help them have the best chances of recovery and break the habitual cycle of quick fixes that bring no cures.

Just Saying.

"We teach children to paint inside the lines then expect adults to think outside the box."

Facts Are Up For Grabs

I have had so many conversations with people struggling inside the construct, or who have left it behind, telling me that they have lost their faith or are losing it. **Without fail, in every conversation, all I hear is people working out their faith and making it their own. Pulling your faith to shreds is a pilgrimage, stepping into a bullshit free zone in search of the real.**

Just this last week I heard about a devout Catholic father's conversations with his child who was asking how Mary was still a virgin. His response was 'you don't question these things, you just have to take them on faith'. You also have to forget that Mary gave birth to at least 4 brothers and 2 sisters without an immaculate conception. Then you look at the church system that requires you to have faith in something irrational like that, something not in its holy book and ask why the perpetuation of a particular narrative is important to its ideology, practices, and the position it wants to perpetuate. Faith isn't meant to be Blind.

There was a great Irish TV show called Father Ted, about three Irish Catholic priests living on the remote windswept Craggy Island with a handful of others. It is the perfect comedy. The main father is Ted, whose goal is to be famous, to end up on TV and spends his days trying to hide their chaos from the bishops. He lives with father Jack, who is always drunk and sitting in the corner on a stained armchair. His only words are shouting, 'Drink – Girls and Feck'. The other is father Dougal, who is a total mummies boy and who knows nothing about anything. A child in a man's body wearing a priest's dog collar, a loveable fool and my favourite scene is where he is sitting in the bath with Mrs Doyle the housekeeper washing his armpits. In one episode there are three bishops coming to the island to upgrade a holy relic from level 2 to level 3 or some other such thing. Ted tries to keep Dougal, who is a constant embarrassment, out of the conversations. With sweary Jack, they manage to lure him into an English lesson donkey style with the aid of a bottle of whisky on a stick, training him to reply 'that would be an ecumenical matter' to all potential questions from the bishops. My most loved scene is Father Dougal walking in a country lane with one of the Bishops, who is asking Dougal if he ever has any question about his faith and his beliefs. Dougal thinks and replies, "you know how God made us all, and is looking down at us from heaven, right? And his son came down and saved everyone and all that? And when we all die, we are all going to heaven and all that?" The bishop replies, "Yes, well what about it?" Dougal says, "Well

that's the bit I have trouble with!" At the end of the episode the closing scene sees the Bishop leaving the clergy in a rainbow covered VW camper van with a big CND logo, along with a pile of hippies, shouting to Father Ted that Dougal had been "really helpful". Ted says, "Dougal - what have you been up to?!"
Full Clip:
You Tube: Father Ted Series 2 The Bishops and Religion

The bits you struggle with as you move through a reframing of seeing what has value, meaning, and substance are the bits you're going to wrestle with. There is no way around it. Why? Because you are now free to question and you may in all likelihood apply that seemingly newfound ability to just about everything. That is okay to do. Even if it is exhausting (the idea of this makes some people go into protective panic that they will be left without a divine being at the end of it), you have to do the work.

Isn't that what it means to be a grown up with anything that you have learned and experienced? You are going to have to work out what is of importance and is still of use to bring with you on the journey. Give yourself permission to question things and to not fear that you're going to fall off the edge of the earth because if God is God, he will catch you. As a human you also have incredible inner strength, resourcefulness, and resilience. The spiritual journey is always about becoming more whole and more fully human (body, mind and spirit).

Again, with grace eyes and not law or exclusion eyes, Jesus said, "It is better if you have not seen and yet you still believe." He did not say, "you're a worthless idiot if you need some substance or evidence." He did say, "here, put your hand in my wounds - see, it really is me". Remember, at that moment most of the Jesus gang will have been thinking, "oh shit, I thought he was going to be King. He was going to usurp the power of the Romans to sit on the throne. But now all of that has gone to shit instead he submitted, lost, and was killed. What the heck was that all about". Imagine their reframing of what was, to now being something very different. It's worth remembering in the post cross narrative that Jesus knew that one of his closest friends would say that he didn't even know him. The pressure was not on Peter to work it all out, resolve all his guilt, but upon the Jesus person to find him in a familiar place and restore him in a deeply personal way.

If it's all fallen to pieces, don't panic and definitely don't rush to rebuild for fear of losing who you are. Too many times people have pulled the wall down, only to rebuild it with a new song and rearranged furniture (I'm okay with repeating myself in hope you will catch it). Allow this process to be all that it was meant to be as you go through your own personal journey of fresh discovery and rediscovery, as you inevitably put some aspects of what was, down forever. Here is something to hold onto. The nature of God man, continues to say to you,

" Some of what you were led to believe was unclean, is now clean. What you were told not to eat can now be consumed." This is still part of the journey and of his revealed nature.

How Many Christians Does It Take To Change A Light Bulb?
"Change?! Chaaaange?!!!"

It's important to know that what you are looking for won't be found in this or any book, though it may give you some tools. You will likely discover your own new frames of reference or language to help you understand the new space being explored.

I remember fondly reading a book which helped in my own deconstructing /decentralising journey. It was about how the church isn't the building and never was. By the end, I was disappointed to find that rather un-imaginatively, the solution seemed to be doing everything you did in the congregation, only in your home. For me, this journey that we are on, it really isn't about bringing the routine, the programme, the alters or even the song singing with you into another context. If that's where you landed then you never really deconstructed. You simply reinvented the house church movement from the 70's and 80's, along with its inbuilt trajectory to grow numerically by addition until all that was organic and treasured is lost as you search for a school hall to move the small into the large (a house church wiki search will show you a picture of a house church in Beijing, in the exact scenario I describe). Perhaps you managed to remain small and multiply, I give all credit to you, but you probably still have micro congregations in their behaviour and function, gravitational pull and programme?

Showing Up (Integration)

In the absence of a thing to look at, we are instead left with stories, so I will tell you one concerning what I call integration, showing up in life. My favourite bar in Athens was Braziliana, a small place on a square close to my doorstep run by a collective of friends. It was a cool place with a group of loyal customers because of its unique vibe, the kind of place where you cannot remain a stranger. I remember me and two guys once sat in the square as we were all low on money and buying cheap beer from the street kiosk whilst fighting the mosquitos, when one of the bar owners came and got us, pulling us into the bar for a free beer saying 'we are friends, we all know hard times'. Wonderful, anyways the story kind of goes like this:
Sitting in the bar with a beer, usually a bottle of Amstel, one of the owners, Takis, is being the barman and playing the background music of his choice from a laptop behind the bar. I didn't really know Takis that well yet but he was a lovely guy and was trying hard with his English for my benefit. A song plays, a classic northern soul song from the 70's called The Snake by Al Wilson and suddenly he becomes animated, moving his feet and arms, we find that our eyes meet, we are both miming the words to the song. He asks, "you know this song", "yes sure" I say, "I really used to be into this music" to which he says, "we must put on a soul night!"
It may come as a surprise but actually Greeks don't spend all their time dancing, they are hard working and in reality go to bars mainly to talk with friends, not dance to music, unless its traditional Greek music, then you can't stop them. Having

said yes to Takis 'lets do it', I suddenly realise what a terrible idea it is if nobody is going to dance. I say that we must get someone over from the UK for a series of dance lessons for its unique moves, then we will launch an Athens Northern Soul Night. As it turns out, I found it impossible to get someone to come and help us and so agreed to do the dance lessons myself, not having really taken it seriously since my twenties. Takis and my 'okay lets do a night' seemed to resonate with a community of people in the city who were big fans of this style of music, so much to our surprise around 30 people showed up for the first lesson and it went from there really. I teamed up with two Athens soul girls and we started Athens Northern Soul Club. The picture in this book was taken for Athens Voice magazine that did a feature on our growing club.

There was a buzz, and a wonderful few years of life happening and also the fun of seeing Takis learning some moves to his favourite music. Sadly, Takis died of cancer not too long after which was truly devastating since I had not been to the bar for sometime. In response to my last message to him, he told me not to worry and he was doing fine. The next thing I know is some mates mention in passing that they had attended his funeral and I was fuming at them, not to have told me he had gotten worse or even that he had died. I share this to say that I still believe the comment to be true, half the battle of getting out of the construct, is to just show up in life, being around stuff. The other reason is that you meet people, find them to be wonderful, feel you let them down by not being around when they are saying au revoir, and then you are not sure why you are crying in the kitchen feeling pretty silly because you met someone who mattered to you, a kindred spirit and you remember that you are human and that you feel! R.I. P Takis.

Integration and being in life also has its comedy moments too. I had brought my custom scooter to Greece with me, as a heavily modified motorcycle called Pussy Riot named after the Russian activists. I parked it outside the Braziliana bar and two guys shouted " Pussy Riot, fuck me, what are you doing here?!", since my bike had been on several international scooter community sites. By accident or by design I made good friends with those two German / Austrian scooterists who live in Athens. We drank together, talked crap, laughed and fixed each other's scooters. I was still working in counter human trafficking at the time and around issues of prostitution, which made this memorable moment all the more amusing. During one night of laughs and beers with John and Ali, John disappeared into the bathroom and returned having removed his members t-shirt from their own local Vespa tribe and bid me to put it on there and then. I was welcomed into membership of their club, which was really heart-warming and special, other than the club was called <u>Pussy Slaves</u>. I asked why this name was chosen and Ali explained how the two of them were sitting in the bar one night and their phones both went off at the same time with their wives asking when they would be home, "see, we are slaves" says Ali. "So it's not a sexual thing?" "Nope"' says Ali. " So why am I wearing a t- shirt with a large back image of a bare breasted woman sitting astride a Vespa scooter touching her private parts?" He shrugs and tells me he didn't really know she was doing that. See, integration can also be fun.

If I have in any way included a 'what's next' concerning such journeys, a 'what it looks like', it will have been entirely accidental, since doing so has not been my intention at all. I feel I would have failed anyone reading this book to have distracted you in any way from your personal outward journey and exploration.

Do yourself an 'adult' favour and trust yourself.
Being a participant in the ever downward and outward flowing kingdom isn't safe, but it's good. Being in the 'keeping you safe till heaven' church construct isn't safe either, and some of it isn't even good for you.

'I send pure love to you and your lovely family' Takis
SOUL BROTHER

Chapter 22

The Anarchist Spectrum &

The Chaordic Path

Apart from a shared gratitude for living through the Sex Pistols years where music collided with a desire to vent at oppressive systems and the institutional elite, I would not have ever sought to identify with anarchists beyond a sticker on my bike. I think part of me considered them to be a bunch of angry tossers who chose being mad at stuff as a lifestyle. I recognise that whilst this assumption was not entirely wrong, it is also a very limited view of a group of people who are consistently (not as a hobby like some of us) resisting broken powers and contributing to change.

One day at the Khora project I was sitting around, eating the lunch that had taken all morning to prepare. Around 12.45 pm the food would be ready and the volunteers from the multiple floors; legal, kids play area, education and others, would get their chance to eat before the semi chaotic 1.00pm distribution of a hot meal to between 700 and 1000 members of the refugee community. As I sat munching on the day's tasty dish, I was having a conversation with a guy who was part of the education floor. He was telling me his story as an anarchist who was looking to discover other anarchists living and working in a joined up and productive manner, having so far been disappointed with projects in other countries.

He asked me what I was about ('about' is better than asking what it is a person does – a waiter in a restaurant may have a reason for being there but it does not express the fact that everything he carries within him is about becoming an influential music producer). I explained my journey in the church world from my late teens onwards, and how I became aware of its limitations from a very early stage. Realising those limitations then grew into my attempt to confront those behaviours and structures, hoping to discover something new. I joked that nobody wants to pay you to pull faith-based structures apart. His reply, 'Oh, so you're an anarchist too!'

"No Them, Only Us!"
Khora inclusive speak

Athens is known globally for an ancient relic called the Parthenon, below it is a small patch of dirt called Exarchia, the anarchist area of the city. Exarchia represents both a symbolic and literal day-to-day fight against what they consider to be oppressive regimes, fascism, and broken systems.

When we began working there it was a police 'no go' area. It simply wasn't worth the opposition's efforts to pass through or attempt to oppose or arrest people there. Greece has many anniversaries, including the student-led revolution opposing the military junta in the 1970's. This resulted in those in power eventually driving tanks through the local university gates onto the campus, causing fatalities. Another would be on every anniversary of the intentional killing of 15-year-old Alexandros Grigoropoulos by police in 2008. Protest marches have a great many thousand people across the age spectrum in attendance.

I guess I was in a semi tourist mind-set when I chose to spend the night at a friend's place in Exarchia on the anniversary of the Alexandros shooting, only to find my hosts were moving out to sleep elsewhere, sick of the tear gas seeping in around their windows on such occasions. I found this whole thing to be one of my more stupid ideas. When I approached their apartment, which bordered the Exarchia 'no police zone' and the 24-hour armed police cordon, which existed around its perimeter, two military clothed policemen were standing on the corner. As I reached inside my jacket for the apartment's door keys I had safely tucked there earlier, I was met with a raised automatic rifle pointed in my direction. I quickly put my hands in the air miming door unlocking and shouting 'Just Getting My Keys'. At the same time I was thinking 'sod this for a game of soldiers.' To be fair, they had been shot at on the previous night, but still, not cool.

We have worked in the area for several years now, and frequent an Afghan bar in the central square (Plateia Exarchia) as the haunt of choice for some of the area's international volunteers. I have DJ'd some solidarity parties there on occasion, which was a total blast with a wonderful bunch of western and refugee volunteers from projects. Exarchia is a fascinating place, but also an unstable place. Clashes with the strongly militarised police could kick off any time, in semi regular push and shove, with tear gas and petrol bomb exchanges. I was not prepared for what we found ourselves in the middle of one afternoon while having coffee with some Iranian friends.

Whistles began to blow all around us as we sat outside our bar. People began shouting, and the refugees who inhabited the square, some selling cheap cigarettes and others having been recruited by Albanian gangs to sell cannabis, were scattering in all directions. Vic and I saw people dressed in black come into the square from all possible entry points to try and trap people as they, the mob, began to walk around menacingly. They were seeking to identify specific refugees selling drugs with their walkie-talkies and people shouting orders. It was a scene of very organised chaos. I saw police steel batons, snooker balls in socks (actually they were made of purpose built woven sleeves like it was an investment), and wooden clubs in many of the hands. The mob consisted of 50 people wearing black balaclavas; one was taller than the others and was wearing a white one. We were told to stay inside. I was specifically told not to attempt to take any pictures, as it would result in a beating. My chest was pounding with adrenaline and anger. My first strong assumption was that this was one of those **planned attacks by the far right, the golden dawn fascists** that I had heard about. Such raids had resulted in the hospitalisation of many refugees who had sought out safety during the night hours in the city squares. I was appalled, no, I was disgusted to find that this was actually the local anarchists, and this was something which happened from time to time as they sought to police their own instigated 'no drugs to be sold in Exarchia' policy, though I am sure their own substance use was pretty normalised. At one point, having identified a young male sitting drinking coffee with two females, they attacked him. They beat him with batons and kicked him on the ground while bystanders remained back. One of the guys was holding aloft a gun to silently state 'don't fuck with us or try to intervene'. I liked what that implied, that without the gun, people might have intervened in the pseudo political violence. They chanted and jeered and continued in scattered groups to harass and seek out targets. As they moved away from the guy they had beaten, I approached to find I knew one of the girls who was nursing the victim. He had blood coming from many places and an open head wound from being struck with a glass ashtray. This had shattered, causing multiple other wounds as he struggled to defend himself laying on the shards. It was clear that his arm had been broken. I found that the bar had no glass ashtrays and that it had been picked up elsewhere with a planned desire to use it as a weapon, which I also found to be sickening. The mob took out his ID and took photos of it as if this would prove to those they were answerable to that they had accomplished their task of locating specific individuals.

Eventually, the anarchists reformed and marched away in front of the bar I was standing in. One lad in black was laughing with his mates about how he had managed to actually bend his metal retractable police baton, which had been used in the beating. You can insert your own feelings and desired response here, I am sure they mirror my own. I would say this is one of those moments where I experienced my own trauma, brought on from helplessly witnessing systematised violence by those allegedly 'for' refugees, the self confessed protectorate of the oppressed and the marginalised. I thought the whole display was weak. They had an inability to actually engage meaningfully with the mafia who were making the money from the drugs, so beat up the refugees trying to scrape a living.

In the weeks that followed, I witnessed some subversive stickering and postering in the area. Images of the anarchists with baseball bats that had been cleverly replaced with large pink rubber sex toys and the phrase 'big sticks - small dicks'. Some posters of anarchists stood alongside Klu Klux Klan that stated Exarchia was for the Whites. Someone else was clearly reacting to the conflicting behaviour of anarchists as inclusive, and yet, targeting people of colour for stepping out of line. Even the guy who had the stand out white balaclava had been targeted with stickers, where in the eye gap he was cross eyed and there was a silhouette of a penis where the nose should have been, suggesting the balaclava was a necessity not a choice. I knew, or at least I hoped that this was the minority group amongst what was, for the large part, an actively inclusive community. Perhaps the norms of policing your own community with a threat of violence had not given enough consideration to the outcomes of beating refugees, for any reason.

You might like to read a book that I found very helpful in the circumstances, and have come to consider to have been my 'book of the decade'.

Blueprint for Revolution - *How to use rice pudding, Lego men, and other non-violent techniques to galvanise communities, overthrow dictators or simply change the world* by Sroja Popovic. My suspicion of the phantom sticker person was that they had read something similar about non-violent confrontation.

Isn't that the best book title ever? Sadly, I don't think anyone who planned the action of that day had read it, nor were they aware of the statistical reality that violence is less likely to achieve your desired outcome, despite the group of anarchists probably being academics under the masks. To a large degree I've put Exarchia in my rear view mirror. The frequently dualistic nature of the place was just way too hectic for this introvert. What I once found to be creatively dynamic and hopeful, I no longer feel energised by, but actively support other friends who do. In reality, I am an outsider who is trying to make sense of other people's worlds and complex politicised cultures, will always be a perspective, which is limited and flawed.

The one golden strand which came out of the mob attack that day was that I was told, as they stood jeering at the guy laid on the ground, the voice of the bar owner and bar inhabitants, anarchists who were much older and longer in the tooth having stood the test of time as neighbourhood founders, shouted back to the mob, "You are not fucking anarchists, you behave like the police." They yelled repeatedly "New Police – Same As The Old Police." That struck me as a good description and critique from the community to the community. I was now aware that even within the anarchist community there were those rejecting others as extremists.

It was some months later that I heard something helpful in a conversation with an Athens resident that was working out alternative living and economies in her own, more productive aspect of anarchy. She said, "I don't relate to many of Athens anarchists, they are the wrong sort, those who perpetually need to find something to be 'against' to validate their own existence and to give a focus to their activism, whilst offering little to no alternatives." This is when I realised that anarchism exists on a spectrum. My own mental picture of said spectrum had angry fuckers at one end, (I've met some who need something or someone to be against as if they are trying to build a portfolio of actions outworked through violence, kangaroo courts and summary beatings). At the other end were those who are contributors towards change, who have things, which they are clearly against, they are using intellect and resourcefulness to pursue alternatives, which they themselves were practitioners of. Having said this, and so I don't entirely reject those who advocate violence, a young activist girl told me, "when you are participating in the front of a legal protest against what is widely considered to be a state led by a fascist far right regime, and the police begin to illegally attack you with tear gas and batons, it's good to look behind you and see 'black block' (an ultra violent element of world anarchism) there having your back."

I have come away from what was a particularly intense period with a deep respect for those in the community who re-tasked several of the area's empty buildings into squats. Those who sought to house hundreds of the refugees arriving in Athens when the state was failing to provide adequate care and accommodation.

We got to spend a year collaborating with one of these makeshift, self managed communities and it has formed one of the primary images in my mind of displaced, desperate people being given a sense of dignity and respect. We met some amazing people there who I feel honoured to consider friends, both those risking creating a home for others and those being housed.

With some Anarchists, like some Christians, you can't really ask 'where are you going and why?' To someone whose main function is to protect a position or belief, since they are less likely to be practitioners, mobile, and forward moving outworkers of ideas

The problem for me and how this relates to my own resistance is that I am offering no alternatives, but am instead giving an invitation to explore far beyond the known.

I'm declaring that in this venture outward and away from; there is more than enough life and dynamism to make the venture worthwhile. It is certainly not to communicate back to the system that a discovery has been made 'out here', something you can draw an image of and make a vision statement for, which is then turned into a new version of the old problem.

I have chosen to convey this 'beyond' place as one of 'holding space' to see what naturally emerges and not jumping into creating anything new, if at all. But I would like to qualify this from another perspective. It comes from something I learned through participation in the Art of Hosting community in their school of participatory leadership. One of the ideas posited there is that of the CHAORDIC PATH.

The Chaordic Path

This is best illustrated as two overlapping circles, one of them Chaos, the other Order. The Chaordic path is the ability to navigate that place in the middle where they overlap. **Trying to explore that space means we are placing ourselves in a context of having to address internal default mechanisms that society has taught us. They are for us to 'fear chaos' and then 'over do order' as we pendulum swing away from the seemingly unsafe towards the over-safe.**

See: (you tube) The Art of Hosting - The Chaordic Path with Vanessa Reid.

The chaordic is the creative nurture/nature place between chaos and order. Seeking to understand and inhabit this place ensures we refrain from following either of the two contexts towards their extremes. One is Order becoming Control, and Chaos becoming the Greek word Chamos , which is destructive.

Control is the place where order becomes fixed, rigid beliefs and practices, authoritarianism, risk aversion, and fascism. A place where there is no life or energy to give space to change.

Chamos is a place where chaos becomes not creative but destructive. A place of despair and hopelessness, a loss of life, and eventual collapse

I have felt, and have also experienced, this Chaordic middle ground as a place of the unknown or over the rigid known. It is a place of sitting and holding the questions, a place of innovation and birthing where emergent patterns can be discovered. Yes, discovered **as you rest and wrestle to remain in the place of what you cannot yet see**.

Read that again till it makes sense because I think it is the actual place of having faith, not a faith in, not a religious faith, but the practitioning of faith. Even the biblical narrative of faith is a faith in what you cannot see, cannot perceive fully.

It could well be a dance with the divine, but more so for the rational. It is a dance with nature and how it can create a sustainable, workable order of its own. A place where seasons are understood and we respect an on-going death of the old and emergence of the new. A sense of order and rhythm will, I believe, find its own way if we can stay there long enough.

Things will take on a flexible form as the unknown continues to become known and as we remain movement orientated, holding onto that which emerges, on this occasion, with a much lighter touch!

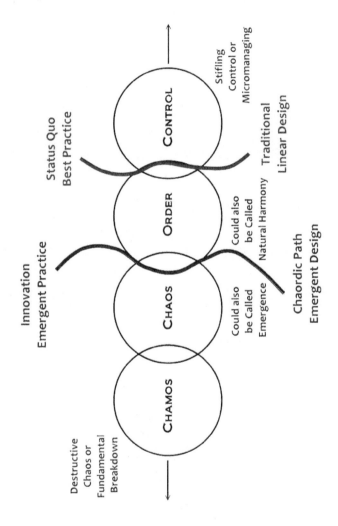

EXARCHIA
'COURAGE HAS NO GENDER'

A REACTION TO EXARCHIA REFUGEE BEATINGS

Chapter 23

The Footnote And Footprint

(A brief reflection before the final chapter)

"Christians often comment on how the Catholics excessive focus upon 'the mother', has 'eclipsed the son'. However, Christians pay little attention to how their own obsession with 'the bride', has 'eclipsed the son'!"

Take Me To Church

I confess that today I did indeed carry my bottom to a building calling itself church. We are in California at present with our family, we were sitting in a bar opposite a generic shopping park building, which turned out to be a church with a conveniently late morning service. I randomly said to my wife 'we should go' and she just said 'okay'. A couple of weeks passed before we had time to go but the intention and desire to do so remained consistent. Checking on myself, it's been a very long time since I've participated in what I am writing about. It would be rude not to take a dip, ahead of putting my less than charming voice out there. Do I still carry the same conviction to speak as candidly and as openly as I have done?

I would say we attended something, which was the best of the best of the best of what church as a construct can be when it has stretched itself to occupy every last corner of the cultural box. There was· A theatre style auditorium with a stage, big screen and multiple smaller screens with dynamic media, full professional worship band, digital tithing tools, beautifully sung contemporary emotive praise music. There was a significant introduction to tithing (giving to get more) but giving to the organisation, not giving as lifestyle. Actually it was a separate sermon on giving, which happens weekly they said. There was female leadership, prophesying from the platform, an alter call for salvation, a sermon which affirmed all the church programmes as being central to life. Relationship and community based on this sub culture, not actual engagement in community. Finally, there was 'and lets not forget... we are also here for our city and to see it change'. I could not fault it on being an exceptionally good version of church as construct.

Without doubt, every person there would have told me that they belong, that it is their family and that it is their home, along with 'this' being much more alive than where they were before. Instead of being something I would delight in, it just worries the shit out of me! "We are a spirit filled church, the spirit is free to do what he wishes here, we are spirit led", as the digital teleprompt clock ticks the speakers time down to zero.

There were a myriad of beautiful human beings present, none more beautiful than 'Pepper', a delightful woman whom despite there being 20 or more people as official welcomers in coloured t-shirts (some to say hi 'actually on the t shirt', some to sign you up for house-groups), she came over to us to welcome us and engage in meaningful conversation, despite only being in attendance herself for three weeks. We got to affirm to her that she doesn't need a t-shirt to be who she is, and encouraged her to be who she is in life, a shepherdess in the field and not to wait to be affirmed in the fold. She shone. This book is not a 'diss' on the beautiful saints, im dissing a half life system - I hope you get that. As a result of this mornings experience, I want to affirm that wine is wine, I love body people, but I would not remove a single sentence from what I have written concerning the human construct called church, the church of elsewhere, church as its own sphere. I witnessed afresh the focus on the organisation, the centralisation of life, a clear hierarchy, the building up and multiplying of what is, community and relationship around programme, God is more here in the gathering. 'God is in the house, this is Gods house' new temple building speak, God is more present in the worship especially our worship, 'Is everyone having a good time?' CHEER!.

I lost count of the exaltations of leaders/pastors by other pastors with the conditioned response of whooping, clapping members and obligatory 'AMEN'. It would have been comedy if it were not so horrifying how people cannot see the toxicity or counter productivity of this, as they play their part in enabling celebrity culture. **The all-encompassing church world cultural air was heavy**. On reading up online following the visit, it seems the churches network has come under fire in the media for 'cash for miracles', bigger giving for bigger breakthroughs. My suspicion is its the prosperity gospel in jeans trainers and a shirt instead of a suit. I just didn't want you to think I'm writing solely from distant, perhaps distorted memory.

" I wonder what the spirit thinks of our being 'spirit led'. I have this idea of a church version of TV's 'So You Think You Can Dance' with the trinity holding score cards showing their 'actual' participation in the performance"

Wrapping Up My Ramblings

It will be of great amusement to me when I find out if this offering of a book and its contextual thoughts have had a wider readership than the three people I have 'guilted' into reading it.

It is difficult to pre-determine who the readership is going to be other than people who are on their way out, or already out of organised Christianity. I didn't want to over-think the subjects or my own writing style as I sought to turn my messy ADD brain into something even vaguely cohesive and legible. I have tried my best and I **thank you** for your resilience if you have read through to this point.

In being needy and seeking affirmation I managed to find some people who read early draft chapters who said I should continue writing. I didn't even have to pay them to say it, either. You have those folks to blame if the reading has not been to your taste. In posting the cover on social media, a friend saw fit to express sorrow for my loss of church whilst stating she is able to take the good with the bad. My response is 'the book will be marmite,' or vegemite if you're in Australia. It will have a love hate reaction.

When I first sought to put pen to paper, having left congregation life, I was approached by a pastor from a large congregation who was pro stuff like; *'city, community, collaboration and unity'*. I hoped that they might have a rich church member who would back this horse called Gaz. They didn't, but they did need a cleaner and offered flexible hours. It was a kind offer, and also a little messed up, but I ate the humble pie. It would at least be a means of paying the bills. I became their janitor, not for one, but for five years alongside my still doing other stuff. Lets just call these the wilderness years of being in close proximity to the congregational machinery, which solidified in my core, that this was not my world.

It was not all gloom. I made some friends and had a little fun too. On one occasion, when the church was hosting a leadership team from a larger congregation to help them explore 'growth', I accidently walked into their meeting with a hoover vacuum in my hand and introduced myself as 'Gaz, the unseen guest at dinner tables and the invisible listener to every conversation'. I also got to say that my job was 'cleaning up church shit,' both literally (and metaphorically) to a number of people over the years.

Getting back to the point, I met a lovely couple there in that group who were relatively newbies, Kirsty and Jerome. Their newness needed, in my view, to be protected since I saw that 'new wineness' slipping away as they took on more and more roles in the church construct. I find the new and old wineskins idea to be deeply unhelpful metaphor, since we fail to see in as anything other than an old construct for old wine and a **hoped for permission** to build new construct skins for new wine. I'm not sure there is anything from that existing concept which is at all redeemable. **I prefer to reference the new skin as the 'skin we are in', it is our own body, our own moment**, not being held back from the nature of on going evolution and relevance by previous generations, no not even the last one.

I wonder if we can do that, I want to embody my faith in my time in my way, not wearing the skin of another, which is a poor fit for how culture and freedoms may have unfolded in the few years which have passed by. New Skin? Our Time! The character Johnny from Terry Pratchett's 'Johnny And The Bomb' has this lovely phrase he repeats frequently saying, he has a real sense of 'The here'ness of here, and the now'ness of now'. This is the space 'we' occupy, our time, to be fully present in our skin in all our newness, unhindered. Jesus speaks concerning church three times... perhaps we need to adjust the attention we pay to such really bloody distracting notions.

25 years ago a family member in Australia gave me a good sized folder on my family history. I have to say it's a little weird when I think that every Kishere in the world is an actual family member. This relative, a delightful man named Dennis, is a researcher and he had really done a lot of work on where we came from. The root of our family name is the name of the person who would have **'fashioned' the leather** thigh armour for the French cavalry in approximately the year 1200. Around 25 years ago I went with a friend called Iain to Texas to stay at YWAM Mercy Ships base and to get the heck out of the UK for a while. One evening we got to meet and pray with a bunch of people, we prayed for them,

they prayed for us as visitors, the usual thing, nothing out of the ordinary except... A guy grabs me, says he has a word for me, prays for me saying 'You will **fashion the leather** for the new wineskins'. Obviously the use of those specific words rang a bell for me, such that I would never forget and yet, I have done little to no leather shaping in the years, which have followed. But if this was a word for me, and if it was divine in nature, then let it be this, that the New Skin, is The Skin We Are In. It is as new and as fresh as every generation, it is the only temple of the spirits abiding and is likely always incarnate, always culturally relevant, increasingly counter culture in actions and one day, hopefully free to 'be', without the hindrance and distraction of the construct.

As for my two friends back in the church where I was the janitor, I felt desperate for them to remain new, to be expanded by the spirit within them, within their new skin. I could tell it was costing them dearly to have their square peg corners slowly sanded off to fit the round ministry holes available. There were definitely other meaningful things that they carried in real life that were not affirmed. I checked in with them recently to find they no longer participate in the church world, but are immersed in the riches of normal life. I will at some point thank them for being the catalyst, which changed my inner deconstruction from being a solely personal journey to being one where I also felt a deep desire to help others who were going through the painful journey of transition. It is they who are still featured in my mind as I have written these past months, as being people worthy of love and our best support. Many more faces have joined them over the years as I have sought to be of use to those trying to move away from organised Christianity, accumulating as few scrapes and bruises as possible. Your ability to resist control, to remain movement orientated, to ask questions, to work out your own faith beyond what was handed to you on a plate, are noble things that need to be applauded.

Apart from edits, today was supposed to be my last day of writing and sharing. That was until I saw what I consider to be a perfect comment on Facebook from my good journey friend called Doug. I know he is someone who gives considerable thought to his journey outward and onwards as he re-explores faith and meaning beyond the inherited systems. I just loved what he said;

"If we move away from our constructed image of God, whatever that looks like, we find that an inner strength emerges. There is no loss, only gain. This truth is hard to take. It can feel very scary. To be alone in a vast universe! Once we achieve freedom from our own constructs whilst retaining our enquiring minds, then we will find there is no separation from anything and our connection with our roots will produce "impossible" fruit! May we stir in one another zeal and energy that releases the Eros of our lives! Life is given meaning by our response to the world we inhabit."

Cast off all that hinders

If there is a bible concept, which fits deconstruction well, it is the concept of casting off things which are a poor fit for you, hinder your walk or cause life to become stuck. It's what I found myself doing and it led to my leaving the church building in pursuit of more. I never left the community of the saints, I still have friends who are Jesus person followers. I simply sought out a prettier, purer idea of the 'bride.' A strange, continued exploration of something lovely, workable and life giving. It never ceases to amaze me that those aspirations led me to walk away from what has self declared itself as 'church'. I mean completely. I completely walked away from it all. I don't say this to be condescending or arrogant. If you can't see it, you can't see it. However, if you have seen it, you can't 'un-see it' and have to act accordingly, lest we die inside a little bit more as the months and years pass. All of that stuff has been replaced by more earthy things **I now have a natural sense of flow, like a gentle river, moving ever towards what was always more, always uncontainable, and limitless.**

I hope that you find the God of the creation (if we can draw such an idea from the retrospective Genesis story dreamer passages), away from man's efforts to contain him in new temples of human design. If you have not, I offer you my sincerest apologies. If leaders and the church machine have literally beaten the living Jesus out of you, as I have already said before now, J man still shows up for me.

If I had never met a Christian, never read the Bible, never had a name to call this thing that I feel or the experiences I have had, I would have to simply say, that I reached out with my insides. I gave an invitation to an unknown spiritual presence that has seen fit to hang out with me. It is an active presence in my on-going movement orientated life of 'becoming'. However, I acknowledge that I did actually arrive here through church world and in stripping all of that back, I am grateful, deeply grateful for what remains and the changes which have taken place in my life. I am especially thankful for the incredibly personal, transformative nature of walking with the Jesus person. *I am grateful, not for being a Christian or a becoming a better Christian,* **but for being more fully alive and complete as a human being,** *more able to participate in society with all of its vibrant colours.*

It is my genuine hope that you continue to find sources of pure water, for your spirit to drink from, wherever these may be found.

This is my truth so far.

See you in the space!

Meilleurs Voeux Et Amour Pour Votre Voyage

G

Happy
In
My Own
Skin

Edward

Links:

Coaching and Therapeutic Support:
www.facebook.com/movingthewalls

Counter Trafficking Work:
www.crossborderinitiatives.org

Donations & Cheering Us On:
www.stewardship.org.uk/partners/20025251

Continue To Journey With The Book
www.facebook.com/castoffculture

www.artofhosting.org

One day you will tell your story of how you've overcome
what you're going through now, and it will become
part of someone else's survival guide

Chapter 24

The Christian Church

'Cult By Degree'

It is important for all people exploring faith to understand how cults operate. It is not a world away from many high street or downtown places you would happily sit on a Sunday morning. I doubt that any reader of this book would believe that cults are a good thing, that they are safe, or that they operate with accountability and integrity. People in cults generally don't know that's what they were joining until it's too late, just as those running the cult don't often realise that they are broken and controlling - the delusion goes in both directions. It is problematic that the Christian church operates from much of the same framework. While cults are, to the outsider, much more clearly in the business of usurping power and indoctrinating us with fear of the outside world, church can, and does, cross over into the same destructive behaviours, some of which, you as reader may have experienced behaviours, which are insufficiently challenged, patriarchal, misogynistic, controlling, and traumatising.

For some reason, while exploring our spirituality and faith, we become over trusting. We are over reliant on the belief that the advertising on the label states exactly what is inside the tin can. We all have the potential to do this. To leave our brain at the door, our thinking mind with its objectivity and critical thinking. **Perhaps so desperate is our desire for acceptance and inclusion that we adopt thinking and behaviours, just as we seek to be adopted and loved.**

The underlying Christian ideology/pathway invites you into a deeply personal relationship with the Jesus person, **a private you and him connection**, and yet, people see it as their duty to put their sticky finger all over that relationship.

There is nothing with the name church or any religion, which can state honestly on its outer label or in the small print, 'Untouched By Human Hands'.

20 years ago, during its first incarnation the chapter was called; Christianity, Cult By Degree. Its original wordy format still exists out there somewhere in the blog world, probably with a readership of three or four. It seems pretty insane to me that I first wrote this while I was still a fan of organised Christianity and a pastor /advocate of the church world.

What I learned was that the church has a methodology for how it seeks to convey or describe cults and their various dangers. Its method of communication on such matters is incredibly black and white. In painting a cult, as something so incredibly far removed from the church, there is no way you would ever consider the church anything other than safe and nurturing.

It places cults somewhere far over there with its unsafe, dark agenda's, controlling powers, along with loony leadership looking to separate you off from normal life, ultimately destructive in nature. In so doing, the church places considerable distance between it and the idea of a cult, perhaps unintentionally protecting itself from scrutiny. Many of the same behaviours and traits operate around us in church world in plain sight and are foolishly applauded.

Remember that cults generally aren't setting themselves up to do something bad, nor are they looking to do anything more than be obedient to their understanding of God, the divine or sources of spirituality and revelation. They see themselves outworking the divine's will for the people, using that as a justification for their building a group with distinct beliefs. They begin with an earnest seeking, paired with a lack of internal scrutiny or external critique.

So, I'll place a relatively shortened version of those identifying factors here where I am trying to highlight that it isn't black and white. We ourselves, as church, do actually live in the grey, occupying the space in between freedom and control.

Positional Leader Culture

Cults often have a dominant, mostly male leader who is sometimes referenced as appointed, anointed, high priest, or father figure (they love family language, just as much as the church does). They are often the founder of the group, or one who has been closely discipled and indoctrinated by the founder, alternatively is recruited on the basis that they will continue the dominant narrative and beliefs of the organisation, whilst promising to take them into an as yet unseen prophetic future. The leader has access to superior knowledge and alleged divine wisdom, or at least he has the edge on his peers. There are few female leaders and if there are, they have few female role models, so they tend to adopt a masculine, dominant, projected, and charismatic approach. The main leader will be the only or most frequent communicator to the group, as well as the disseminator of most or all of the information and sacred texts to the group (specialist). Others close to him will also be given opportunities based on their ability to sustain or progress the existing and agreed narrative.

In a cult your role is one of obedience as a follower. Be obedient to the vision, occasionally agreeing to it as a personal covenant. It is possible that you have no direct or meaningful contact with said person, though it will be much desired. Your view of self will often be measured by how you perceive this person views you, the success of your gaining proximity to them, or a list of identifying factors which mean you are performing the implicit or explicit expectations of the group. Those outside the group will have increasingly less influence on you or perhaps less access to you. I could name one large seemingly successful evangelical church in my home town that ensures submission of the wife to the husband in the marriage vows, and that annually members renew their covenant and beliefs as members of the group - dodgy as F.

I met someone recently who told me about their adult single mum being rejected and cast out from a Christian community because she met a guy without a chaperone present. It seems the tightrope walk of pleasing God is alive and well out there in 'cultsville'.

To be fair, my own entry into the church world was kind of welcoming in that I had a whole bunch of people stroking my love deficits and need for affirmation. Cults, churches, use very similar grooming approaches, which draw upon your likely love deficits and frequent lack of father figures. I don't say that to shock you, it's simply true. It's a proven methodology that is used to appeal to your needs and is all too familiar to me in how traffickers recruit people.

I very quickly left my tribe and culture group, dumped my own distinct dress style, bought some beige corduroy trousers, and began to give up my 'The Cult and Burfield Shits Scooter Club' t-shirts in favour of things somewhat less interesting. In truth, I felt a bit of a celebrity as my presence affirmed their success and street appeal to have reached another young person, though in reality, me as a new joiner was an anomaly, not an affirmation of anything much. I was blissfully unaware that I was becoming 'churched', that I was adopting inherited thinking and behaviour as I sat weekly, open eared, staring at the special ones on the platform. It took me a great many years to recognise the loss and removal from my cultural peers. Shit, what I mean to say is the loss of 'my friends'. The problem was, I had people here who were committed to telling me I was a good guy, which was great, but also incredibly seductive, though some of it was clearly genuine.

In a cult your personal development, training, or mentoring will come via trusted people who have a model for you to adopt that best reflects the beliefs and values of the organisation. Structural accountability to the group is the only valid place of sharing, disclosure, or help.

The leadership will have the greatest understanding of religious writings, they will be the specialists and experts, whilst any insights you might have are likely to be less considered, especially if they are counter to the party line. Questions about the organisation are not welcome, and questions concerning its practices? You are there to behave so that you can belong.

Whilst some church groups seek to experiment with on trend notions such as non-hierarchical leadership or flat leadership, these are essentially a squashed hierarchy where everyone knows who the high priest is. Cults almost always gravitate around charismatic leaders, even if your group is a distant subset and the leader is in another country or location at the 'hub'.

Mathew 23:9
And do not call another on earth 'father', for you have one father and he is in heaven. (I don't think this has anything to do with 'dads' but people and positions)

Proximity To The Group

You may just show up and sit at the back, or you may have been invited or recruited, but at some point you will be offered a passage of entry, both into the beliefs and to the 'higher valued' activities and practices of the group. Your loyalty is measured by your proximity to the group and the roles you undertake in the organisation. Your faith is measured through the same checklist, whether this is the measurement from the group or your newly adopted measurement of yourself.

The concept of Ecclesia as the ever evolving contextual concept of church came into Europe via Greece and was the occasional gathering of the believers for things of significant importance for the whole community. Everything since this inception has been counter to this idea in every way possible. The development of a programme for religious input, for socialising, for forming relationships within the group over relationships with those outside of it, and even a programme of entertainment. All of these underscore a desire for you to remain as a full participant in the organisation and if this is not explicit enough for you, ask yourself how much of your time outside the group, outside those relationships, is expressly valued and encouraged.

Working with girls in street prostitution, friends have asked the girls if they are trafficked and some of them say they are not. But, when you ask more questions about their ability to walk away from what they are in, it is clear that they cannot. They are controlled and live in fear of consequences. That is trafficking, even if you've forgotten that you are not free and your being controlled has become normalised.

The world of life and work progressively become a place that you visit, not where you abide and have your being. Sacred texts, teaching, and narratives are often chosen to reinforce your need for the group, your participation in the group, and your proximity to it. Anything concerning the ever-decreasing world beyond this is often a token gesture or referred to as OUTREACH, which in and of itself cements the notion, that out there is somewhere else. Life, work, and relationships with those outside begin to become part of a programme or project. The world, and our life and work in it, becomes a place to survive, to be fearful of, and increasingly safety is in the beliefs, practices, and involvement in the group. The section on dualism unpacks this more contextually. It is also called 'boxed' thinking; inside the box is safe, outside is not, inside the box is biblical... etc.

James 5: 12
Above all my brothers, do not swear – not by heaven or by earth or my anything else. Let your 'yes' be yes and your 'no' be no, or you will be condemned (up shit creek).
(In case your primary frames of reference continue to be the story book)

People generally begin to lose their ability to disagree. The group has a narrative already worked out as to why your concerns or questions are an indication of weakness, temptation to sin or a lack of character (back sliding).
Disagreement leads to being shown the door, or through necessity, finding it yourself and walking through into the preferred unknown. If you're a woman, all your ills are a result of Jezebel spirit (which is not and was never a spirit). The guys, well I don't know about the guys, they don't seem to have a slanderous male version of Jezebel, but it just goes to highlight that much of the scrutiny and control is towards the women as submissive 'ribs'. Let's face it; Adam was the first narcissist, unable to take responsibility for his part and so pioneered blame.

Shall I continue? This is cults right? Something we would never consider becoming involved in. We'd never allow ourselves to leave our critical thinking and our own unique connection to God's voice at the door, would we?

One True Church or Revelation

In brief, cults are established on the basis of having had divine revelation on who God is and how we are to be as his people. Even if one cult bears several similarities to others that already exist, they will have an aspect, which is deemed to be a progression on what is already there. It will express itself as being able to take you into a deeper truth, which then leads to a deeper understanding of God and purpose. In terms of feeling or your tangible experience of the spiritual, it will offer more than you have had to date. It will at its inception have built itself, in part, not simply upon what it uniquely is, but on a narrative of what it is not. That it is better than the others, and as a result of your participation, it will take you into 'Truer Truths' and 'Greater Freedoms' than others can. It isn't that different from marketing. Someone has an idea for something, then creates in you the idea that you need it more than what else is available. The only difference is this idea for the next Dyson hoover is said to have come straight from the top. As with the Dyson ball, being able to readily go around corners, your actual experience is likely to be an improvement on previous products and experiences as a consumer. Therein lays the hook. This new thing does quite possibly give you more, but it is deep in the foundations, in the inherited thinking, and the repetition of the immovable controlling root that lays the alternate reality you will experience or adopt.

Yay!

In return you are grateful that you have this opportunity to participate in something more life giving than you have known before. You are a person, but you are also a demographic which has been studied and offered a progressive feel good product whether you like it or not, regardless of how you will spiritualise it, or how spiritual it may actually be.

I have given almost zero thought to church world over these years but I have a continued regard for people and it would be uncaring of me to celebrate my 'being out' and not have a regard for those still in. I want to remember that a great many good people live in these contexts, having bought into a promise of something where the contents don't stack up to the description on the outside of the container. They have simply taken this to be the point of arrival and have lost the ability to question and journey onwards. We should not be ok with such things. I want to have a deep respect for those who remain while also wanting them to know there is more.

" *I Feel Much Happier With What I Don't Know, Than With What It Is You Think You Do Know.*"

Earning or Sustaining Salvation

Unlike actual Christianity, where the idea of salvation is framed clearly as a gift without expectation or rejection, some groups will want you to still work for it, earn it, or if you have successfully attained it, sow seeds of fear and doubt that without strict observance of their list it can be lost. Even if salvation is conveyed as a free gift expressing the nature of God's heart, pretty much everything else surrounding it takes work.

Community Ethos

At this point I want to remember a guy I met called Chris Bulpitt who, whilst immersed in the depths of man flu, wrote a paper called 'Ethos, Ethos 1 and 2 to be specific. He wanted to create a line down the middle of different approaches to, or teaching on, our Christian faith that will either liberate or inhibit our experience and journey. I found his thinking transformative back in the 90's and some of us used to meet from across the country with this as the basis of an open dialogue together.

Some examples:

e·thos
noun
noun: **ethos**
the characteristic spirit of a culture, era, or community as manifested in its beliefs and aspirations.

Ethos 1
God's will is a tightrope, on which we walk with fear and trepidation lest we fall.
Ethos 2
God's will is a field, in which we are invited to confidently explore with the Holy Spirit.

Ethos 1
Catholic/ Protestant approach to church, heavy on teaching and adherence to the bible as holy scriptures. People are built up, fed, maintained. Safety
Ethos 2
Celtic approach to church
Biblical narratives are a launch-pad/backdrop to an on-going fleshing out of God's story in us and through us, in the here and now. Exploration

Ethos 1
Statements and answers for everything. Questions are not encouraged or are to be avoided as dangerous
Ethos 2
Questions and dialogue are highly valued and are a vital part of continued exploration and of the faith journey

Ethos 1
Structural approach to making stuff/life happen
Ethos 2
Relational approach to making stuff/life happen

Sadly, I can't remember many more of those truly helpful frames of reference but you get the picture. So many questions were asked back in the mid to late 90's. There is a counter approach, a counter narrative, a counter version of the story, which is still being written and can be explored as a new frame of reference for living.

Cults have little interest in you discovering Ethos 2 as a worldview or as a lens through which to view your faith and practice. However, Ethos 1 with its fear and need of performing for acceptance will remain central.

Conformity

It is difficult to argue that the basis of cults is the adoption of an alternative way of believing and behaving. As such, we are becoming participants in, and shaped by, a culture. You are likely to inherit much in the way of culture and behaviours, being encouraged to be prompt adopters of new ideas, thinking, and practices. Some of this will be explicit, you will need to do certain things and believe certain things if you want to belong. Some of this is implicit. As an example it is possible that nobody told you that you had to dress in a certain way to attend a gathering. Also more than likely, nobody said you can't put your hand up and ask questions during the weekly download from the specialist or chosen one. We are both conscious and unconscious sponges ready to soak up our new surroundings, especially if it is offering the promise of something we want and have been earnestly longing for, having now seemingly found it. Along with new behaviours there will come the adoption of new words, language, or frames of reference. In reality these frames will further alienate you from society or 'normal' humans. We become recognisably different, but we would be foolish to believe this is in a good or more approachable way.

Selective Knowledge

In Christianity this is called 'proof texting' and I'm guessing it exists in other groups with a sacred or holy text as a script for its play. It's where something is communicated in part but not fully, perhaps not in context of the passage, the cultural setting or the issue it was specifically intended for. I will take a slightly amusing approach to an example and you can fill the space of the horror stories where proof texting creates control or abuses. On a recent visit to my oldest daughter in California I was bracing myself for a diet of all things healthy when I saw a loaf of 'biblical bread' on the worktop which I assumed had been bought for pure comedy reasons, not just for its stated 'Food of Life' holy recipe. The loaf of bread reports to be a 'biblical recipe from Ezekiel 4:9', which is its actual name, written loud and proud on the package of the bread. I thought it would be funny to post it on Facebook with the words 'only in America' so I did. The best part was someone's reply post, which asked if it was also baked with authenticity of the rest of that bible text, with **a fire made from human shit**!!

That's just a loaf of bread, where the marketing team felt they could get your buy in with the selected part of the story. Imagine how much it happens when people want your obedience, attendance and money, for you to take things that they say on face value of their being accurate, trusting them as the specialist.

Creation of New Family

Whilst I was studying to become a counsellor, I began client work, I remember working with a girl who had been part of a church community and was going through a deep crisis in regard to her past and family. She was drifting back towards the created family as avoidance. I actually chose this as the subject of a thesis on how the created family within religion and cults can give us an 'out' for dealing with our biological family. It can, in fact, play a part in further isolation from them and create blocks to recovery and wellness where this is involved.

Cults will be quick to use family language like 'welcome to the family, join your brothers and sisters, here are some spiritual mothers and fathers and ultimately father God'. It is saturated with such language, which can be a welcome relief, and is meant to instil a sense of safety and belonging. However, it can also perpetuate or create a considerable hindrance to your development as a unique individual, defaulting still to your identity being who you are in the eyes of others, in proximity to others, and fulfilling the spoken or unspoken criteria of sustaining acceptance and conditional love from them.

There's the saying that there is the family you are born into, then there is the family you choose. It is not meant to be an either or scenario, though in a cult that's exactly what begins to happen, unless your family is a part of the cult too (add your own 'oh shit' emoji here).

Someone rightly pointed out that Jesus uses 'inclusion into family' language himself, so are we to disregard this? My answer is no, but **it is my consideration that the Jesus person had no concept of what we today call church, where that language could lead to counter productive, counter freedom, counter growth behaviour**s.

Lack of Privacy

I remember working with some grassroots communities in the U.S.A who were looking to break free of institutions and experience more freedoms. I'm not sure that's what happened, as it was the first time I heard the term 'invasive community'. This means that leaders and other community members afford themselves the right to participate in your life in ways that they see fit and at times when they desire. It may also mean that you have been 'required' to give permission to such activity in becoming a member or follower. Rarely does the member of a community invite or initiate such actions.

Invasive community and invasive relationships are very rarely rooted in love, kindness, and thoughtfulness of others (even if those who use such behaviours consider it so). They are far more likely to be flowing from insecurity, a misplaced 'imposed' ideology of community, or the need for control by those in positions of power. This kind of invasiveness is not in the nature of the Jesus person. Much of our relationship is built around our invitation to him, not his barging in with dominance and force. A friend once preached with great passion about the nature of the Jesus person, and at the peak of communication he stated in a loud voice that 'God is a rapist - not a lover', which is of course not what he meant to say, but I'm pretty sure everyone will remember the point he was trying to make.

There will also be an idea promoted, that to be godly, you must also be known fully by others. Being fully known by someone can be a deeply enriching experience, though in reality, it is not very often that we find those rare, beautiful people who are worthy of such disclosures and trust. Generally, it is a misguided concept, an idea about spiritual relationships, and one that is rarely done naturally in the flow of a normal healthy relationship. 'Confession is good for the soul', perhaps at the right time and to the right people, yes. ' A problem shared is a problem halved,' or doubled, depending on the power that your honesty and vulnerability has given another in your life, or the positional dependency it perpetuates, or the role of others around you as parent, and you, the never self actualising child. People have ideas about community, about relationships, and about being on a shared journey with others. But, these are often just ideas. They are not meant to be a religious ordinance that we sign up for, or give away our rights and privileges as unique individuals in order to belong to them. 'Well meaning' can still be abusive. I asked a co worker is he was still hanging out with someone we both valued in terms of the dynamic work they were doing, he answered, "No, not for a while now, the trouble was that they kept speaking the truth without an ounce of fecking kindness!"

We had a generally positive experience of working with others in youth work back in the 90's. There was a genuine sense of being in something together, of gathering around something with a sense of purpose. From my engagement with those working alongside refugees in Greece, this is best described as solidarity, a shared sense of what you are gathered around and sacrificing for together but with cults, you end up feeling like you signed up for something in blood. The sad reality is that some in church world feel the same. There was a clear way in, but there is no clear way out. There will also be those, who unwittingly hold you to that invisible blood signed contract,
"But you made a commitment!"

I still have a diary somewhere of our work and meetings schedule from when we were young youth workers in our early twenties. We were the only marrieds in the group for four years, and then the only people with children for seven years. We had one afternoon off in the week for housework and shopping, then two evenings off a week, but you were still explicitly encouraged to do 'natural' relationships with the same people you worked with. This was on top of other weekend church activities or youth based work. I remember one evening we had put our then two children to bed and had that two hour magic period of being alone before falling asleep, when there was a knock at the door. Someone wanting to be 'naturally relational' from our team/organisation was standing on our doorstep. In reality, if it's an expectation, encouraged by the organisation to be with organisational people, then there's pretty much fuck all that's natural about it. On another occasion, we put a note on the door, which said something we deemed to be reasonable, limiting rejection or confusion. It simply said 'Please Do Not Disturb.' You can't wait for people to be happy with your boundaries, that's why you have boundaries. Oh my, the guilt we were 'enabled' to feel when questioned about this and if we felt it was appropriate to create private space when we were seeking to be a dynamic community. I remember the mountainous challenge of being honest and pushing back at the leader on it only to be told " Hey, I'm not the enemy, the enemy is the enemy". And that is where the healthy boundaries get blurred and visionary father figure steps into controlling critical parent.

The inability to create truly safe spaces, to feel you have rights, that there are clear edges to where you stop and other people begin, that's where the erosion of trust creeps in. I could write about cult leaders who displace attention away from themselves, how they exhibit traits of narcissism, and where things are often a result of someone else being the problem, but I don't think that's necessary. Especially since, as I write this chapter, the delusional followers of Trump have stormed the U.S Senate building. I think we understand those things much better, at least I hope so, for those who have ears to hear and those who have eyes to see when behaviours or agenda's are out of wack!

Outside of cults, I believe the faith aspect of our community flows out of our walk with the Jesus person. The nature of our interactions flow from his spirit, and it can be indeed fruitful and helpful and rather nice to be around, till we fuck it up again because we didn't recover from our toxic defaults.

That's all I want to say about Cults and how the church has educated us concerning them in very distant, black and white terms. In reality, we are not that much different in approach and practices, certainly not as much as we would like to think. For some, the experiences have been exactly that of a cult.

I doubt that many have walked away from organised Christianity without feeling an aspect of rejection, forced outside the fold, being viewed as unwell, rebellious, bruised or uncommitted. This is where the lines more than blur, this is where we can find ourselves in need of recovery from cultic behaviour, abusive leadership, overbearing or agenda informed relationships. We become destabilised as we seek to re-establish truth and not feel we just left God in the building or with the group we were part of. Real community, genuine relationship with absolute beautiful gems of people, can continue beyond the life in the container. There may have been some friendships which survive your distancing from the programme, but sadly for some, they journey forward alone, having been actively excluded.

In spending time with wonderful people exploring faith and relationships beyond the construct of organised religion, I got to travel a fair bit. Our having a 'new thing' meant our rave/bar/club/ church explorations popped up on people's radar. One group I spent time with was in Savannah Georgia, a place where I experienced both the pain and joy of people finding a way to explore again. I am a big fan of simple food, for all the Michelin stars out there, I don't really do pretty, and so the South's 'low country boil' was a fabulous experience for me. I heard about a friend's wedding where the food was all cooked in huge pans, smoked sausage, blue craps, with huge amounts of shrimp, corn and potato (not to forget heaps of spicy old bay seasoning). It would then be tipped out onto paper in the centre of the table like a true help yourself feast.

We went to visit a wonderful family who lived in a big wooden house under trees with an estuary at the bottom of the garden where dolphins could be seen feeding as you approached the muddy waters edge. We exhausted ourselves jumping on the massive trampoline and waited for the shout of 'foods ready' as the huge pots bubbled away on gas burners in the garden. The aroma when you're hungry was simply painful and torturous, but eventually the 'tip it out and feast' time arrives, and you've got your beer in hand. I think I must have eaten at least a pound of shrimp dipped in hot sauce.

I can't remember when in the evening's activities this happened, but I definitely recall a whisper in my ear that I shouldn't be alarmed when a particular couple arrived, and that we should all hide our beer, as they were religiously 'non' drinkers whatever that meant. I didn't think much of it at the time.

Does anyone know what mud bogging is? I didn't, but one of the family's sons invited us out in his open sided jeep, under cover of night, to a field where we began to rip through the mud and puddles. We were covered in, well, mud, and we laughed hysterically and cheered regardless of the reality that none of us had a change of clothes. It was just awesome, until the hiding police car turned its lights on, gave a flick of the siren 'wooooooh' and halted us in our tracks. Now, as kids in England, we had been brought up to see the police as an extension of the family. As you were stealing apples from the neighbours garden you could expect the local 'plod' to catch you, grab you by a twisted ear and haul you off to your folks where they were expected to hand out the relevant punishment for the crime. This was not my experience here. You'll have to imagine your own southern drawl on the sentence " *I oughta be haulin your ass into jail right now,*" and I will spare you the lengthy, highly parental lecture that seemingly went on forever. Suitably ass whipped, and feeling oppressed simply for the amount of times we were required to respond, 'yes sir or no sir,' we returned to the party at the homestead.

Cultural Faux Pas #1
On walking into the home, in reaction to the verbal ear
battering we had just had, I began to share my best southern
accented impersonation of pretty much all the bullshit things
we had just endured from the police. I personally think I
nailed the *'haulin' your ass'* bit, totally! I think I was
encouraged to keep going for a little too long by those
laughing at the English guy having experienced true
Americana. I'm a little slow sometimes, I take these things to
be an implied encouragement that I should continue, like the
first time I tried to dance like a Greek as people clapped,
missing completely that we were all meant to take turns.
That's called grandstanding right? Heck, I should become a
pastor, no wait I already did that!

Cultural Faux Pas #2
'Hey, where's my beer, actually where's all the beer?'
Having failed to notice the late arrival of our abstaining
guests.
I thought no more of it as it was a fabulous evening with
great people, a combination of blood families and chosen
family. A few days passed before the email arrived from said
couple. If I might paraphrase, essentially 'they were
disappointed by my mocking of authority figures and not
showing police the respect that their position deserved.
Moreover they were disappointed in me, a Christian, and
apparently a leader, in how I spoke and carried myself.'

Reversal is a beautiful thing ...

Some days later, I was invited to join the couple in some
coffee house where I found out that they were being
brutalised in the church. It was an unusual get together, me
thinking I had been a bit of a dick while also thinking they
were also a couple of dicks. What they shared cleared all that
stuff straight off the table, as I was faced with two beautiful
human beings. They were wrestling deeply with how they
had been told how they should be, what they should think,
and how they should behave as part of a system in which

they sacrificially and lovingly served, and yet it was abusing them, personally defaming them and causing them to step back from the community, or at least the religious construct they were a part of. As part of the leadership, she was being let go, shown the door and had in no uncertain terms been told that she was demonised along with serious issues she needed to repent from. Why? Because she brought a critique! She challenged the conflicted belief and values decision that the leadership were making. Decisions that were being made about, of all things, the church looking to spend hundreds of thousands of dollars on a gymnasium. The conflict for my soon to become respected 'friend' was that this gym was to be built primarily or solely for the use of the church members as an extension of the church building with its majority white membership whilst located in a poor majority black neighbourhood. What fuckery is this? The worst kind!

In the months that followed they wrote to me and apologised for what they had said to me about my behaviour. How awesome was she to call it out with her peer leaders? To discover that awesome sense of personal authority where she would allow her yes to be yes, and her no to be no, while both risking and experiencing extreme rejection. Still, she said 'hell no'.

I wonder what will be the thing for you where you might need to say, 'Actually that's not ok,' or even simply 'No'. It's shocking to me how difficult it is, within the inherited and adopted Christian culture with its hierarchy and power positions, to say such things. To challenge authority and ideas, to remain true to yourself and your convictions, perhaps even to the point of voting with our feet, risking the great unknown of the world outside which we have been taught to fear.

But do you know what? Very little of this matters if you're a happy camper church consumer and its programme is scratching your itch pretty well.

Thank You, Au Revoir, Stay Safe, But Not Too Safe!

Ok, that's the end of reminiscing for me concerning my exploration of cults. There was actually a much longer list of behaviours and beliefs in the old version of this, but even I got bored reading that version. The main thing is that you get the idea, if we lose our ability to question and critique, there are a great many contexts, which will take advantage of that, or are actually counting on that. The common ground of all groups forming a community around an aspect of beliefs should have a health warning which enables us to choose to smoke their tobacco or not. Why not! TV in America has a 'potential side effects' disclaimer with every advert for medicine, to heal the body, why not for things, which declare that are a salve for our spirit and mind? We should be afforded the objective insight of knowing what something truly is before we sign up in blood. Exploring this subject cemented my love and desire to see people set free from such things, to detox from their inherited or born into cultural addictions, and to lose their high dependency upon a sustained production of feelings and experience.

Ultimately, to help deprogram inherited or indoctrinated thinking which was life limiting.

My personal experience, and that of those I have stood with, is that **every aspect of this cultish behaviour exists to some degree, or even thrives, within Christianity** as an organisation.

I would say that one of my deepest areas of sadness is the degree to which I have employed these cult and addiction terms, as well as these processes to help people heal, find joy, and the freedom to further explore the idea and/or experience of a person God beyond the construct which has the name Church. It's difficult speaking with people who want to journey out and do something else with their time, since we may have one 'counter' narrative conversation, but the established doctrine and culture has them every week or more, assuring them of the truth, their version of the path, the importance of attendance, of sustaining spiritual covering along with stating the vital purpose of the church as a

building, as a separate sphere, as sacred centre, but perhaps never stating that its an organisation with a business model and a need of you to perpetuate its brand and its future
That's a lot to deal with over a coffee or beer.

Again, this is my truth.
What's yours?

Please note that any images used in this book, which show children, were included with the written permission of the parents, my friends.

350

About the author

Gaz has spent much of the last three decades working in community development, project funding, mentoring, counter child trafficking and supporting people who are displaced. The last few years have been spent investing in grassroots projects with leadership and strategic development, alongside giving therapeutic support to frontline workers who are dealing with stress, trauma and burn out.

Having spent close to 20 years in the congregational system, 15 of these in leadership, he has now spent the same amount of time outside of its walls and confines. Gaz no longer considers the church a useful context for learning, with the author feeling he has done his time in church school, an educational context that even Jesus could not graduate from.

Gaz has spent a considerable period of time learning what is transferable from church culture into the real world and has, along with others, found it necessary to detox and recover from a the conforming operant conditioning which exists there. He is now delighted to be working in real life settings where restrictive inherited thinking and adopted organisational cultures are more readily addressed.
Gaz no longer affords this 'separated off from life' system the name that it has given to itself, the Church.

2021

Printed in Great Britain
by Amazon